A Sea Blue Boat

ALSO BY IAN BROOK

Novels
Jimmy Riddle
The Black List
The Golden Bull

Non fiction
The One-Eyed Man is King

A Sea Blue Boat

And a Sun God's island

Ian Brook

With photographs by the author

Adlard Coles Ltd   London

Granada Publishing Limited
First published in Great Britain 1971 by Adlard Coles Limited
3 Upper James Street London WIR 4BP

Copyright © 1971 Ian Brook

All rights reserved. No part of this publication
may be reproduced, stored in a retrieval system,
or transmitted, in any form or by any means,
electronic, mechanical, photocopying, recording
or otherwise, without the prior permission of
the publisher.

ISBN 0 229 98635 8
Printed in Great Britain by
Northumberland Press Limited,
Gateshead.

To
Nofokerphtah who, by incantation, gave life to puppets he had made and with their help found the book of Thoth.

> He who tempers his gales
> Unto men as he will;
> some shake out glad sails,
> Some in sorrow sit still
> Fate-fettered: these speed from the haven, the white wings of those never fill.
>
> Euripides

This book grew out of a series of articles for *Yachts and Yachting*, to whose editor my thanks for allowing me to use some of the original material

I

You can do it in all sorts of ways. Some men hit the bottle. Others go overboard for women, take up gambling, go on the needle or spend their spare time hitting a small ball mercilessly across expanses of country and into artificial hazards. There are those who send pigeons on errands over vast distances or devote themselves to labouring in gardens. Men sit in exposed, windy and uncomfortable places watching trains go by, or fish, stamp collect, write to the papers, do a little shoplifting, bully their wives, beat their children: they watch blue films, an occupation which has the advantage of being more comfortable than bird watching, which many prefer. Pub crawling has its enthusiasts and there is always church-going to fall back upon—there is no limit to the things men do to escape.

But there is one sport which, while offering men escape and hazards in plenty, doesn't do a ha'p'orth of harm to anybody or anything: sailing. The sport's scope is infinite. It can satisfy the aspirations of the modestly timorous as well as cater for the suicidally foolhardy. It has a range extending from the awkward hilarity of youths taking their birds out in dinghys hired by the hour to the enduring skill of men making long and lonely passages across oceans. Between these extremes there is room for everybody, from the powerboat owner dispensing cocktails aboard his splendiferous chrome and varnished glory to the family with their beloved and exiguous tub, to the racing dinghy sailor acrobatically trying to sail a given course faster than anyone else—or the loner living aboard a craft that might have come off a cartoonist's drawing board. But, whatever they sail in or live on, people in boats deal with an element which requires of even the most casual among them certain skills and some understanding of its nature —and there is nothing more wayward, marvellous and ever changing than the nature of water, sea water especially. No one who has dealings with the sea can avoid acquiring some understanding of the mysteries which govern the universe. And a man can take to the sea surrounded by familiar things to comfort him, in as much or as little ease as his means and tastes will allow. But without certain skills he is doomed.

There are vast areas of land left in the world to challenge men, but meeting the challenge usually demands resources beyond the means of individuals: elaborate vehicles, aircraft, a complex supply service and help which can only be provided by powerful corporations or a government. But the sea can be challenged by a man alone in a boat modest enough to be within the means of many people.

> 'I struck the board, and cry'd, No more.
> I will abroad.
> What shall I ever sigh and pine?
> My lines and life are free; free as the rode,
> Loose as the winde, as large as store.
> Shall I be still in suit?'

The need of men to get away, to escape to responsibility, is shown by the enormous increase of interest since the Second World War in sailing—its greatest attraction is that there is no limit to its scope. A man can begin by building a canoe in his back yard and progress over the years to solo crossings of the Atlantic, or, even a shot at going round the world.

Man came from the sea and is now turning back to the sea. Driven by necessity, he has begun, in the space age, to try and adapt himself again to an element he left in his long climb up the evolutionary ladder. The sea is in the blood of all of us. No wonder that, under the pressures of present day life, men are turning for relief from their frustrations back to their original element.

Each year people in their tens of thousands come to the Boat Show at Earls Court in London to dream of escape—the long and the short and the tall, the rich, the artisans, the young and the very old, couples desperate for somewhere to be alone together, people in wheelchairs. They gaze for hours at boats, objects which offer at least the dream of release from office desk, mortgages and the spew of restrictive legislation spawned by mediocrities in parliaments. To go round the Boat Show, hot, jostled, foot-sore and enthralled is for increasing numbers of people a glimpse of hope. Gullivers staked out and tied up by Lilliputian bureaucrats, the Boat Show gives them hope. One day ... they promise themselves. A win on the Pools.... Something, anything—somehow.

Commander Cousteau keeps constructing new marvels to search the oceans. Films are shot in colour under water that bring the wonders of the unknown waters into every home. Girls in city offices fly to the Mediterranean, or hitch there, and, by covering their faces with a rubber mask and sticking a tube in their mouths, find underworlds of aquatic splendour. Men are training porpoises for service as messengers between working parties on the beds of seas. Devices of ever-increasing ingenuity plumb the precipitous deeps, probing and evaluating. Engines of strange design grope along the beds of seas and men live for long periods under water in special houses.

Great and growing as is the activity under water, it is only a fraction of that going on upon its surface. All over the world yacht marinas are being built to cope with the growing boat traffic. Men are taking to the water in everything from a Minisail to elegant marvels of the yacht builders' art, poems in wood and laminates, stainless steel and Fibreglass, buffed and polished to gleaming perfection—toys designed to eat money and provide occasional pleasure. Some of them inevitably find their way to places like Malta where they lie, commanded by paid skippers, awaiting in expensive idleness the brief visits of their owners. These are boats not made for ordinary mortals, and only too often provide remarkably uncomfortable sailing in warm waters like the summer Mediterranean, where a boat must be roomy and have plenty of ventilation if it is not to be a floating sweat box. Most of these boats have been designed for cold seas and become ovens in the seas of sun. Time was when I would have bought one of them if I could have afforded it. I know better now.

The war gave me my first opportunity to muck about in boats. After that, my addiction for them became incurable.

A Guards officer, asked what it was like at Dunkirk, flipped a boneless hand deprecatingly and said 'My dear, the noise and the people!' He might have added '—and the boats!' They came in all sizes to save the Army from that assailed beach. I, by the luck of the draw and after a certain amount of waiting, was taken off by a minesweeper HMS *Skipjack*. Immediately after getting aboard I asked her captain where it was. He offered me the use of his private one. No sooner had I settled than I went to sleep. And asleep I stayed through air and surface attacks. Only prolonged and increasingly violent hammering at the door after we docked at Dover aroused me from my Rip van Winkle slumber. I was not popular. The incident has left me inordinately sensitive about making gaffes on boats.

My next military encounter with boats, apart from an eternity aboard a floating hell ship the Army was pleased to call a trooper, upon which I, in company with what seemed like ten thousand others, was shipped out to the Middle East, was when I joined the 1st Special Air Service Regiment, the SAS.

The SAS, conceived and created by David Stirling, one of the great irregular soldiers of the last World War, drew its collection of staunch individualists from every regiment in the Army. David Stirling started out with a single, simple idea—to create a unit capable of going anywhere by every conceivable means of transport that came to hand, and attempting anything that was even remotely possible—or having a go at the seemingly impossible if the stakes justified it. Boats figured largely in these plans.

I went one day to Kasr el Nil barracks in Cairo to order a new uniform. David Stirling was there doing the same thing. I had for some time been a liaison officer with the Free French, a force which reflected much of its leader, de Gaulle's, intransigence. I felt I needed a change, something less acrimoniously wearing. 'Could I,' I asked David Stirling, 'join your regiment?'

'Yes,' he replied.

In due course I reported for duty at the SAS base at Kabrit on the Bitter Lakes. I was met by the adjutant and told that I was to be attached to the Boat Squadron. My Walter Mitty dream had been fulfilled with not a string of any kind having to be pulled. This was a happy bonus. A moment after, he said 'By the way, I wonder if you'd very much mind getting off to Kufra as soon as possible?'

'How soon is as soon as possible?'

'No need to push it. You might as well have some tea first.'

I thought the news about the Boat Squadron was too good to be true—the chances of having any boats to play with in Kufra would, I knew, be pretty remote. Kufra is an oasis, or rather a string of oases, each with its huddle of palm trees clustered round a small expanse of muddy water. Kufra lies on the other side of that vast stretch of nothing which has so admirably been named the Sand Sea. The SAS used Kufra as an advance base from which to strike behind the enemy lines. My going there wasn't quite such a total loss from the sailing point of view as it appeared to be—crossing that emptiness was in many ways like finding one's way across a sea: one had to navigate.

I returned to Kabrit in due course and was sent to learn parachuting, something everyone in the regiment had to do if he was to remain a member. Even that has some resemblance to sailing—especially when the wind blows you somewhere quite different to the place you intended to land. After that, I was taught to handle explosives and other devices before being sent to join the Boat Squadron in Palestine, as Israel then was. Boats at last! Foldboats—slender skins on a collapsible framework—MTBs, Jellicoe intruders, submarines—every conceivable kind of boat capable of taking soldiers across water: and not a shred of sail among the lot. We paddled vast distances, dived deep to pick up weights from the sea bed, swam endurance tests, landed on rocks during Stygianly dark nights, scaled cliffs we approached from seaward, and generally learned how to handle boats without coming to disaster before reaching our target.

And then boats passed out of my life for a long time. A submarine spawned us off an enemy island one night. We paddled ashore in a rubber dinghy. Some days' marching later we hit our target. It promptly hit back. After eighteen days in the mountains I, with my remaining companions, accepted an invitation to be the guests of a foreign government. And that was that for what seemed like eternity.

After the war I went out to West Africa and in the course of time was posted as District Officer to a water division where I had a launch all to myself. She was a long, shallow draught, flat-topped, raffish *African Queen* of a boat and had no sails—but she was enough to revive half-forgotten yearnings.

When my territory got self-government (an odd description for the genocidal process now replacing the rule of law all over Africa south of the Sahara) I returned to England and got a job in London. My chances of ever owning a boat, a sailing boat, of my own seemed more remote than ever.

2

Time slipped by. I travelled from my home in Kent an irregular number of times a week up to London in connexion with my job, by courtesy of British Railways. One day I got home five hours late. For a journey of fifty miles it must have been some sort of record. I was the only person in my carriage who was not a member of British Railways. As hour after hour passed and our journey showed no sign of ending I made a disobliging remark about the service. One of the railway officials leant forward towards me, pointing a wagging finger for emphasis. 'Let's get one thing straight,' he said, 'what you've got to realise is that passengers are more bloody nuisance than they're worth!' That was the straw that broke this camel's back. The admirable official had made much that had puzzled me clear. I now understood the reason for all the slovenliness that we, the public, put up with with such totally unadmirable and sheep-like patience. We moved to London.

There was a sailing school not far from where we settled, in Barnes. I took a course in Enterprises and concluded it by capsizing in the dying moments of my last lesson. It was winter. But not even immersion in icy water dampened my growing resolve that I would, somehow, acquire a boat of my own which I would by hook or by crook sometime sail in beneficently warm seas. I admire enormously those stalwarts who, muffled up like Arctic explorers, perform feats of competitive skill in icy and restricted waters. But not for me. Sailing as far as I am concerned means cruising. I even enjoy cruising in the Solent—windy, morose and overcrowded as that place always is when I have been there. No, for me, joy means cruising wearing a minimum of clothing and with a hot sun beating down upon grateful flesh.

My appetite whetted by brief excursions into the world of boats, I became increasingly conscious that even the earth itself is a prisoner in London, held down by a smothering scab of concrete. I sometimes travelled by tube to get to my work, an experience which strengthened my resolve to sail clear of urban civilisation when I could. How pointless speculation about the existence of heaven and hell is. A glance at the faces of people travelling in the Tube is enough to establish that Hell at least exists, and that most of them know they are in it.

I worked as an Examiner for the British Board of Film Censors. The effects of the permissive society were just beginning to be felt at the Board at that time, and increasing pressure was being brought to bear upon it to allow shots which, until then, had been taboo on the screen. And then the spate of nudist films started. These posed problems. How nude could a nudist be? My own belief was that if you were going to have a nudist film then it should be nude, but I found hard to stomach some of the wretched little efforts we saw; films clearly designed for those cinemas whose patrons are men carrying shabby white mackintoshes over their arms. Why do nudists spend most of their time playing ball games? Netball seems to be the favourite and must, surely, be the least suitable of all. Leaping around to put a ball over a net is not an activity designed to present the sedentary human body to its best advantage. Gradually, and only after much discussion, a policy about these films emerged: breasts, it was decided, were OK. It was remarkable how few were, aesthetically. Bottoms were OK, too—and what sad sights the majority of them were! Pubic areas were out but could be tolerated at a pinch in the very young. Arguments raged in the darkness of the Board's beautifully equipped miniature theatre. How nude could a nudist be? The hours we spent spotting the impermissible! 'There!' someone would exclaim. 'Where?' another would ask. 'I missed that one. Let's run it again.' It was like a television panel game. I can't imagine why the BBC never filched the idea to replace Stop the Clock. I suppose because Spot the Cock would have been the only possible title and they hesitated to print that in the *Radio Times*.

As an exercise in fatuity our nudist film activities were sublime. They convinced me that there should be no degrees of nudity in a nudist film—the only thing that worried me was that seeing them might put susceptible people off sex for life. Nudist clubs seem to attract a high proportion of people who should, at all costs and on every occasion, remain totally covered. Large numbers of men and women are simply not made for public exhibition. When they play ball games naked, things flap and flab and quiver, a more distressingly unerotic spectacle couldn't possibly be devised—and what better reason is there for not allowing the spectacle? There might be something to be said for these films if sex offenders were obliged to spend their sentences watching them as a form of corrective therapy.

The early nudist films contrived to shoot people in such a way that their parts were always covered by a towel, a providentially placed shrub or a bent leg assisted by a coy hand. But this simple phase didn't last long. We soon had a spate of American quickies with titles like *Not Tonight Henry*. But other films which had nudity in them were pure joy, and when Brigitte Bardot first walked naked across our screen she lit a squib amongst us which burnt and sputtered for many a month. I wonder what she would have thought of one of our senior member's observation: 'I can't think why these fellows want to shoot women's backsides. Never been able to see anything in them myself.'

I was fortunate enough to see a Robert Dhéry film in which he plays the part of an impresario. He is casting a new revue and is sitting in the stalls with his mistress, auditioning. He has a part to fill and can't find a suitable woman for it. A stark naked one walks down the aisle towards the stage. 'There,' says his mistress, pointing, 'what about that one?' He cocks his head and studies the retreating figure and then says decisively, 'Non, elle a les fesses tristes'. How many 'sad' bottoms I had to look at when I was a member of the Board. Looking at them did nothing to diminish my wish for a boat in which I could escape from a world grown so fatuous that men can make fortunes showing films any man with a reasonably sensible sexual education would pay not to see.

I went to Corsica to write a book, temporarily released from the Board, and took with me an Avon inflatable dinghy and an Evinrude outboard, the model with a folding shaft which is so convenient for carrying in a car. A year later I went to Greece and again took them with me. That was a fatal trip. It convinced me that, somehow, I would have to get a proper boat and go sailing in the magical seas of Greece. Before taking the final plunge I went off for a cruise in an Audacity. It was early in the season. We were abominably cramped on board, cold and very uncomfortable. I enjoyed it for all that and decided the time had nearly come. I took the first step by leaving the Board. I was now adrift in a world over full of people trying to make a living with their typewriters. Anyone who tries to do so is certifiable. On the other hand, anyone who remains too long captive in a concrete jungle will certainly become certifiable. I began to look around for a suitable boat at a suitable price.

Boats come in all shapes and sizes—and at all prices. But the ones cheap enough to be possible were, even to my tyro's eye, unsuitable for the purpose I had in mind. Besides, having got a boat where did one moor her? Mooring on the Thames costs a king's ransom. And there was the small matter of sailing her. The sailing I had done had at least served to show me how little I knew. And there was another difficulty. I am a mathematical illiterate. I even have difficulty in counting change. But, sooner or later, I was going to have to face up to the problem of learning navigation—for the sort of sailing I wanted to do it was an essential. The prospect filled me with both gloom and alarm. Difficulties are easy to create. On the other hand it is as well to recognise one's limitations. And yet ... The SAS motto, WHO DARES WINS, has a great deal to be said for it. I decided the navigational hurdle could be left to be taken later.

My ideas about the boat I wanted gradually crystallised. She had to be seaworthy and at the same time of a size and weight that I could tow across Europe. Finding a suitable boat wasn't easy. I read every yachting magazine I could lay my hands on. Why are they all so alike? I bought books on navigation. Time passed and the prospect of finding a suitable craft seemed to become more and more remote. I began to flag in my search. Then I read an article about a boat which seemed to fit the bill. The Drascombe Lugger was the somewhat improbable name of the one which caught my eye and my fancy. She was broad in the beam, had two masts, an outboard well and roomy side thwarts. There was ample stowage space aft as well as in the bows. Jutting out from her stern was a bumpkin, which gave her the jaunty, gallant air that its tail gives a bull terrier. I was enchanted with her. She looked like a boat. Her lines had the unity that any good functional object has. I wrote off at once for details and got back a pamphlet which did nothing to diminish my enthusiasm, pedestrian document though it was. Why is so much advertising literature about boats so tediously presented? She was, I learnt from her builders, to be shown at the Boat Show. I staked a claim on her and said I would be there to see her the moment the doors of Earls Court opened. But that was still months away.

Stimulated by the prospect of at last owning a boat, a proper boat with sails and which could go to sea, I decided to take interest in the occult art of navigation. I bought books and discovered, among other fascinating things, that an Admiralty *Pilot* was not a nautical person of distinction and wide experience but a reference book full of vital information. Deviation, I learnt was not merely something one encountered in certain kinds of films and in those notices Soho newsagents display in which French Lulu promises 'specialities to those genuinely interested' and Rosalie 'red-headed model, 19', invites you to 'just ring and walk up' if you want something 'different'.

I have known Soho since my student days and for several years walked regularly through its seedy, constantly changing and vicious acres as I went to the Board, whose offices are in the heart of its sleazy sprawl. I have a nodding acquaintance with many of its inhabitants. One runs a string of bookshops of a fairly special character. He is a man who also runs strip joints and who considers himself something of a social worker. 'Look at those girls,' he once said to me, nodding in the direction of a scrumble of strippers spilling out of a club, 'if it weren't for me those girls would be on the game. What else can girls like that do?' But it was his literary activities which interested me. Why not, I thought, as I laboriously tried to understand the mysteries of navigation, try writing a sailing cum navigation book with a difference some time? It was the similarity between the terminology of navigation, seamanship, and that of certain Soho occupations which first put the idea into my head. Who better than my bookseller acquaintance to advise on the proper adaptation to my purpose of such terms as whipping, laying, lashing and pink stern, whose definition, as everyone should know, is 'a narrowing after part with a rising sheer'. Suitably illustrated, such terms could enlighten the baffled comprehension of the navigational student, I felt.

It was just as well nothing came of the project. I abandoned it because my flagging efforts to understand the writings of highly competent, but orthodox, writers on maritime subjects received sudden encouragement when I read in one of my books 'Don't be discouraged, however. Navigation is not an exact science, and you must make what allowance as accurately as you can: and when you come in sight of your destination, forget about the compass and steer for a known point.' Heartened, I continued my studies with renewed persistence and abandoned my intention of trying to enliven the instructional literature of the sea. But I wavered in my resolve when I read in the same book later '—the deviation will definitely be different from when she is upright.' And when I come across terms like Paddy's Purchase I am tempted to revive the project.

I had virtually committed myself to buying a boat. The prospect gave me twinges of uncertainty, most of which sprang from my conviction that navigation was going to remain a closed book to me for ever. I knew nothing about it and was fast coming to the conclusion that I never would. The SAS had a very sensible rule that no one above the rank of corporal should do routine navigation—necessary for units operating off the beaten track in vast stretches of nothing like the Western Desert's inland reaches. By evasions of sometimes questionable morality I took care to do none at all, routine or otherwise. Had I ever been obliged to do any I hate to think what might have happened. And the Sand Sea, that extraordinary waste, was, compared to the sea proper, a stable element: there were no currents, no tides —but there were dunes and soft patches, rocky outcrops and broken ground that forced vehicles off course, obliging them to turn and twist, double back on their tracks and make sweeping detours.

The prospect of having to exercise on the sea an art I had not mastered on land alarmed me. I decided to redouble my efforts to learn at least the rudiments of navigation and the use of the simpler navigational aids, in spite of a friend's assertion that 'all one needed to find one's way anywhere was a spoon and a piece of string'. I once set off with him from Lymington in his boat to sail to Ostend. We ended up in Ramsgate, so I felt I was justified in treating what he said with a certain reserve.

Canned music, pretty girls and the smell of paint and varnish fill Earls Court. And boats, boats, boats—boats of every possible kind, some as incongruous as a transvestite seen in broad daylight, others as beautiful as anything conjured up by the fevered imagination of adolescent youth. The outside world, inside Earls Court, fades away.

For two weeks Earls Court is the mecca of everyone even vaguely interested in boats; a place where a man can enjoy the bliss of being surrounded by as many beautiful boats as a Muslim hopes to have women in Paradise.

But where was she? I knew she had tan sails. They ought to be easy enough to spot. I knew the letter and the number of the row and stand. I searched and cast about like a hound that has lost the scent. And then, ahead, emerging out of a tangle of rigging and masts, tan sails! Earls Court suddenly became filled with obstructively slow-moving people.

Her hull is blue, her decks and thwarts grey. The upper strake, inside, is white. She seems very big in the confined space she occupied beside one of the moving staircases. I circle the stand and examine her from every angle. No Italian wolf could have put on a more concupiscent show of sizing up his prey. A man approached her. It was obvious he was going to put his hands on her. On my boat. I cut in on him and headed him off.

I was introduced to her designer, John Watkinson. Her lines, I said to him, seemed to me to have behind them a solid ancestry. There was a familiar look about them.

'—and partly Mediterranean' he finished his account about the sources upon which he'd drawn for her design. He had, he explained, served in the Navy in the Mediterranean during the war and been much struck by the design and lines of local boats.

'Did you ever by any chance come across a submarine called *Severn*?' I asked him in the way one does.

'You were in the SAS, weren't you?' he countered.

I looked at him in surprise.

'I was navigating officer in *Severn* when we put you and your lot ashore to do some skulduggery before the Sicily landings.'

With a coincidence of such magnitude how could I fail to buy her? Besides, I knew that there were other covetous eyes upon her.

I had bought a boat, a real boat, one with sails. Is there any other kind?

3

Owning a boat is just a beginning. Problems confronted me—and the knowledge of my lamentable ignorance about boats burdened me.

Robinson Crusoe built a boat big enough to 'carry six and twenty men'. But when he had completed the task he couldn't get her into the water. Try as he would, he found no solution to the problem. I had at least given some thought to that particular aspect of owning a boat. I would tow her out to Greece, I had decided. Sailing her there was out of the question. The more I thought about it the less I relished the prospect of towing an 18-foot boat with a beam of 6 feet 3 inches across Europe. There were so many questions to which I simply didn't know the answers. What, for instance, was the most suitable kind of trailer? At least one problem had been solved, that of moorings. Until I was ready to take delivery her makers, Kelly and Hall of Newton Ferrers, were going to keep her for me. I would have time before taking delivery to go into the mechanics of getting her to Greece.

Then there was the question of a name. A boat without a name is still just a hull, however much character that hull may have. But finding a name for a boat is as difficult as finding a name for a child—and how many children's names turn out to be suitable? There is, in my opinion, a good deal to be said for giving children temporary names until they are old enough to choose ones for themselves. But that can't apply to boats. Once a boat has been named the name, I feel, should remain with her. To change a boat's name is to remove some of the *vertu* which makes it a personality.

After a great deal of effort, agonising, and making a nuisance of myself to family and friends, I settled for *Aeolus*. For those who, like myself, are not Greek scholars I pronounce it A-o-lus. There are those who insist it should be I-o-lus, and others who assert vehemently that it should be Ee-o-lus. I prefer A-o-lus.

I had my reasons for choosing the name. Greek waters, the pundits assured me, and my own limited experience bore them out, were tricky and full of perverse humours, windy tantrums and moods designed to plague the sailor—as Ulysses found. It seemed to me a good idea to ingratiate myself with the custodian of the winds—the main source of trouble. Aeolus, I recollected, had been kind to Ulysses and had gone to the trouble of tying up the bad winds in sacks for him, and had then presented him with fair ones to speed him on his way. Ulysses only ran into trouble when members of his crew, eaten up with curiosity, opened the sacks and let the ill winds escape. I still can't imagine why Ulysses didn't tell them what was in the sacks in the first place. But he was a wily one and no doubt had his own very good reasons: he usually had some devious motive for each and every one of his actions.

Another good reason for choosing the name was that, during the course of centuries, Aeolus never achieved more than the status of a minor deity. This was an important consideration. I would be unlikely to incur the jealous wrath of more senior gods who might be angered by a powerful rival's name being chosen instead of theirs. And how Greek gods battled with each other over matters of prestige! One couldn't, I felt, be too careful when sailing those wine dark seas which have cradled so much splendour in human history—who knows with the help of what strange powers? It was, after all, only recently that the awful cry 'Great Pan is dead' was heard across these waters, announcing the triumph of the single Christian God over the deities of antiquity. But is great Pan dead? Was there ever a time when he was dead? Are there not clear signs today that the old gods are rousing themselves and claiming again the allegiances of men? Better, if it is so, that it should be the resurrection of these inspirational Mediterranean ones and not the dark, scowling spiritual hosts of Scandinavia, Germany and Britain—whose return is presaged in the reviving interest all over Europe in black witchcraft and dark cults.

The question of a name settled, I relieved the tedium of the remaining months between the Boat Show and when I was to leave for Greece in March, occupying myself with all the things to be done before I could get *Aeolus* there.

One of *Aeolus'* great virtues is the simplicity of her tackle. She had been designed for ease of handling and, as a result, could be sailed single handed. And the more I read about handling boats, making a passage, the art of navigating and the complex of skills needed to get a boat, any boat, safely from A to B the more forcibly I realised that simplicity of handling was a very precious asset. I had already found out what a far cry it is from wanting to sail and being able to without being a potential danger to oneself and other people. Handling a dinghy or a small cruiser under instructions is one thing, preparing to sail one's own boat by oneself is quite another. So, very early on, I decided I would resist any temptation to introduce refinements into *Aeolus'* sail plan or layout. But I did have one modification carried out, and often had good reason to be thankful for it. I had the stowage spaces for'ard and aft made into lockers. These later proved to be worth their weight in gold.

Deciding to tow a boat across Europe involves a certain number of problems. However, if the towing vehicle is of the minibus type the operation is simplified and a good deal less expensive because it makes one entirely free of hotels or even of camping sites. Most of these vehicles have cooking facilities so the cost of food on the way is no more than one would spend at home, or very little more.

The vehicle with which I was going to tow *Aeolus* was a Volkswagen Kombi. It was fitted up for sleeping, washing and cooking. It also had a roof that could be raised—and what a blessing it is to be able to stand upright in a vehicle.

I bought a trailer. The makers guaranteed its suitability. When I came to marry trailer to VW I hit a snag. Volkswagen make an excellent vehicle and an equally excellent towing bar; but for some no doubt good reason which escapes me, the two together reduce the road clearance drastically. I might as well have been driving one of those low-slung supercharged monsters that burn up the road with a snarl of contempt as they pass you. The complications that lack of road clearance, increased by the trailer's construction, was to cause on the way to Greece!

The time came to collect *Aeolus* from Newton Ferrers. I had never towed anything before and the prospect of making my debut with an 18-foot boat through the traffic maelstroms of London filled me with some trepidation. One thing I did know, you had to turn the steering wheel of the car in the opposite direction to the way you wanted your appendage to go. Knowing that was at least something. There is a good deal to be said for diving in at the deep-end when setting about a new enterprise. I had no alternative, but the prospect reduced the euphoria I felt over at last taking possession of *Aeolus*.

Kelly and Hall's yard is at Bridgend, hard by Newton Ferrers. The houses in the village are built of stone, grey, lichened and immemorial. They grow out of the ground, spring from its essence, and are sited with that felicity in relation to their surroundings which was, once, the glory of English domestic architecture.

There is a dream quality about Devon. I MARRIED A MONSTER and

RAVISHED BY A BEAST announced a cinema poster I passed on my way out of London. What had these narrow, high-banked and tidy hedged Devon roads twisting through an ordered countryside of green fields, lovely villages and noble houses got to do with what London had become? Did I really know a place in Soho called St Anne's Court, whose short and furtive length contained three strip joints, a Muslim butcher's shop selling those pretty vegetables, ladies fingers, besides sticky sweets and lumps of meat, two 'educational' bookshops and a larding of doorways to which were pinned invitations to 'ring and walk up', a place filled with the blare of jukeboxes, the voices of importuning touts and stale odours whose provenance it was better not to speculate upon?

The boatyard smelled of varnish and paint and the sharp bitter sweet flavour of newly cut wood. *Aeolus* sat on her trailer, and her lines were as graceful and confident as I had remembered them. I realised again with pleasure that she would not look out of place among those lovely Mediterranean craft, the Greek caiques.

'The Owl and the Pussycat went to sea in a beautiful pea-green boat. They took some honey and plenty of money wrapped up in a five pound note.' But my boat was blue and exchange control regulations would not approve of 'plenty of money', or of a five pound note disguised as wrapping paper. Anyway, before I could go to sea I had to tow *Aeolus* some 2,000 miles across Europe. But, first, I had to get her to London. This proved to be easier than I had expected. As is so often the case, a task is more formidable in the imagination than it proves to be in the execution. Besides, British motorists when they see a boat on tow do everything they can to help.

Bridgend is not the easiest place to escape from with something on tow—it is a place of narrow roads and steep hills. My uneasiness at the prospect of negotiating them expressed itself in too many questions put to the men in the yard about stresses and loads a trailer-borne boat could safely bear, and so on. One of them, in answer to yet another question, replied, 'Well, you got to remember that boats are made for water.' His reply put things into perspective. The thing to do was to see that *Aeolus* and trailer were soundly married to each other, supervise the union with care, and make as good a pace as possible towards getting her into her own element.

Coupled to the Volkswagen, *Aeolus'* bows were only a few inches from the rear window, a looming V shape that was to follow me like an implacable familiar, a doppelganger, and which obliged me to fit large side mirrors to the VW.

I had been fortunate enough to find a garage big enough to house *Aeolus* in London so one difficult problem was solved. All that remained to be done now was to assemble my gear and arm myself with the necessary documents. A friend, Aelred Bartlett, was coming with me as far as Athens. He had, he assured me, very little luggage. I seem to remember something being said about a 'couple of small bags', accompanied by a gesture of diminishment with his hands. This was a relief because I had an enormous amount of paraphernalia—the VW was going to be asked to do a man-sized job before we got to our final destination, Rhodes, capital of the Dodecanese.

For some reason, none of the necessary documents arrived from the AA. I have been a member of the AA for years and, always, with smooth efficiency, they have supplied me with everything I needed and without delay. What had gone wrong this time? Letters and telephone calls had surprisingly little effect. Time was getting short. More telephone calls and confusion: and then, at last, I got a voice on the line as soothing as a benediction, full of assurances and reassurances. The documents would be got off straight away by special messenger, the voice said. They arrived late that night. They were all wrong. Crisis. We finally put off our departure for a week. This at least gave me time to tie up loose ends.

Determined to make sure that, this time, the documents were in order I went up to the AA to collect them myself. There was a curious atmosphere of disturbance in those usually bland premises in Leicester Square. Were my documents ready? Brief referring to a list and a smiling 'Yes, they are here.'

I checked them. They were incorrect. There was an air of baffled uncertainty when I pointed this out, and worried consultations took place. No one seemed to quite know what to do. Eventually, I was told the corrections would take about two hours to make. Could I come back?

'But why should they take so long?'

Vague, murmured replies.

I went back two hours later and, after an interminable wait, was handed my documents. They were still full of mistakes. To describe a trailer as a caravan, I pointed out, was to invite trouble from Customs officials.

'But, surely, they will see for themselves that it is a trailer and not a caravan? It will have a boat on it won't it—sir?' The 'sir' had a distinguishable edge of it. If only Customs officers were guided by reason!

17

'Correcting the documents will take at least two hours, sir.'

'But all you have to do, surely, is strike out the mistakes, correct them, and initial the corrections—that shouldn't take more than a few minutes. And while you're about it you might rubber stamp the corrections to make them look nice and official.'

'That is quite impossible, sir.'

This was impossible.

'Why in heaven's name not?'

'We just can't do it, sir.'

'Look, just change the word caravan to trailer. Forget the rest.'

'I'm sorry. We just can't do it now that . . .' His voice tailed off.

He was a middle-aged man and it was clear this was hurting him. I was beginning to simmer. He could see this and clearly felt I had grounds for not being altogether pleased. He glanced over his shoulder. It was the surreptitious, fearful movement the citizen of a police state makes when he is about to commit an indiscretion. In a whisper he said 'You see, sir, we have been computerised.'

I couldn't get out of the place fast enough, taking my mendacious documents with me. To this day the trailer is described as a caravan and *Aeolus'* value is given as £63. Why £63, I wonder? As I left I had a vision of a little black box, somewhere in a secret place overhead, inexorably depriving men of their initiative. And after that, what? It was evident that the little gathering of staff that had collected about us as we talked shared my feelings of horror.

'We have been computerised'. With a shiver I remembered something I had learnt when reading constitutional law at the London School of Economics. Parliament, I was taught, was sovereign. The example given to illustrate *how* sovereign, taken from Bagehot, was that, should Parliament so decree, John Smith, a man, could be declared to be a woman and, whether he liked it or not, a woman he became—whatever attributes nature might have bestowed upon him to indicate the contrary, and whatever the unfortunate John Smith's (or whatever his name was) feelings might be about the matter. Anyway, that was the gist of the waggish proposition—British lawyers are no less ghoulish than those of other nationalities, but they are more cunning and try with the help of humour to disguise the wolf beneath the skin.

Now that computers were creeping into the seats of power, what wild and irrational fantasies might they not dream up to inflict on men —and not merely as an exercise in legal fantasy? It made me feel more strongly than ever that it was high time I escaped to the sea and sanity.

When I got home I decided it might be wise to check *Aeolus'* insurance policy, just in case. I unfolded it with distaste. I have a disability which prevents me reading officialese, especially when it has a legal taint. Glorious words caught my attention. I read on eagerly: 'Be it known that IAN BROOK ... vessel called *Aeolus* ... whereof is Master, under God, for this present voyage until the said ship, with all her Ordnances, Tackle, Apparel ... Touching the Adventures and Perils which the said NATIONAL EMPLOYERS MUTUAL GENERAL INSURANCE ASSOCIATION LIMITED, are content (content, mark you) to bear, and to take upon them in this voyage; they are of the Seas, Men-of-War, Fire, Enemies, Pirates, Rovers, Thieves, Jettisons: Letters of Mart and Counter Mart, Surprisals, Taking at Sea, Arrests, Restraints and Detainments of all Kings, Princes and People, of what Nation, Condition or Quality soever; Barratry of the Master (Barratry! Me? Never!) and Mariners and of all other Perils, Losses, and Misfortunes ...'

When I next looked at *Aeolus* she had grown bigger, leaner. There was undoubtedly a Viking sheer to her. The row of scuppers looked like gun ports. Was it not a Dutch admiral, Van Tromp, who hoisted a broom to the mast of his ship, proclaiming that he would sweep the English from the seas? And had not an English admiral, Blake, riposted by tying a whip to the mast of his ship, saying he would whip the Dutchmen from the seas? Why was I not getting ready to sail out of Plymouth, all sails set and looking for trouble?

I used to ride a miniature bicycle round London at one time. One day, as I rode past a strip joint in Soho, a group of strippers spilled out in a *klatsch* from a doorway. They were in identical uniform: wide brimmed sou'wester type black PVC hats, black PVC raincoats and black leather knee boots. They were evidently off duty and so had left their whips behind. One of them spotted me as I passed. She squealed, clutched at the others and pointed at me. 'Coo,' she said, 'look at 'im. Ain't 'e kinky!' I was wearing one of those hats with a peak back and front so she had some justification for calling the kettle black. Recalled, the incident cheered me. At least I would know where to get hold of a whip should I need one while sailing with *Aeolus* upon our 'Adventures and Perils'.

4

We were ready to go. Aelred Bartlett's 'couple of small bags' had pupped into a caravanserai of loads and he was taking along an Avon inflatable dinghy and a Seagull outboard motor. He was going to Greece to build a house on land he owned opposite Methana. The sensible way to get building materials to his site was by sea. The only way to do so by land was along a narrow, difficult track winding across steep maquis-covered slopes. Using this track meant enlisting the services of a mule—and the mule which, for complicated social reasons, had to be employed was the nastiest tempered beast in Hellas. The Avon and the Seagull would get him out of both physical and social difficulties. Parts of this track were almost certainly once stretches of the road Theseus used when going to visit his mother at Troizen. A stream which springs from the hillside above Aelred's property is faced with a marble slab upon which is carved the time-eroded figure of a horse and rider. It gives substance to the Theseus tradition. Perhaps he had a rest house here? Beside the water source stands an immense stone vessel polished to smooth, worn away perfection by the ages.

Aelred's place is tiny, a mere patch of land, and of great beauty. A row of cypresses stands beside the sea, a line of pointing feathered spears flexing in the wind. There are two walnut trees which give shade and some olive trees. Lemon and orange groves surround it. There are fig trees. One of them grows out of the sea wall which stops the sea gnawing away the land, and its branches dip and sweep down to the stony beach, stretching out across the water. And on one boundary of the land there is a chapel. Within its white grace a lamp always burns. Inland, bleached and craggy heights tower against a flat blue backdrop of sky. Birds, reduced to mere black accents by the mountain's mass, float with infinite and formal motion in Olympian space.

Two days before leaving there was a crisis. The makers of the trailer rang up and said that, on thinking things over, they had decided the model I had bought would not stand up to the job ahead. They would, they said, supply another, a more suitable one. But *Aeolus*, crammed with carefully packed luggage bedded together like crated tomatoes, was happily and securely snugged down on the present trailer. How was I going to effect the transfer without unloading everything?—a redoubtable prospect. It would not be difficult, I was assured. All I needed was a 'strongback'.

I had no idea what a strongback was. It was described to me over the telephone. I was none the wiser. I rang up boatyards for help. It was just before Budget time. 'Too busy,' they said. 'It's the Budget, they're buying boats like hot cross buns: never seen anything like it.' In desperation I began to mobilise friends and family. If I had to, I would lift *Aeolus* bodily from one trailer to the other, somehow.

The rule that ordains something will turn up if you press irresponsibly on, hoping something will turn up, worked. The man who delivered the new trailer had served in the Navy and knew where he could get hold of a strongback. With his expert help the transfer of *Aeolus* from one trailer to the other was done easily, but with caustic comments on the way she was balanced on the old one. Certainly, set as she was on the new trailer, I could lift it without difficulty to attach it to the VW's towing bar. I now not only knew what a strongback was but how to balance a boat properly on a trailer.

We got up at dawn on the day we were to leave. It was still dark. We rolled *Aeolus* out of her garage and at once hit trouble. The old trailer had been a fraction shorter than the new one and the lighting cable wouldn't plug in to the VW's socket. I gave a sharp tug. Something parted. There was nothing to be done. We would just have to drive without rear lights on the trailer, which would invest our journey with an agreeable tang of the illegal. The coming dawn would, however, soon transform us once more into law-abiding citizens, or nearly so— for we would still be without stop or indicator lights.

We said our goodbyes, waved our farewells and moved off in ponderous good order. Gently I eased the coupled and heavily laden vehicles into the dip where the garage lane joined the road. Coming in, the trailer's jockey wheel had stuck here but I had managed to force my way over the bump with nothing worse than a nasty rubber mark left on the surface of the road. I revved the engine and tried to repeat the performance. No result. I eased back and accelerated again. Nothing. We were firmly stuck. It was no use cursing. That would come, justifiably, at any moment now, from irate householders. We uncoupled the trailer and manhandled it to the middle of the road. When I had complained to the trailer's makers about the jockey wheel's lack of clearance, I was airily assured that it 'wouldn't take a second to whip it off' to clear an obstacle. It sounded simple enough. But try 'whipping off' the jockey wheel of a trailer after a long day or in filthy weather.

We coupled up again and moved off. Our farewells were more tentative this time. 5750 miles on the clock. London was still asleep. The streets were as deserted as those of a conquered city in the hours immediately after its investment. Their desolation increased the melancholy which, for me, always accompanies the start of a journey, infusing the texture of anticipation with a chill of doubt.

To take car and *Aeolus* from Dover to Ostend cost £20 15s. The cost of shipping them from Athens to Rhodes, a sea passage of some twenty hours, was £15 12s. The travel agent who had done the bookings for me had, I discovered when it was too late to do anything about it, reserved for me the only single-berth first class cabin on the Greek ship. This cost £6. But, even with this (I could have travelled deck, sleeping comfortably in the VW—the Greeks are very accommodating about dossing in cars on board their ships—for under thirty shillings) it cost less from Athens to Rhodes than it did to cross the Channel, and this not counting my fare from Dover to Ostend. Running a Channel ferry must be as profitable as having a licence to print your own money or running a TV company. I'm for the Channel Tunnel.

At Ostend the Customs disdainfully waved away the various carnets I offered them. Not interested, they said, and with expansive gestures indicated that Belgium was ours. As we crossed Europe, we were to find no one was interested in my computerised carnets—except the Yugoslavs and they, because of that infernal word caravan, were too interested.

Flying is without doubt the dreariest of all forms of travel—but has agreeable and often decorative hostesses to beguile the tedium. Next to flying in the order of travel non-interest is a journey by autobahn, autostrada, autoput or whatever name the ribbon of unfurling concrete may have. Once on one of them, like a rat on a treadmill, you are obliged to keep going for mile after mile, forbidden to stop except at authorised parking places, your needs served by inhuman amenities as soulless as anything Kafka could have dreamed up.

Highest on my list of undesirable roads is the one from Brussels to Liège—an artery flanked by almost continuous, and entirely undistinguished, rows of dreary houses. For mile after mile we pounded on through a sad drizzle more despairing and grey than anything London could put up at its worst. We looked with growing despondency for somewhere to stop. To anyone thinking of towing a boat across Europe I would suggest avoiding Belgium—it is too built-up a country and the road surfaces are awful, especially for a trailer.

We eventually managed to find a place to park on a broad, muddy space in front of an abandoned factory whose hulking squareness, shattered windows and mysterious assemblages of overhead pipes running from building to building would have made an admirable location for a murder film. As a night stop it was hard to beat for undesirability, even for travellers with their house with them.

It was as well that we had stopped when we did because *Aeolus* had canted over to one side. To rely on the simple pressure of a nut bearing on a shaft to hold the side supports of a boat trailer up may be sufficient for short distances over good British roads, but is less than adequate when road surfaces are bad and over long distances. Anyone buying a trailer for towing a boat to the wider sailing vistas of Europe should make sure that the supports steadying the boat on either side, and these are meant to do no more that that (the main weight should be borne on the shoes along the axis of the keel), are easily adjustable and held either by a ratchet system or by holes through which a split pin can be fitted. Tightening a nut while crouched uncomfortably under a trailer is not conducive to good temper, especially in bad weather. The trailer, apart from this irritating and easily remedied fault, behaved admirably, and I was never conscious of any extra strain being imposed on the VW by having it in tow.

All night long heavy lorries rumbled past us and I worried about *Aeolus*. What if one of those gargantuan transporters, to which were hitched equally immense trailers, skidded? It was a wet, foggy night and the road was greasy. We were, it seemed to me, dangerously vulnerable, hostages to fortune with not even a low kerbstone to protect us.

In the cold light of a dismal dawn our factory acquired a new dimension of chilling sombreness. No wonder industrial disputes in Belgium sometimes become so vicious and violent, I thought, with jaundiced ill humour.

I was glad when we finally left Belgium. I have never been fortunate in that country. On the 10th of May 1940, when the 'phoney' war ended I marched across the French border into Belgium. Women threw flowers at us. Women kissed soldiers. There were no kisses for me. Is there some atavistic instinct which guides women in these matters? I was getting worried. The sun was shining. The dogs of war had been slipped and our hearts were high. Above, German aircraft had already insolently possessed the sky, but our turn would come—we hoped. A kiss would have been a pleasant accolade to fortify the spirit and arm it for what might lie ahead.

And then I got my kiss. She must have been one of the biggest women in Belgium. She came straight for me, head on. Her bosom hit me with the impact of a bulldozer and sent me staggering back into the ranks. It was—literally—knock-about stuff. She stretched out an arm like a pine tree and her hand grabbed me by the back of my neck, drawing me towards her. She kissed me and left as abruptly as she had surged forward. We halted and I straightened my cap. As a romantic prelude to war it was disappointing. Then a Belgium man asked me to have a drink. I accepted, relieved that the day had some roses for me. When we had finished our drinks he shook me genially by the hand and left me to pay the bill. No, my associations with Belgium have not been happy. Only recently, on Brussels station, I went to the Gents. On leaving, the lady in charge emerged from a small cubicle and thrust her hand out. 'My tip,' she demanded. 'Madame,' I replied, 'I did entirely unaided what I came here to do. You haven't had to lift a finger.' She pursued me outside, mixing contumely with her mendicant invective. Not even the rapacious French go to such lengths. Even French cinema usherettes at least flick a light on for you before demanding largesse. And yet I am sure Belgium is an admirable country. It just never smiles for me.

Although motor roads isolate a traveller from the country through which he is travelling, they nevertheless reflect in some degree its character. The German autobahns, such a revolutionary development in road communications when they were first built, are today less impressive than the superb Italian autostrada—which even achieve beauty. But the German autobahns are well maintained and provided with excellent lay-bys which have picnic facilities: tables and chairs precisely set out and with marshalled rubbish bins handy. But when you park in one at night you must leave your side lights on, although the lay-by is well withdrawn from the road. We didn't and, as we were settling in for the night, a police car arrived with its amber roof light flashing angrily. The crew tumbled out like infantry going into action. 'Would we be good enough to switch on our lights?' they asked politely. We would. We did. They thanked us, saluted, and charged off as though they were after a bandit car. All that energy expended over a matter of parking lights! No wonder there is an economic miracle going on in Germany.

German drivers have a reputation for being inconsiderate and aggressive. I found their standard of driving and road manners very good, except in Munich. It was a weekend when we drove through and the citizens of that jolly city, so beloved of Hitler and his gang, were hurling themselves towards the Alps with murderous zest, skis strapped to their cars and wives, girl friends, mothers, babies and elderly relatives stuffed into the spaces left unoccupied by luggage and food. Bumping, boring, cutting in and bandying rude exchanges with each other, often in furious mime, they drove with resolute disregard for anyone else on the road. Those shaving brushes the men wear in their hats made their behaviour appear even worse than it was. They are objects so ineradicably associated with *gemütlichkeit*, song, and a landlord-fill-the-flowing-bowl kind of good fellowship. But they always remind me of the days when I was a prisoner of war in Bavaria. I used to see those shaving brushes in the headgear of gentlemen markedly devoid of any signs of good fellowship. Certainly forget the past—some of it. Let bygones be bygones. But, when confronted with the insane ruthlessness of Munich's drivers it is difficult to prevent fearful memory stirring.

After Munich (Aelred and I were probably suffering from jangled nerves after our passage through the city) we mistook the wrong end of an indicator arrow for the working end and found ourselves embarked upon an idyllic tour through a countryside of wooded hills and lakes. Men sat, stripped to the waist, sunbathing in chairs beside calm waters, or puttered about their gardens. Women wore light summer dresses—in March! And on the heights around there was snow. It was a delicious respite from pounding down interminable miles of autobahn. This was a reminder of that other Germany, the country of industrious people, vast farmhouses, ordered life and majestic reminders of a great past—on our journey we had glimpsed Aachen's Dom in the distance, a massive extrusion of masonry conjuring up the Carolingian past.

Reluctantly, we found our way back to the autobahn and before long were in Austria: and soon got glimpses of that other Europe, Eastern in flavour, which had already been foreshadowed in Germany by the onion domes of churches. Here, the presence of a Byzantine world is felt already. And, as one travels eastward, a flavour of Islam emerges, for we are approaching the region where bloody encounters took place between Christians and Muslim. One forgets how far the Turks drove into Europe—after all they laid siege to Vienna, an event which led to the creation of that delectable article, the croissant: that felicitous commemoration of Islam's terrible crescent banners.

In England I had wondered about the VW's ability to haul *Aeolus* up that steep, winding hill before Folkestone. Then I had worried about negotiating the Pätschen pass. But in spite of the snow which covered it it gave us no trouble. My only remaining worry about steep gradients now lay far ahead, in Rhodes. But we had other worries. When we got to the Yugoslav frontier the computerised carnets came into their own.

'Where is the caravan?'

'There isn't a caravan.'

'It says here'—a portentous forefinger taps the carnet with loaded menace—'a caravan.'

'It should be trailer. Caravan is a mistake.'

'It says caravan.'

Other officials arrive and circle us, stiff legged of gait and narrow eyed.

'But look at the measurements given,' I plead. What caravan could be only 18 inches high? 'And how could I carry a boat on a caravan?' I add.

Silence. Piercing glance from X-ray eyes under the pulled down peak of the hat.

'It says here caravan.'

'That was written by a particularly silly computer.'

Mentioning a computer, I realised when it was too late, might introduce incalculable thoughts. The word recalls the world of olives containing microphones, and other ingenious devices designed to discover the guarded secrets of men and nations. I smiled ingratiatingly, slid off the subject and bent to attend to one of the trailer lashings. That was a mistake. The official's wary suspicion, far from being disarmed shifted to the Seagull Super Century Plus projecting out through *Aeolus'* outboard well. The shaft and propeller were carefully swaddled in blankets and covered in cellophane wrappings, as was the top. Luminous strips were stuck all over and a piece of red cloth dangled from the propeller for good measure. It was the most obviously unconcealed outboard ever carried by a boat across Europe.

'What is that?'

'An outboard engine.'

'An engine?'

The officials glanced at each other, heavy significant looks, but no one spoke. No one was going to give a thing away.

I circled my hand in the air in a wild attempt to convey the impression of a propeller churning water. For two pins I'd have had a go at

There is never any shortage of crew in Greece; and a boat as beautifully mannered as *Aeolus* presents no problem even to inexperienced helmsmen.

Rhodes City is littered with cannon balls, claimed to be relics of ancient siege. They are for the most part probably unsold stock from the days when Rhodes supplied armaments to other Mediterranean powers.

Fish blocks are still used by both Greek and Turkish vessels of traditional type — which most small working craft in the Eastern Mediterranean still are. These blocks, as functional as they are decorative, are, sadly, becoming rare.

Most fishermen in Greece work for themselves, combining their fishing with some other occupation. Wherever you go in Greece men in their tiny boats can be seen culling a meagre catch from the overfished sea.

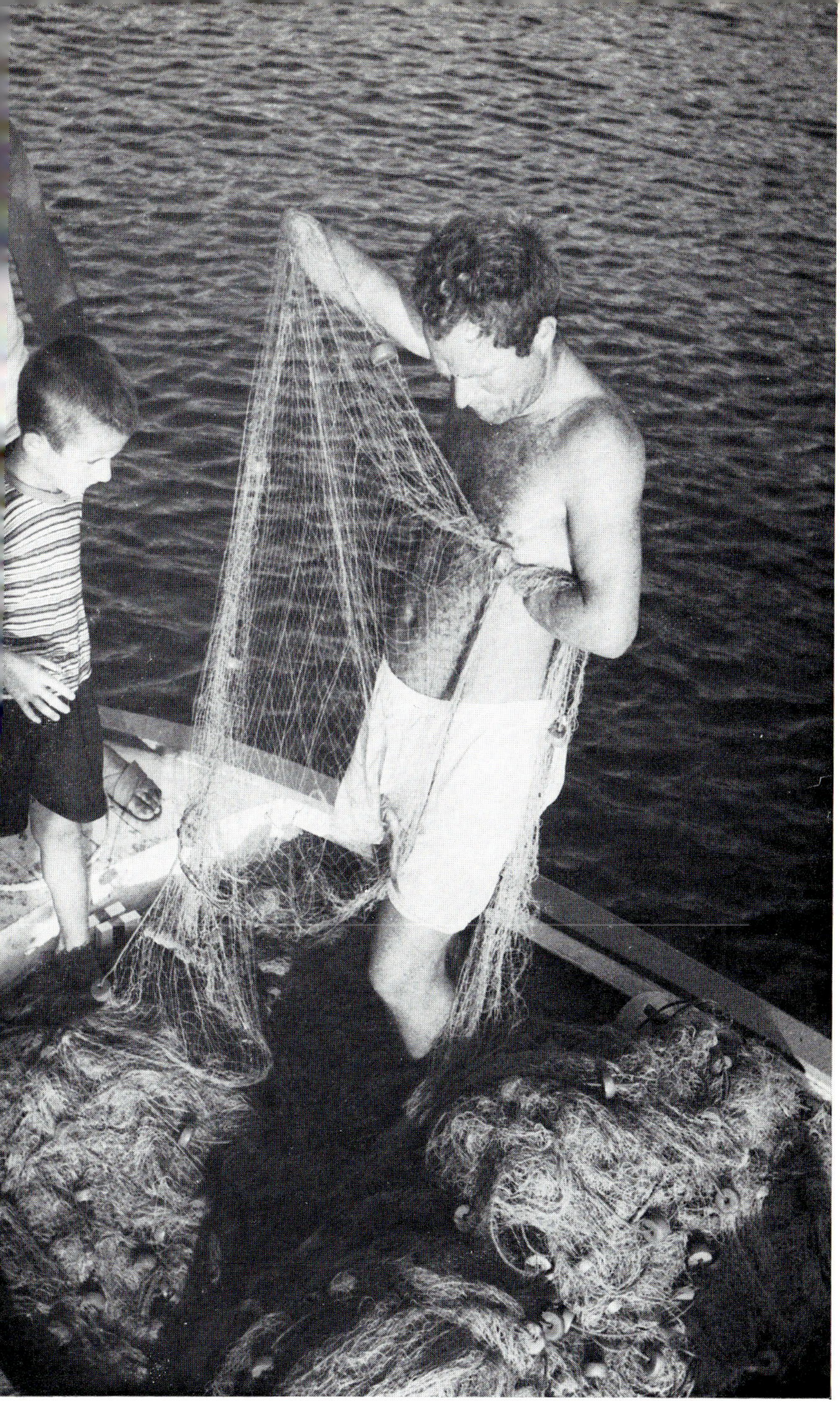

Sleeping out of doors is one of the delights of Greece. To do so under a canopy of vines in a courtyard pebbled in traditional Lindos fashion with black and white pebbles is to sharpen that delight.

Greek boat builders use for the most part the simplest of tools—wielding adzes with extraordinary skill—but power tools are increasingly used. Most of the men are independent craftsmen working on daily rates.

Plastic sponges have ruined the Greek sponge industry. But crews survive, supplementing their income by doing mixed fishing—lobsters being their most profitable sideline, one which old diving suits allow them to go deep enough to take.

Greeks have an almost mystical enjoyment of the fruits of the sea. Strong as this is it never matches the zestful enthusiasm and knowledge Italian holidaymakers show for all that comes out of the sea.

A Greek master shipwright sighting to establish where the waterline of a boat about to be launched should be drawn. The accuracy achieved by this empirical method is remarkable.

imitating the sound of an outboard engine.

'But it says here a sailing boat.'

Fingers flip the pages of the carnet triumphantly. Now we've got the dangerous brute cornered. Let him explain that bit of duplicity away.

'It is.'

'But that is an engine.'

'It is a sailing boat with an auxiliary engine.'

'A boat with an engine is not a sailing boat.'

I can see him thinking he's hit me for six with that one. I resist the temptation to answer 'and by the same token a boat with sails is not a motor boat.' But it is better to tread softly with Customs. Provoke them and they are liable to turn their attention to anything.

Then with capricious suddenness the whole subject of boat and engine is dropped.

'Do you have any transistor radios or television sets?'

'No,' and we are waved on our way into Yugoslavia.

Obsessed with the idea of getting to the seas of Greece and launching *Aeolus* upon them as quickly as possible, I was tempted by a line of red dots drawn on a Yugoslav tourist map. It indicated a projected autoput. In reply to our enquiries, a policeman assured us with vehement and smiling certainty that it had been completed. Abandoning the Ljubljana-Zagreb road I took the shorter way the new autoput offered. It turned out to be an unsurfaced nightmare of corrugated, pot-holed vehicle-destroying ruination. With every thud and judder I bled for *Aeolus* as we crawled painfully along. The trailer's jockey wheel kept hitting the road so we 'whipped' it off. This did nothing to improve our tempers. One of the trailer's mudguard mountings snapped under the strain. We stopped at a garage to have it welded. A cheerful mechanic guided me into the wall of the garage with urgent beckonings that all was well in answer to my doubtful hesitation. It was the only mishap during the whole trip and the damage was slight, a fractured tail light, a dent in the metal number plate and a small hole punched in *Aeolus*' transom by a protruding screw.

I had crossed Yugoslavia for the first time some years before, when one had to carry supplies of petrol with one to cross the great Yugoslav plain. Now there was no need to do this, petrol stations and camping sites line its whole length. There was no doubt that Yugoslavia was turning towards a non-socialist economy—the appetite for making a fast buck was positively American in its unashamed capitalist greed.

The only advantage this dreary route across the Yugoslav plain offers is speed. There is nothing else to recommend it: flat, featureless and littered with the wrecks of accidents, it is a bore to drive on and frightening—great lorries tear along, driven with reckless incompetence. A much more agreeable away of getting to Greece is through Italy to Brindisi and from there by car ferry (and very good ones they are too) to Igoumenítsa in Greece.

We drove through Belgrade during the mid-day rush hour. At the sight of us every Belgradian in a car turned into a hot rod kid and tried to burn us up—something about *Aeolus* seemed to fill Belgrade motorists with the suicidal frenzy of moths drawn towards a light.

After the frenzy of Belgrade we felt we needed fortifying so we spent the night at a camping site. Aleksinac is an admirable place. Besides being a camping site it is a hotel, or rather, a motel. There are good facilities for campers: showers, washbasins, lavatories and electric light. We were the only car using the camping area but the restaurant was well patronised by Yugoslavs, and deserved to be. An enormous meal with slivovitz, an assertive plum brandy, to start off with and wine came to £2 for both of us. This was the first meal we had not made for ourselves during the trip.

It was bitterly cold next morning. The frost covering everything was so thick that it looked like a fall of snow. We were both glad we had eaten a glutton's meal the previous evening as, still sustained by it, we scraped the car windows clear of its coating of icy frost.

Shortly after we started off next day the second mudguard mounting snapped, followed soon afterwards by the repaired one. I lashed them both in position with those expanding elastic things with metal hooks on each end—essential bits of equipment on any journey. We got the mudguards repaired at a garage which expressed furious contempt for the work done by the other one, and promised we would have no trouble with theirs. We didn't until I got almost to my destination in Rhodes. We set off, heartened by their confidence, assuring each other that we would soon be across the border and nothing else could go wrong before then. But fate had another slap in store for us before we left Yugoslavia. It had been a long time since we had passed a petrol station and we were getting very low. Then we saw one on the opposite side of the road. There was no other traffic on the road. I slowed down. A short distance ahead was a policeman watching us placidly. Immediately I started to pull across the road he went into action, peremptory action. It was, he informed me angrily, forbidden to cross an autoput. That miserable stretch of bumpy tarmac an autoput? No one would have guessed it. He demanded I pay a fine of 3,000 dinars on the spot—the equivalent of a pound. I told him I had no dinars.

How could I then buy petrol he demanded, not unreasonably. I showed him my remaining petrol coupons, bought in London from the Yugoslav Tourist Office. By an odd coincidence there was exactly 3,000 dinars' worth. He tried to take them from me.

'Oh no you don't,' I said firmly. The reason I had no Yugoslav money was that on a previous visit, finding I had rather a lot left, I had tried to change it for Greek money at a Yugoslav *Bureau de Change* on the border. The official in charge smilingly said I could do that more conveniently in Greece. When I got to Greece I found the Greeks wouldn't accept the money as a gift let alone change it for drachmas. I had no intention of being caught again. The petrol coupons were the only currency on me that would be accepted in isolated Yugoslav places. No policeman was going to take them from me.

The policeman began to shout and walk up and down, tapping his revolver holster with the palm of his hand. He demanded my passport. Foolishly, I gave it to him. He thrust his hand out demanding the petrol coupons, sure that he now had the upper hand. I refused. He muttered angrily. Impasse. I demanded that he take me to his senior officer. That did the trick. Sullenly he handed me back my passport and jerked his head at us in dismissal. He wouldn't let us fill up with petrol. We just made it to the next petrol station. The motto for the motorist in Yugoslavia should be at all times behave as though you are walking on eggshells.

As if to make up for the policeman's one-man anti-tourist drive, the Yugoslav Customs on the frontier with Greece dispensed with all formalities except the ritual (and surely virtually meaningless) examination of passports, waving us through with smiles and salutes.

A short no-man's-land to cross and we were in Greece. To one side of the road, in a sentry box raised up on a whitewashed dais, stood an Efzone, one of Greece's élite kilted soldiers. He smiled when I took a photograph of him. When we drove on he set aside his rifle, leaning it against the side of the sentry box, and drew from his tunic a pan pipe, reminding us that this was a land whose history stretches back to legends and myths that are still alive.

We were in Greece! Only a short distance away, where we had just come from, even the air was heavier. Soon now the waters of the Aegean would wash *Aeolus'* travel-stained hull, a sea which got its name, some say, from Aegeus, a king who threw himself to death from the heights of the Acropolis at Athens.

5

The feel of Greek soil, the first sight of her arid, scrub-covered hills lifts the heart, drives out thought of tragedy. There is a madness in the air of Greece, an intoxication of the senses which can disturb the balance of a man's mind, so there is danger in forgetting past tragedies. The Greeks of old knew this. Was not their guiding maxim moderation in all things? To withstand the force of Greece's impact it is necessary to hold on to reality, and to remember.

Aegeus, according to legend, threw himself off the great rock which dominates Athens, upon which his palace stood, in the belief that approaching black sails conveyed the news of Theseus, his son's, death. But Theseus, who had voluntarily included himself among the young Athenian youths and girls sent annually as hostages to Crete, had vanquished the Minotaur, seduced Ariadne of the ball of twine, who had helped him find his way out of the maze and escape from Crete, and was returning to Athens flushed with triumph—so carried away that he forgot to hoist the white sails which, he had agreed with his father, would announce victory and his own safety. A Greek tragedy indeed. But it is as well to look under the surface of things. Kings in those days were men in whom the power of the God resided. When their powers began to fail, the God, acting through his agents the priests, usually indicated that the time had come for the king to die. This is done to this day in parts of West Africa, where a chief is presented with a clutch of parrot's eggs as a token that it is time to kill himself. Should he fail to do so then he is killed by his chiefs. Of what use is a ruler whose potency is diminished? The only result of his continuing to live will be failure of crops, barren women and other disasters—the prosperity of a people is directly linked with the power of their ruler to create life. Perhaps Aegeus, who was an old man, felt the blow of his son's death was a gift from the gods which served to ease his way out of life. Who knows? But it is tempting to speculate, and who could resist doing so with a boat pressing close behind him which would sail for the first time in her life in the waters named after Aegeus?

Remembering the old story, and all the other legends that people this country with heroic memories, it didn't seem too fanciful to imagine *Aeolus* was crowding the Volkswagen, anxious after her long and captive journey for the freedom of her own element. No sea had as yet touched her hull. It was time I brought a term to her earthbound captivity.

There is a very good motor road from Greece's northern border to Athens, along which one can travel nearly as fast as one's impatience demands. And our impatience was great, Aelred's to get to his house building and mine to get to my sailing. Besides, our spirits were fortified by oozo and retsina, those two drinks which each in their very different and distinctive ways evoke Greece. Oozo is a spirit distilled from grapes which, when water is added, turns milky white. It contains aniseed and is found in all the countries of the Eastern Mediterranean: arak, zebeeb, raki are some of its other names. Pernod is its cousin and absinthe its lethal blood relation. Retsina is a white wine to which pine resin has been added. It is an acquired taste and some people never take to it, but once you do it becomes an addiction—beside it other wines seem lacking in body, spiritless. Like all wine, it can be very good or very bad depending on where you buy it—its quality rarely depends on price. There is also a red retsina, strictly seasonal and difficult to get, called kokineli.

Strong as was our urge to press on—mine was as driving as the force which must possess a lemming as it rushes, in a press of thousands of its fellows, to its plunging death in the sea—we found it impossible to pass Thermopylae without paying our respects to Leonidas and his glittering three hundred.

A memorial to the Spartans has been built by the Greek government and stands close beside the motorway. It is of some size, grandiose and of little architectural merit, unworthy—but it has a certain impressiveness for all that. On the opposite side of the road is the mound the Spartans raised, a monticule of earth covered in spring flowers. At the summit a plaque set in a low circular bed of marble pays tribute to the three hundred who fought to the death against the Persian Horde under Xerxes.

> GO TELL AT SPARTA, THOU THAT PASSEST BY,
> THAT HERE, OBEDIENT TO HER WORD, WE LIE.

It is a moving experience to stand at the top of the mound and look across the terrain where the battle took place. The sea is much further out now than it was then. But it is not difficult to set the scene and people it, to imagine the Spartans, not content to stand on the defensive in the pass, making wildly gallant forays into the plain—taking on time and time again, always at overwhelming odds, and under the eye of the Great King himself, the cream of the Persian army—and defeating them with heavy slaughter. Only as the day wore on, and their losses grew, did the Spartans confine themselves to the pass and to fighting on the defensive.

It is striking how, across time and distance, the human spirit finds similar ways of expressing resolve and endurance in totally dissimilar circumstances. Before the battle of Thermopylae the Persians were astonished to see the Spartans bathing and nonchalantly combing their hair, to all intents and purposes unconcerned at the prospect of the coming encounter with the vast panoply of Persia.

Among the Fulani of Northern Nigeria it is the custom, when youths are about to enter manhood, for the whole village to gather. The girls of marriageable age form a circle. Within this youths take their place in turn to be flogged by a companion who will himself later suffer the ordeal, until the girls say 'enough' and accept that the youth has endured sufficiently to prove that he is a man. It is a point of honour for the youth while he is being flogged to hold up a mirror and study himself in it, while combing his hair to demonstrate his indifference to pain. There are many similarities between customs found among people of petty West African kingdoms and those of the kingly states of ancient Greece—but the Greek passion for individual freedom with all that that has meant in the history of Western civilisation, is not found anywhere in West Africa.

The road to Athens for much of its length skirts the coast. It winds and twists, lurches inland and gives sudden, lovely glimpses of stretches of blue water. A Frankish castle crowns a hill. Mountains rise into clouds which cover their peaks, lending them mystery. A long dreary straight stretch of road has a petrol station standing at a road junction. It is like petrol stations everywhere but even more of an eyesore because it stands in isolation. You stop to fill up and realise with a shock that the mountain in the background is Olympus, home of the gods. That is Greece, a country where the fabric of legend jostles the pedestrian, a land where the plastic plague, expressed in articles of horrendous vulgarity, invades places venerated throughout civilisation as shrines to man's greatest aspirations and achievements.

Before you are really aware of what is happening, you find yourself being sucked into the swirl of pre-Athenian traffic. It takes hold of you and funnels you into Athens. Then, above the sea of buildings which the Attic plain has thrown up to make of modern Athens a metropolis, you see the Acropolis dominating the city from the heights of its rocky massif. You are almost in the place whose memory is engraved more deeply in man's history than any other in the world.

Athenian traffic has a life of its own, avid and concentrated, it has a rhythm unlike that of any other capital. To drive in Athens requires a special flexibility. To the driver of a car with a boat in tow, a combination which takes up some 35 feet of road, it could be nerve-wracking, but isn't. The Athenian is amiable and has time to give directions, and does so with a smile: he is a helpful man and friendly. A taxi driver, if appealed to, will signal that you should follow him and will put you on your way. The traffic police wear white helmets and make curiously stylised, hieratic gestures as they give their commands. If you fail to do what their signals require of you you will get a look of outrage, a shrug—and be waved on.

The old part of Athens is concentrated in a maze of streets and squares at the foot of the Acropolis, the Plaka. There are restaurants galore here, tavernas and joints—most of them catering for the tourist. The world and his mistress, the weird and the square, the beautiful and the grotesque, young, old, flower people and the vacationing businessman, young Greeks on the prowl, girls from all over Europe and the United States waiting to be picked up, touts and pedlars, even good bourgeois Greeks, jostle each other in this warren. And the Acropolis dominates it all, lends dignity to the hybrid swarm. When the visitors climb the hill and enter its precincts they exchange the hustling of the bazaar, the vitality of the fairground, for the peace of the sanctuary. The spirit of the Acropolis lays its calm upon the visitor —and no matter how many pullulate within its precinct, dominates them. This is something common to all the ancient sites of Greece. Even small Tyrins is never diminished by the shoals of visitors. Put to the sack, occupied, reduced, its buildings torn down and its people refugees, Athens has survived and resurrected itself through clusters of centuries: and the stones of the Plaka tell its story in their shattered, surviving remnants, glimpsed among an overlay of more recent building. Themistocles, Socrates, Pericles, Demosthenes and Alcibiades, that brilliant scoundrel, were citizens. Phidias, the painter, was an Athenian and so was Praxiteles the sculptor. Plato taught here—there is no end to the roll of distinction and honour emblazoned with the names of remarkable men.

Modern Athens, like New York, is a city consumed by a frenzy of building. Blocks of concrete go up and blocks of concrete come down, seemingly overnight. The city expands and bustles with activity. It is filled with the offices of great international companies, chic shops and urbane places where you can watch the swirl of life go by as you sit at your pavement table. Modern Athens has elegance and sophistication—and it is new. Its theme music is the chatter of pneumatic drills. And beneath the activity lies an Eastern languor, a feeling of leisure.

The Piraeus is something quite different. It is joined to Athens by a suburban sprawl as, once, it was linked to it by the wall Themistocles built against the investing Persians. It has a character of its own, a separate identity. The Piraeus has none of the elegance of Athens, and all the expansive, vital, rowdy vigour of a fishwife. There are no pretensions to gentility in the teeming streets surrounding the port. The place is a mart, a trap for sailors and a tourist clip joint. Boats from all over the world fill its harbour, from which Greek ships shuttlecock to and from the islands—busy maritime hustlers going about their business in a cacophony of noise from transistor radios and ships' loudspeakers. The Piraeus is clamorous, brash and on the make. It is a bazaar whose shops, stalls and booths burst with sacks of food, piles of fruit and goods piled high on shelves that climb to ceiling height. It is noisy and full of colour, a place of exotic smells, sweetmeat stalls, nut sellers, lottery vendors and peddlers, where melancholy men fingering a string of worry beads sit heavy-eyed over cups of Turkish coffee. There are little tavernas in side streets where you drink in a room lined with giant barrels and where the floor is strewn with sawdust. And there are the prostitutes, magnificent opulent women, some of them, whose eyes are shadowed with khol, and whose ringleted tresses—hair is an inadequate word for those dense, high-piled, black masses—give them a Byzantine look.

> La langoureuse Asie et la brûlante Afrique,
> tout un monde lointain, absent, presque défunt,
> Vit dans tes profondeurs, forêt aromatique!

They favour black satin, sequins and jet ornaments and stalk along, hips surging, on tiny feet in black patent leather shoes with stiletto heels. Making their way singly, in couples and groups through all this activity, are the kids of Europe and America. Men and women alike in jeans, packs on their backs, dishevelled, sweating and eager. They have the hungry look of people searching, and the lost look of those who don't know what they are searching for.

Even in a place like Athens where many languages are spoken, there is one great drawback to communication—as everywhere in Greece—the alphabet. Not to be able to read street signs and notices gives one a terrible feeling of helplessness—the feeling, in fact, that it's all Greek to one. A great effort is being made to help the tourist by introducing signs using the Roman alphabet, but it is well worth the effort to learn the Greek alphabet before going to Greece, and a few words of Greek. Better still, learn a few simple phrases. They will repay many times over the effort made to acquire them. Greeks are always appreciative when anyone makes an effort to speak their language. Learn to count and things become even easier. And, while on the subject of making life easier, carry with you a supply of toilet paper and a plug for wash-basins. Also, if you don't want to suffer from stomach upsets in Greece, eat moderately and only a little fruit at first. Stomach troubles may be caused by the olive oil in which Greek food is cooked, but more usually they are simply due to too much food and drink suddenly imposed on systems used to plainer fare.

An agreeable custom in Greece is that of walking into the kitchen and choosing what you want from the dishes cooking on the stove. Greek cuisine is limited—Greece is not a country for the gastronome. If you go to first class hotels—which means hotels in Athens and, possibly, Rhodes—you will get first class food—and it will taste more or less the same as food in first class hotels anywhere else in the world. It is one of the great mysteries of travel how large numbers of people are prepared to journey far and pay heavily to get the sort of food they can have at home. For those who want to eat and drink the food and wine of the country, Greece offers food that is good and cheap, some of it interesting; and a lot of it of Turkish origin. But nowhere will you find any of those little places which specialise in a dish so renowned that gourmets will travel a hundred miles and more to eat it, as people do in France: and there are no *circuits gastronomiques*, none of the literature, mystique and chichi of eating that you will find in at least the capital city of most countries. The Greek is simply not interested in food—and it is just as liable to be served cold as it is hot, or in the wrong order as not. What does it matter? The Greek eats to live and this perhaps stems from the days when a Greek citizen served the polis, and part of that service was to take the field at a moment's notice in defence of the city-state. Fat burghers make poor soldiers when Shanks' mare is your transport and fighting hand to hand—the continuity of a nation's basic traditions is persistent. Fish is usually the most expensive item on the menu—a surprising fact in a country which is so surrounded by water. But the fact of the matter is that these parts of the Mediterranean have been over-fished. Things are not helped by the Greek enthusiasm for using dynamite for fishing and of taking anything, however young and small.

I had booked my passage from Athens to Rhodes well in advance, but it is a good thing to check your sailings—if only because Greek shipowners, never too keen on publishing sailing lists, are very flexible about changing them. Anything can happen. Luckily, bad weather had delayed sailings from the Piraeus and there was no need for me to wait for the ship on which I was booked. I could leave the next day. One of the advantages of flexibility is that it works both ways.

Aelred's gear had to be got out of *Aeolus*. We couldn't unload outside his hotel so I parked on a convenient flat space near the harbour in the Piraeus. I took off the boat cover. This attracted a few spectators. A boat in a coat is not as common a sight as all that in Greece. The amount of stuff stowed in *Aeolus* caused a stir of interest even among the Piraeus's blasé inhabitants—people who through the centuries have seen it all. I found the sight of that grossly overloaded interior comforting. If *Aeolus* could carry all that weight the distance she had without straining anything there could be no doubt about her structural strength, not that I had ever questioned that. It was my own competence in stowing things that I doubted. Had I got the weight distribution right?

I left Aelred at his hotel and decided to spend the night in the Volkswagen somewhere near the harbour. Athens has a parking problem as acute as anywhere else and so has the Piraeus. The only vacant places I could find were near scenes of noisy activity which I felt would probably go on most of the night. Eventually I found a quiet backwater and settled down for the night.

I was woken by a violent banging on the side of the VW. I peered through a crack in the curtains. The street outside was swarming with lorries and men. There was a good deal of shouting going on. I gathered I was parked right in the middle of the access to one of the docks. I was, in fact, holding up the collection of a significant part of Athens' fresh produce. I dressed and emerged apologetically to confront the lorry drivers and stevedores. The place was by now a bedlam of expostulating, protesting men and honking horns. But the dockers and drivers were good-humoured. When they glimpsed the interior of the Volkswagen they became interested. Athens could wait a bit longer for its produce, they decided. Urged to demonstrate, I pulled out the cooker from its housing and lit it. I showed them how the fridge worked off both the battery and a gas supply. I pumped water into the washbasin, which swings cunningly up and out from under one of the seats. I let the roof down. By unanimous demand I raised it again. This sent them. 'Orea!' they exclaimed, 'Orea!' Beautiful! Beautiful! *Orea* is a very useful word and covers every shade of meaning from that's a beautiful girl to see how well your lavatory flushes. The two pipe cots, available when the roof is up, they found an enchanting bit of ingenuity. We played happily together. Thank God *Aeolus* wasn't there. If she had been Athens would probably have run out of supplies.

The ship on which I was to travel to Rhodes was the *Miaoulis*, named after a general famous at the time of the War of Liberation, and is a veteran of the run. *Miaoulis* has done the Piraeus-Rhodes run so often that she could probably find her way without benefit of captain or crew.

The crew, directed by a bosun weathered to chestnut brown by sun and weather, lowered *Aeolus* and the VW to the deck after some passionate altercation and fitted them somehow into impossible positions. The bosun even found time to make occasional soothing noises in my direction. *Aeolus* finally came to rest perilously close to a large bollard. With assurances to me that everything would be all right and not to worry, the bosun, humouring my anxiety, finally ordered a seaman to wedge a fender between bollard and *Aeolus*' side. I still wasn't very happy. Some naval ratings, who were much taken with *Aeolus*, told me to go to my cabin and not to worry: they would keep an eye on her. I left reluctantly for my small cabin. It was to be the last time I travelled in one in Greece. I now always travel deck. It is cheaper and if you have a sleeping bag, some food, wine and other comforts, a very agreeable way of spending a happy, gregarious time. Travelling deck, you come into contact with aspects of Greek life which, immured in the grander parts of a ship, you never see. On deck, everyone is your neighbour and you soon meet Tom, Dick and Harry or, in this case, Stephanos, Yani and Dmitri.

The Greek is by nature a traveller, a man forever on the move. If he is not off to some far country to make his fortune then he is travelling between the islands of his homeland. And when Greeks travel they don't travel light, they go with a good part of all their worldly goods with them. They also take along most of their family: grandma is there, sitting on soft amorphous bundles wrapped in cloth. Mother is there indulgently spoiling a covey of children and feeding them non-stop; and then there are cousins, aunts, retainers and friends.

Strewn about among the passengers are consignments of furniture, melons, baskets of red and green peppers, boxes of tomatoes and fish —dried, frozen, or so freshly caught that they are still flopping limply. At every port of call hawkers selling peanuts and cakes, lemonade and dried melon seeds, cashews and roasted almonds, thread their shouting way through the confusion, a basket slung over their arm and their bodies leaning steeply against its weight. And all these goods and people are stirred into violent movement every time the ship stops at an island. Caiques come alongside, take a gaggle of passengers off and replace it with another—accompanied by shouts, advice that no one listens to from anyone that has a mind to offer it, and occasional spurts of histrionic and very local anger. But the quarrels which appear about to flare into angry violence always dissipate in good humour.

The amenities of travelling deck are not distinguished. Simple food can be bought from a hatch in a space below, which at times looks like a scene from Dante's Inferno, and so can drinks. There are lavatories which make one long to be able to suspend natural functions for the duration of the voyage. There are primitive washing facilities. In compensation, and it is compensation enough, you can sleep in the open air and look up at a sky unbelievably studded with stars, and you have a grandstand view of life.

Travelling to Rhodes with a boat of my own on board held a particular savour for me. For anyone who had been in the SAS these waters were full of associations: landings in rubber boats, forays off submarines, raids with Foldboats and caiques. I had played little part in all this but it was with the Boat Squadron of the SAS that I had learnt something about handling boats, so there was a special appeal in returning to Mediterranean waters to learn something more about them.

6

The approach to Rhodes harbour is made more dramatic by the grey, raking shape of an American destroyer lying, immobile and helpless, fast aground on rocks close to the entrance. She was a total loss. It was the best possible warning to anyone of what can so quickly happen in these deceptively calm and smiling waters. The captain, so local reports have it, ignored advice about the dangers of the anchorage he had chosen. The wind shifted. The anchor dragged and the ship was lost. Even to a layman it looked an unsuitable place in which to moor. I resolved then and there that I would always listen to local advice—though I soon learnt to treat it with a certain caution. Advice which may be good in one place can be worthless only a few miles away in the temperamental Aegean.

All that remained now, before *Aeolus* could be launched, was the journey from Rhodes to Lindos. There are one or two curves and gradients on that road about which I was uneasy, but practice had diminished the misgivings I felt in England about towing a trailer. I knew now that, should the worst come to the worst, I had enough experience to face most manoeuvres I might be called upon to perform.

The VW was slung over the side of *Miaoulis* and deposited on the wharf. *Aeolus* followed. The sky was an even blue and the sun blandly hot, without the biting power it would soon have. People and goods poured off the ships lying alongside the wharf. Small three-wheeled trucks ran about among them with disturbing, bustling élan. *Aeolus* had survived the long journey virtually unscratched and I wanted to get her to Lindos that way. The angry buzzing of the little trucks was a threat which filled me with anxiety as they tore past.

Only one thing remained to be done before I could leave the docks and head for Lindos. There is a quaint custom in Greece—a levy imposed by the dockers on every car on and off a boat. It is perfectly official and there is no use protesting about it. But it is an irritation—especially when you are importuned for a tip as well by men who have done nothing but watch as you drive on and off. When you are slung

39

on and off the ship they do at least do something for the money they so imperiously demand.

Rhodes is a town of the Knights of St John of Jerusalem. The walls and bastions which ring it are their work. The harbour is protected by the defences they left behind. Into these they put the military genius of their age and of their Order, an Order of Hospitallers dedicated to the service of the poor and suffering: an aspect of their vocation they never totally forgot, unlike the Templars. Even in their heyday, when they became rich, noble and as proud as Lucifer, they continued to maintain a hospital where they tended the sick. Today, the one they maintained on Rhodes is a museum.

Rhodes became the headquarters of the Knights after they were driven out of Cyprus and, from 1309 to 1522, the Order remained master of the island and used it as a base from which to harry the Turk. What, I wondered, would the redoubtable Knights have had to say about a boat which had travelled from England and yet never once touched water? Whatever their comments might have been, they would have been well qualified to voice them for they were notable sailors as well as redoubtable soldiers.

The walls and bastions which they built are not only miracles of military engineering but things of beauty, whose stones glow biscuit gold in the sun. They stamp the Knights' seal upon Rhodes. Above them, minarets thrust to the sky their triumphant lances of faith to proclaim the final downfall of the Knights and the one-time supremacy Islam established over the island.

Sultan Suleiman the Magnificent conquered Rhodes after a siege which lasted six months. He is said to have used 200,000 men (some accounts put the figure at 100,000), supported by 300 ships, in the assault, and to have lost 90,000 men. The defence consisted of 500 Knights and some 6,000 Rhodian Greeks, many of whom were put to the sword when the Knights evacuated the island. Suleiman was so impressed with the tenacious courage of the Knights that he allowed their Grand Master, Villiers de L'Isle Adam, a man of over seventy, to lead the surviving Knights out of their fortified city with honour, permitting them to take with them all their belongings. Had it not been for the treachery of a Spanish Knight the siege would have lasted longer: the island might even not have fallen—on that occasion. But the rise of Turkish naval power in the Mediterranean made its fall certain sooner or later.

The Knights, when they left, took with them one of the wonders of the medieval world, one that rivalled that other, the Colossus of

Rhodes, all signs of which disappeared centuries before. The Great Carrack was a vessel of eight decks, so large that it carried a frigate on board and had another in tow, besides other craft carried on board. It was sheathed with six layers of metal below the waterline and never suffered a defeat. It could stay at sea for six months at a time and had a bakehouse on board which could make 2,000 loaves a day. It was fast, easily manoeuvrable and bristled with cannon. Like the Colossus of Rhodes, it disappeared without trace.

There is so much to draw the eye and stir the imagination in Rhodes that it is a temptation just to stand and look about, to absorb the place through the pores of one's skin. But standing and looking about is not an occupation of profit for anyone who has a boat to look after. I coupled *Aeolus* up to the VW and slowly made my way out of the dock area and towards Mandraki, the yacht basin and centre for small commercial craft.

I had intended to move off at once for Lindos but the temptation to stop and look at the yachts lying in Mandraki—a name which means the sheepfold—was too strong to be resisted. It was early in the season and yet there was plenty to see—there always is in Rhodes. And in the mind's eye one can see more, for this was the place upon which so much of Rhodes' life hinged from the earliest times. It was probably close to here that the Colossus stood until an earthquake destroyed it in 224 BC. Here, the galleys of the Knights of St John lay when not harrying the Turks (they were not above harrying other Christians too upon occasion, sometimes going so far as to ally themselves with the Infidel in order to do so); and it was upon the fort of St Nicholas, still standing on one of the breakwaters, that the Turks, in 1480, when they made their first attempt to capture Rhodes, directed the main weight of their assault. Sometime in the possibly near future there may again be something unique here to arrest the visitors' attention. There is a persistent rumour that American interests propose to build a new Colossus of Rhodes—one which will have a revolving restaurant in its head. Perhaps as the idea evolves it may become more ambitious. Why not stand the new Colossus on its head and make a helicopter landing place on the soles of its feet? Whatever form the project eventually takes I am for it. Anything to jolt architects out of their attachment to buildings looking like biscuit boxes is to be encouraged.

It is about 35 miles from Rhodes to Lindos. The road is good but difficult and narrow. Great tourist buses juggernaut along it at speed and the driver of a car can never relax his attention. The road was built by the Italians during their occupation of Rhodes as part of their policy of developing the island as a holiday centre. Its surface is good but it is surprisingly badly engineered, not a fault usually found in roads built by Italians. Italy occupied Rhodes in 1912 when she took the island over from the Turks, and gave it up in 1947 when the Allies, under the terms of the Peace Treaty with Italy, awarded Rhodes and the other islands of the Dodecanese—the twelve islands—to Greece.

Rhodes lies on a NE-SW axis and is about 45 miles long and 20 wide at its broadest point. The mainland of Turkey is only some 9 miles away. A mountain range, rising to its highest at Mt Attayoro, 3,986 feet, divides the island along its axis. Rhodes, in spite of its mountainous terrain, is fertile and has as a result, throughout prehistory and the historical period, seen the coming and going of wave after wave of conquerors and occupiers. Unlike the majority of Greek islands it is verdant the year round in spite of the fact that, like the rest of Greece, all its rivers are torrents. In summer these become dry boulder-strewn channels whose aridity is brightened by stands of oleanders on their banks, rich green clusters of foliage crowned with bursts of pink and white flowers.

The road to Lindos runs for most of its length along the coast, but occasionally swerves inland to pass through villages. These all have a character of their own. The biggest, Archangelos, is crowned by the forbidding, shattered remains of a great castle. Like most Rhodian villages Archangelos sprawls on either side of the road, the glare of its whitewashed walls broken by the purple and scarlet of hibiscus and bougainvillaea. The women of the village are of notably sturdy build, the older ones still wear enormous neutral-coloured leather knee-boots so shapeless that at first sight the wearer looks as though she is suffering from elephantiasis of the legs. They are, it is said, worn for protection against snakes when working in the orchards and fields. The island used to be infested with reptiles and was for this reason once known as Ophussia.

There is a legend that a king's daughter, suffering from an unsightly and incurable disease, was banished to Rhodes in ancient times. While on the island she was cured of her affliction and her father in gratitude sent Rhodes a herd of deer as a gift. Deer are the natural enemy of snakes. And so Rhodes' scourge of snakes was removed. There are still snakes on the island—but they are so scarce now that they are no worry. The legend is probably commemorated by the adoption of the deer as the symbol of Rhodes in addition to the rose. The entrance to the harbour of Mandraki is flanked by two columns. A deer surmounts each. Where these columns stand may be where the Colossus once stood—according to ancient belief it bestrode the harbour. Modern scholars maintain that there is no foundation for this belief. But scholars are constantly having their scepticism proved wrong by later research. One reason advanced for rejecting the possibility that the Colossus bestrode the harbour is that it would have been impossible for ships to sail under its legs. But the ships of those days were small and unstepping their masts would have been simple—and the statue's height was 105 feet. If one accepts the canon which established the proportion of the human body as being of 7 head lengths, this would give a height between the legs of the Colossus of 15 feet, more than enough for ships of the time with their masts down. Perhaps somewhere in some obscure repository of documents is a record of exactly where the Saracen conquerors of Rhodes found the Colossus lying. All that is known is that the pieces were still lying around in AD 656, eight centuries after its destruction, and that they were sold for scrap. Nine hundred camels were needed to remove the pieces.

Occasionally in small villages in the mountains of Rhodes one sees a set of antlers, the universal symbol of cuckoldry, nailed to a door. The snake is a symbol of fertility. The association of ideas is a thought for those interested in the universality and interplay of cultural beliefs and folk myths. In Italy to this day a woman being pestered by a man can get rid of him by thrusting out her hand at him with two fingers extended. The fingers used for this gesture of sympathetic cursing magic are the index and fourth. I am assured by an American woman friend of mine that it works. I once, as a ham joke played on an impulse, called out to her when she was looking in a shop window in Rhodes, using what I hoped she would mistake for a Greek wolf's importuning voice. 'Mees,' I called. 'Mees.' She is nearly six feet tall and athletic. She whirled round and threw her arm out like a javelin at me, making the sign. The fire in her eye alone would have been enough to put me to flight—so I can't wholeheartedly vouch for the sign's effectiveness: freely translated it means while you're making a nuisance of yourself to me your wife is at home putting horns on your head.

Except in Crete, I am told that the Greeks on the whole are not pesterers of women: and when they are it is usually merely verbal accosting of a fairly light-hearted nature. Bottom pinching, goosing and the rest of the male sexual skirmisher's tactile sampling armoury are not used. Even in a place like Rhodes, corrupted by tourism, a woman has little difficulty in shaking an admirer off. It is something which astounds me, for the come-on incitement to molestation offered by many female tourists has to be seen to be believed. Some of them appear possessed by a lust as consuming as that which drove the Bacchante to their excesses. Ariadne, it will be remembered, took part in one of these Bacchic orgies on Naxos, according to Marie Renault. Was that why Theseus abandoned her there?

Before leaving the subject of deer, and the power a two-fingered evocation of its antlers has to ward off prowling wolves in Italy, it is interesting to remember that the Hand of Fatima, Mohammed's daughter, a symbol to avert the evil eye, is represented with two fingers raised. Egyptians use the sign not only to ward off the evil eye but to curse people. By an evolution it would be fascinating to trace this two-fingered sign became one British soldiers adopted as a ribald and derisive insult, substituting the index and second finger for the index and fourth—an easier gesture to make. They also changed the thrusting horizontal movement which accompanies the sign's use into an upward vertical one. The gesture later spread to civilians and is still widely used in Britain. Churchill, by immobilising it, converted it into the V for Victory sign and made it respectable, on occasion deliberately employing the faintest of upward movements to restore the original military significance.

After Galathos, the last village before Lindos, the road dips, makes a steep crotchet inland, and then begins to rise again and run within sight of the sea once more, a sea of a colour not found in nature—a miracle, here, of hues that range from deepest ultramarine, through limpid greens and butterfly wing blues, to pale straw where the sandy bed slopes up to sweeps of beach. The road rises again, twisting; switchbacks up, and there, below, is Lindos. The Acropolis, enclosed within fortified walls, crowns a massive upthrust rock which rises sheer for 400 feet on the seaward side. The town clusters beneath the gentler sloping landward side of this. The foliate shaped expanse of Lindos bay is enclosed within embracing horns of rock which terminate in dominating heights, one surmounted by a tomb, that of Cleobolus, and the other by the Acropolis. Two islands guard the bay's entrance. The elements which form this panoramic view have an individual beauty, but it is as an assembly, something which takes the eye as a whole, that the sight is one of the most beautiful in the world. However many times one sees it it retains its power.

The road dives in steep curves into Lindos village and comes out in the Platea, the village square. A large shade tree growing out of a circular whitewashed plinth dominates this. The steps of the plinth are a favourite place to sit and lounge. Two tavernas face each other across the square, one with a vine-covered trellis inside from which bunches of grapes hang down, waiting to be cut and served to customers. On the landward side, facing the sea, a stream of water spouts from the side of the hill as it has done for thousands of years. A stone retaining wall, put up by the Turks and decorated with cursive inscriptions, holds the hill in place. Donkeys water from a trough filled by the spring's overspill. Every evening women come here with amphora-shaped earthen jars to get their household drinking water. Water for rough domestic needs and cooking used to be delivered in petrol cans slung across the backs of donkeys. There is now a piped water supply in Lindos but the women still come to fetch drinking water from the spring. The clay pots they use are slightly porous and cool the water by evaporation. The coming of electricity and the prosperity brought to the village by tourism is now displacing these. As households acquire refrigerators they take to plastic water containers, and so effectively throw away the advantages of one of Greece's greatest blessings, pure untainted water.

On the seaward side of the Platea is a low protective railing to stop the unwary, the careless or the drunk from stumbling over the drop to the land below, which runs down to the sea, a sweep of ground covered with lemon orchards, olive trees and vines. The main beach is a wide crescent throw whose expanse is never crowded even at the height of the season.

The sun was setting when I arrived, turning to red-gold the tops of the remaining columns of Apollo's temple, which project above the walls encircling the Acropolis.

People were strolling in the Platea. They glanced round at the sound of the VW's engine, indifferently. Just another car. In summer Lindos is invaded by vehicles and no one would have paid any attention at all. But this was still the off season and the sound of a vehicle drew attention. A man spotted *Aeolus*. This was something new. Interest quickened. A friend recognised me. People converged. My hand was shaken. I was embraced. *Aeolus* would soon be in the water. I felt as though she had come home. It seemed to me wholly appropriate that she should meet the sea here, 2,260 miles from the island where she had been born. I took the boat cover off her to satisfy people's curiosity. Admiring hands stroked her sides. Questions spurted. 'Plastic?' An indignant answer from me, 'Wood.' Astonishment was expressed and admiration of the finish, and a measure of doubt about whether she really was made of wood. Discussions started. Pundits began to hold forth about her. Even the donkeys which take

45

tourists up to the Acropolis turned in their stable and looked at her, wondering at the stir.

I sensed a growing uncertainty in the climate of appraising admiration for *Aeolus*. I soon discovered the reason. A fisherman was the first to voice it openly. 'How,' he asked, looking at me and then at the outboard well, 'can a boat with a hole in the stern sail the sea safely?'

I learnt later that a meeting was held afterwards in one of the tavernas to see what could be done to help me. Clearly I had been sold a pup. Such a pity—a beautiful boat in every other respect but just not seaworthy: any fool could see that.

7

It was too late to unload *Aeolus* that night, or even to think of establishing myself in the house my friends the Manus's had found for me. I had supper with them and, later, we walked into the village from their house overlooking St Paul's Bay and had a drink in one of the tavernas, Lindos by Night. Willard is American and a writer. Mavis, his wife, is a Scot, small and a dynamo, the focal point of much of the life of Lindos. They both speak Greek and are devoted in their efforts to reconcile the sometimes outrageous ways of foreign visitors with the customs and cast of mind of the Lindos people, about whom their fellow Rhodians have some disobliging things to say. There are equally many said about the people of Archangelos and other villages on the island. For my part, with a single exception, I have found the people of Lindos agreeable, kind and remarkably balanced in face of the pressures to which they and their children are subjected by the rising tide of tourism, which increases yearly. And what pressures they can be.

There are three different elements in the life of Lindos: the villagers themselves, a colony of permanent expatriates and the visitors who descend on the village in swarms during the summer, who are divided into two groups: the coachloads who come for a few hours, tourists, and those who stay for a few days, weeks or, like myself, a few months. The permanent foreign residents are British, American and German for the most part: painters, writers, sculptors and those with enough money to live abroad, who claim to be painters, writers and sculptors—the inevitable fringe found in any expatriate colony and which is so important to the development of any holiday place. Among them is a high percentage of the spiritually numb and the emotionally unbalanced, as is the case with many of the visitors too: they are the people who help give Lindos its peculiar summer flavour.

There was dancing in the taverna that night. When I had last been in Lindos the place had been a shop owned by the mayor. Now there was a new mayor who had built a pension—the use of the word was itself a sign of the changes taking place—right on the water's edge at the Boat beach, a small beach on the right of Lindos bay, in the lee of the Acropolis, used by local fishermen and residents with boats. The old mayor now had a shop further in the village and was constructing a new taverna at the tourist beach. The taverna which on my first visit to Lindos used to attract the liveliest elements among the visitors had gone. Its owner now owned Lindos by Night, a name coined by visitors. So Lindos was stirring and, I suspected, the pace of change would quicken. Another new taverna, a large concrete structure, was due to open soon at the tourist beach, I was told.

We drank our retsina and our brandy, exchanged greetings with Greeks and visitors, and clapped our hands in time to the deafening music from the jukebox to encourage the men dancing in the exiguous space in the middle of the floor. Dancing in Greece is almost entirely a male affair, though foreign women sometimes join in. I have never seen a Greek woman do so in a taverna, but then one hardly ever sees them in one. Men usually dance in a line, arms about each others' shoulders, and moving in a formal measure broken at intervals for a solo performance by any man who feels moved by the spirit of the dance. There is a strong narcisstic quality about Greek dancing and a total lack of selfconsciousness. If a man feels like it, he will get up and dance by himself. When he has had enough he will stop and quietly regain his table. Sometimes, the atmosphere will become charged and the quality of the dancing will change, become more athletic and exhibitionist. It is then that a dancer, encouraged and aware that he has the concentrated attention of the taverna's patrons focussed upon him, will give everything—he will leap and twist and spread his arms out, alternating passages of action with moments when his body, after slow stylised movements, remains poised, and then bends, snaps upright and leaps in the air. Sweat pours down his face. The clapping from the audience in time to the music grows louder and then the dancer stops, smiles and becomes awkward as he returns to his table to receive the congratulations of his friends, who glance triumphantly around, and the applause of the foreigners.

Tired, I excused myself and walked slowly to the Platea. I had decided I would take *Aeolus* and the VW down to the open space, a sort of hard, at the Tourist beach and spend the night there. Tomorrow would be time enough to unpack and settle myself in the house Will and Mavis had found for me.

There was not a soul on the Tourist beach or in the taverna in the corner by the rocks, which was dark and mysterious. The street lights of the village traced the outline of its streets, revealing how it was built on various levels—their shining brightness subduing the glow from the windows and open doors of houses, flares of life against the empty lampblack void of the night. The great rock of the Acropolis loomed, a dark presence sensed rather than seen against the sky.

The night air was fresh, stirred by a zephyr. It was 30 March and it had taken me seven days to get from my home in Barnes to my resting place for the night on Lindos beach. The only sound was the stir of leaves in the surrounding olive groves and the soft sluther of little waves on the beach.

I swam next morning in a sea the same colour as the pastel grey dawn. I had been too tired to make the effort last night. There was no one else about. Soon now the bare neutral whites and greys of the rocky heights surrounding Lindos would change to amber as the rays of the rising sun suffused them.

A fishing boat put out to sea and broke the cotton wool silence with the stacatto sound of its outboard engine. Then a donkey greeted the coming day. The donkeys of Lindos are a special breed. They take tourists up to the Acropolis and they transport produce, building materials or anything else they are called upon to carry. The donkey boys of Lindos—men around whom much of the life of the village revolves—speak to them in a language of trills, grunts, aspirated chokes and raucous 'ho, ho's!' assisted by wild leg movements and rooster-like flappings of the elbows. The donkeys appear to understand and can be controlled from a distance, their owners' voices exacting obedience in much the same manner as a model boat is guided by remote control. But the thing which distinguishes the Lindos donkey from all others I have known is its bray. It has a bray like no other donkey on earth. It starts with a prolonged wheezing. This is interrupted by a choking, followed by a series of swallowed gulps of wind which appear to provide the initial impulse for the beginnings of a bray. But this is short-lived. Then a series of distressing gulps and gasps seem to foreshadow the beasts' imminent and painful death. A forerunner of a bray emerges from this travail, gets going and is cut off as soon as it shows signs of coming to fulfilment. I have never yet heard a Lindos donkey achieve anything like a sustained, full-blooded, wholesome belly-expelled mother and father of a bray such as other donkeys all over the world produce. And even to express the eccentric, abortive sound he does make the Lindos donkey has to work his flanks in agony, heave with distress and stretch out his neck like a camel scenting water. And just when you think the poor animal has given up in frustration and sorrow, the whole performance begins all over again; or else the beast emits a plaintive mew like a kitten, sounds like a scolding woman, a child whining, a man groaning in his sleep. The noise like a ship's hooter is reserved for the night. It is made by donkeys stabled next door to your house.

I am told there is an explanation for the vocal disabilities of Lindos donkeys. Whether or not it is true I don't know. It is due, self-styled experts assure me, to the dustiness of Lindos. Perhaps. I don't think Lindos is particularly dusty. I have certainly been to very much dustier places. And yet the donkeys there appeared to suffer no impediment in their speech. But the donkeys of Lindos are as full of grace as any others. To prove it, they are just as prominently marked on the back with the Cross of Christ as their more vocally fluent brothers elsewhere. Curious, that the most exploited and generally ill treated animal in the world should be so honoured. Not that Lindos donkeys are ill treated. Far from it, although the unwanted young are left at birth to die on the hillside from exposure.

Taken by and large the Lindos donkey's non-bray, unsatisfactory as it may be in Ass's terms, is the most devastating comment on the human condition that I have heard, its painful frustration an appropriately incoherent description of the indescribable. And the human condition in Lindos at the height of the season at times shows characteristics as painful as any sound the donkeys of Lindos can produce. Only the male donkey brays. This, I am told, is connected with his erotic fancies and certain physiological dispositions attendant upon them. Should these not come to term before he brays fifteen times it is believed the beast will collapse and die. I should have thought if he couldn't make it by then he deserved to. No Lindos donkey that I have ever heard has shown the slightest sign of getting near even one decent bray so they are evidently a more than ordinarily virile lot.

I drove up to the Platea, already astir with lorries from Rhodes bringing in supplies. Mavis had given me the keys of my house the previous night. I got hold of Savas, one of the two odd-job men in Lindos, and with the help of his carrozza, a box on drunken bicycle wheels, we transported the mountain of luggage *Aeolus* and the VW had carried to my house.

Most Lindos houses are welcoming and pleasant. This one had a neutral coldness about it that I found depressing in spite of the glimpse of the sea one got from its courtyard. I made up my mind almost at once that I would move.

A peculiarity of many Lindos houses is that when they are let the landlord keeps one room for himself. In this he stores effects which, unless one is firm, he, or more usually she, inspects from time to time, although the room is securely locked and the landlord keeps the key. My house was no exception to this rule. The landlady's reserved room, the best in the house, was crammed with furniture. On being asked if some items could not be used to furnish the almost empty house she gave the classic Lindian reply: everything in the storage room belonged to her son in America and it was as much as her life was worth to touch a stick of it, though she did as a favour weaken and extract from the hoard a bucket with a hole in it which she presented to me—the only water supply was from a well in the courtyard. The son/uncle/cousin/daughter in American gambit is the one invariably used by Lindos house owners to excuse the paucity of furniture in premises let as furnished.

In fairness to them, landlords in Lindos have had some nasty experiences. In the house I had on a previous visit the tenants before me, an American painter and his Belgian mistress, had demolished the carved balustrade of the traditional raised platform found in Lindos houses to use for firewood. I knew of other examples of senseless vandalism, and had myself seen walls daubed with paint and houses reduced to a shambles after turned-on occupation. Similar treatment might at least have given this house character, I felt. But the first priority was the launching of *Aeolus*. Installing myself in a house, or finding another, could wait. I left everything lying piled in disorder and went to get help for what I anticipated would not be a simple task.

The Boat beach was out of the question for the launching because the only access to it was along a narrow, winding street through the lower part of the village and down a steep slope. There were only two practical alternatives: taking her to a place some miles away where there was a concrete ramp or to get her, somehow, into the sea from the area above the Tourist beach, where there was a drop of several feet.

Lindos, like so many other towns and villages in the Mediterranean, turns its back on the sea. As a source of fish the Lindiot accords the sea an almost mystical devotion, as do his fellow Greeks. But Greeks have none of the love of the sea for its own sake that is found in northern European peoples—nowhere in Greek literature is there to be found any of that appetite for mastering the sea in its fury that one finds in Norse and Saxon saga: and none of that temper which led Saxon pirates to raid at the height of a storm, confident in the prowess as seamen which allowed them to take advantage of the fact that no one would expect an attack in such conditions. No Greek will put to sea in rough weather if he can help it. Greek seamen, when the wind gets up, make for the shore, ignoring the fact that they would be safer if they stood out to sea. And this has been so all through Greek history. The Greeks have always stayed close to the shore and avoided stretches of open water if they could. This apparent excess of caution is partly due to the construction of their vessels. Made to pull up to a beach (in ancient times, as today, boats only sail at night if constrained by circumstances) they are of shallow draught. No man could endure for more than a limited time the violent motion of these craft in a rough sea—they roll fearsomely but will never go over.

In common with most other Mediterranean people Greeks associate the sea with trouble. It is from the sea that, more often than not, disaster came. Throughout history corsairs, raiders and invaders surged across it to commit their depredations. As a result the configuration of many Mediterranean towns repulses the seabord, as does Lindos, which huddles on the landward side round the Acropolis rock, protected by its steep cliffs from the threat of seaborne menace. No house in the village is sited close to the water except places recently built to cater to tourists. Corsica is a place where, notably, the inhabitants built their towns far from the sea. In parts of Africa similar reasons kept men from building near a water supply. There are villages where the women have to walk five miles and more each way daily to fetch their water. This caution is understandable: slavers and other enemies could easily follow a watercourse until it led them to a village, but the thick bush far from water offered sanctuary and a formidable barrier to those ignorant of its secret paths.

I discussed with Willard how best to get *Aeolus* into the water. He decided the thing to do was to consult friends in the village about the problem. We hadn't gone far when we met one of the donkey boys. We presented him with the matter. It should be understood that Lindos donkey boys are men of parts: farmers, shoemakers, mechanics. They are independent and self-reliant. After giving the thing some thought he called one of his friends out of Lindos by Night. Soon we had a group round us arguing the pros and cons of this or that solution proffered. Voices rose and tempers seemed to be getting heated. Then, in the way things have a habit of doing in Greece, agreement was suddenly reached. We all made for the Platea and piled into the VW. Enquiries shouted after us, about what we were up to received shouted replies. The enquirers said they would follow on down to the beach and give a hand.

By a general consensus of opinion it had been decided that the Tourist beach was the place—and the best method, to lift *Aeolus* bodily off the trailer and carry her to the sea. No one was interested in anything I might have had to say. Things had been taken out of my hands. Leave it to us they said. This did nothing to diminish my unease.

The straps holding *Aeolus* to the trailer were quickly undone. Discussions broke out. Orders were given. A great deal of frenetic bustling about and shouting went on. Then there was a lull, a paralysing moment of indecision, uncertainty and inaction. Suddenly, without any visible signal being given, a concerted advance was made on *Aeolus*. She was lifted off the trailer, manhandled down the wall of the hard, taken across the beach at a stumbling run, and lowered with triumphant shouts, laughter and formless self-encouraging approbatory gasps into the water.

And so, borne upon the arms of men, *Aeolus* was carried to her meeting with the sea—the first in her life. It was an appropriately reverent form of transport for a boat named after a deity—even if he was only a minor one.

There had been something incantatory about the cries attendant upon the launching. *Aeolus* now floated on a calm blue sea, affectionately touched by those who had carried her there, and surrounded with proprietory admiration. By invoking local help she had established herself as belonging to Lindos. The people of the village now had a stake in her. She was already no stranger.

8

Aeolus lay at anchor in shallow water off the Tourist beach, in full view of everyone in Lindos. But I felt the Boat beach would be more suitable and more private for her fitting out. It would be less disconcerting to go about unfamiliar tasks as unobserved as possible. Like *Aeolus*, the Seagull outboard engine was also new. It also had never been near water. My only previous experience with outboards had not been happy so I took care to see that the oars were ready for use. Most of the local fishing boats are powered by Seagulls and I was not anxious to fluff this maiden operation, which would have to be carried out under the eye of experts. The Seagull started at the second pull and the short trip across to the Boat beach went off with gratifying smoothness.

Other friends of mine, Polly and John Hope, came down to the Boat beach and, with Williard, gave me a hand in rigging *Aeolus*. With their help things went very easily. The main mast was stepped with only a minimal amount of indecision over what went where—cordage and stays were wrapped around it in a cat's cradle of, at first sight, alarming complexity. The mizzen mast presented no problem. Its erection roused the interest of watching fishermen. Such a small boat and yet it had two masts! The bumpkin slid into place and caused a puzzled ripple of speculation. The Wykham-Martin self-furling gear on the jib raised a surprised and admiring murmur which gave way to expressions of concern. Our preparations were interpreted as an intention on our part to go out for a sail. It was then that I learnt about the meeting in the taverna to discuss what could be done about the 'hole' in *Aeolus* stern.

The fishermen need not have worried. I had no intention as yet of going out sailing. There would have to be a period of restraint, of working up, I had decided on the way out to Greece—a time to familiarise myself with *Aeolus* and to get to know local conditions. I also had to have a good mooring and would have to prepare it myself. That would take time. The only place where I would find the things needed would be in Rhodes, at the junkyard there. There is no chandlery of any sort at Lindos but the village is well supplied with ordinary necessities: fruit, vegetables, tinned foods, groceries and drink are in good supply. Even Rhodes, for a town so much used by yachts, is poorly off for chandlery—and what there is is mostly for caiques. But visiting yachts can get diesel fuel and take on water at Lindos and there is talk of putting in a petrol point for boats. Surprisingly, there is none available in the village for cars in spite of the heavy traffic in the tourist season.

Anyone needing anything but the simplest things for boats must rely on Athens. There, most things can be got—if you are prepared to pay the prices asked and if you hunt long enough. But Rhodes has what is probably the cheapest petrol in Europe, the result of the special status accorded the island after its return to Greece. There is a great deal of talk about Rhodes being a free port with all the advantages that such a status has to offer in lower prices. I confess I haven't noticed that it makes much difference apart from petrol. Drink, both local and imported, is cheap, good and easy to get: oozo, retsina and local brandy are found in even the smallest tavernas. The most expensive drink is imported beer. There is a Greek brand, Fix, which is very good and much cheaper than imported brands, but waiters increasingly try to push foreign beers. A good and thirst-quenching long drink instead of beer is a mixture of white wine and soda water. Add a few cubes of ice and a slice of lemon and it is delicious.

One of the things which dissatisfied me about *Aeolus* was her cordage. I couldn't help looking sourly at the fused ends of her nylon sheets, warps and lanyards as I sat in her contemplating all that had to be done. They should all, I felt, be neatly finished off with a back splice, served and whipped. I knew nothing of these arts. And how to find out about them in Lindos?

The solution to various problems would have to wait for the next day. The sun was setting and I was invited to dine with Polly and John that night. I had not yet unpacked anything. Clothes worn in Lindos are far from formal and virtually anything goes—but dinner in just a pair of bathing trunks might be a bit chilly, though wearing nothing at all is perfectly acceptable on occasions. The practice of 'skinny dipping' at night was becoming fashionable. Occasionally a family of Scandinavians, Swedes for the most part, will strip to the buff and try to prance about during the day. The Greeks are not keen on this. They will put up with the most exiguous of bikinis and men may wear the sort of trunks that serve to advertise their masculinity, but total nudity offends Greeks and they won't put up with it. This is not surprising. It is only very recently that some of the younger Lindian men have taken to appearing in bathing costumes on the beaches—none of the older men would dream of doing so. No Lindian woman does so. As everywhere in Greece, except Athens, what goes for foreign women most certainly does not go for Greek women. The Greek likes his women modest and makes sure they are, but he is quite happy to enjoy the chances afforded him by the greater freedom foreign women enjoy—indeed it would be difficult for him to avoid doing so.

Polly and John Hope have a 'captain's' house—the sort of house the people of Lindos call a 'knight's' house. But most of the houses in the village which people call 'knights' houses are in fact ones built by sea captains. When the Knights of St John were in Lindos the garrison was almost certainly never commanded by more than two knights at a time—certainly never by enough of them to have occupied all the houses claimed to have been knights' ones.

You go up a set of curved white-washed stone steps to the Hopes' house. It is a rule in Greece that houses must be regularly whitewashed. The outside door in its ogival arch was, once, painted by Polly Hope in a pattern of geometric shapes in subdued earth colours. Unfortunately a Rhodian legislator has introduced a law obliging every door and window in Lindos to be painted brown. Protest as they might, the Hopes' door, like every other in the village, had to conform. The result of this unfortunate rule is that some of Lindos' bright beauty has been eclipsed. Nowhere now are there any of those splashes of colour, faded beautifully by the sun, which used, before, to point the buildings' harmony of line and mass. The dun rule is all the more regrettable because it springs from a misunderstanding. Lindian houses probably did have 'brown' doors and windows in former times, but it would have been the natural brown of oiled wood, not the excremental one of cheap paint. Only one door in all Lindos has escaped the ban. The reasons for its immunity lie in the reluctance of the police to challenge ancient powers believed to be possessed by the owner.

The outer door of the Hope's house gives onto an arched space and shallow steps leading up to a courtyard set with black and white pebbles patterned in a bold design and embowered in vegetation: banana trees, bougainvillaea, hibiscus, plumbago, and a frangipani in a pot. The feathered leaves of a jacaranda are etched against the white garden wall and the blue sky. A canopy of vines gives shade and the odour of watered, cool earth is permeated by the smell of damp earthenware pots and the perfume of flowers. A large main room leads directly off the courtyard. The room's high ceiling is painted and beamed. A long wooden platform running its whole length divides it. This, a reminder of the Turkish occupation, is a common feature in Lindos houses. Smaller platforms often surmount it and like it, have an ornamental balustrade. The main platform, carpet-covered, serves as a sitting-out place and the smaller, also covered in carpets, were used for sleeping. The space beneath is used for storage and is a very effective way of increasing the available area of a room. Steep steps led off the Hopes' main room to a smaller one, and an outside staircase from the courtyard to upper rooms giving off the flat roofs of the house, each separated by a low wall.

Inside the big room sea shell encrusted amphorae stand on the main platform, against a wall hung with John and Polly's paintings: coloured statements, uncompromising—his geometric, spatial: hers less stark but disconcertingly positive for all their representational elements.

Inevitably, over dinner the conversation turned to boats. The Hopes have a boat, a local one, brightly painted and decorated with oculi, which they sail—almost the only people in Lindos, Greek or foreign, to do so, everyone else uses power alone. Even when the wind is fair the local fishermen don't use their sails. As we ate our roast lamb and dolmades—meat and rice wrapped in vine leaves—we talked of the islands and the sailors of Greece, discussed their eccentricities and habits, speculated about the Homeric legend and drew parallels with modern Greek sailing methods. Towards the end of the meal, over coffee and strong Greek brandy, we talked of foreign yachts and yachtsmen. The Hopes told the story of a British yacht, a large and magnificently appointed one, making for Rhodes in almost a full gale. The owner, who knew Rhodes harbour well, decided to sail straight into Mandraki—not the easiest of entrances at the best of times. As the yacht raced forward under sail she hit rocks at the entrance, the same ones which had destroyed the American warship. Pounded by heavy seas she started to break up almost straight away. There were guests on board and a large crew. Some of them struggled ashore and, bleeding from their injuries, their clothes in shreds, made their way towards an establishment at the end of the mole where a fancy dress dance was being held. Laughter and applause greeted their appearance and it took some time before it was realised that the survivors were not people who had gone to elaborate lengths over their fancy dress. It was a sombre note upon which to end a pleasant evening.

After the warm comfort of the Hopes' house my dark and empty one was less inviting than ever. I examined the bed's lumpy, stained mattress by the light of a torch and rejected it in favour of my camp bed. It was typical of the house that the platform upon which I set it up was a wretched affair of cheap planks, and meanly proportioned. All the money had gone on making the house appear a desirable residence from the outside. It was a sorry example of what would increasingly happen in Lindos, a sad portent of the results of growing prosperity too suddenly come by.

Now that *Aeolus* was in the water and safe enough for the time being, I resolved I would begin my search for a new house in the morning. There seemed little point in living in one of the most beautiful places in the world in quarters as undistinguished as a seaside boarding house.

9

'Boats are made for water,' the man in Kelly and Hall's boatyard had said. What he didn't say was that once you've got a boat in the water you've only just started—it is then the real work begins and the problems present themselves.

The days that followed *Aeolus'* launching were busy, too busy for house hunting or to put the house I already had in order. I used it merely as a camp while Mavis, always patient in spite of her electric energy, looked for another for me. I spent most of every day on *Aeolus*, pottering—getting to know her—and marvelling at the number of new things there were to discover about even a boat of her small size.

One day I got an urgent message from Mavis. She had heard of a house that might suit me and would I look at it quickly in case someone else took it first: the demand for houses in Lindos was becoming intense. As soon as I saw it I knew I would take it. It was only a few doors up from one I had occupied on my first visit to Lindos, in a narrow lane. It had a courtyard with vines and consisted of two large rooms, one with a balustraded platform running its whole length. There were three platforms in the other room, one of them a double-decker. All had carved balustrades. Both rooms were divided by wide arches across them—possibly this feature of Lindian houses originated as a strengthening device against earthquakes—and the high ceilings were of mud and lath supported on beams. There was a kitchen and a separate lavatory—in many houses in the village this is often virtually part of the kitchen. An added attraction was that the landlord promised to install running water as soon as possible. Above all, the house was a welcoming one and belonged to a cousin of a friend, Tsampiko the grocer, whose shop was only a short distance away. At the corner of the lane was Dmitri's taverna—an advantage when there is a sudden call for more cold wine.

Anyone thinking of taking a house for the summer in Lindos need not worry about house agents. There may be difficulty in finding what is wanted at first but something will turn up even at the height of the season—though this may not be the case for much longer. And you can usually find a room. These cost around thirty drachmas a night and often are fitted up with a gas ring so that you can do your own cooking. It isn't a bad idea to first take a room and then look round for a house at your leisure—this will give you a chance of learning something about your future landlord's reputation. House agents should be avoided. The only ones on the island are in Rhodes. Friends of mine who used one found themselves involved in all sorts of complications and friction as a result of the agent playing them and the landlord against each other to his own benefit.

Lindos has a native population of about 700. All of them are more or less related. Spread the word that you are in the market for a house and the news will get around in a flash, almost before you have properly thought of it yourself.

One of the curious illusions foreigners in Lindos have is that their clandestine activities are unknown to the village: that, provided they confine themselves to their houses and courtyards, they can turn on, freak out, and be as kinky as used knitting wool without anyone being any the wiser. Folly. The police and the inhabitants of Lindos recognise the smell of hash floating over a wall as well as anyone, or a fair enough number do. They also know that foreigners go to Turkey not merely out of archaeological interest, or because their permitted period of residence in Greece has expired and they have to qualify for a further period by 'going foreign', but because a man can easily replenish his supply of hash there.

The people of Lindos are remarkably tolerant of foreigners' behaviour, as they are in most of Greece, but it is as well not to overstep the wide limits permitted. If you want to sunbathe naked in your courtyard, or loosen up with extrovert practices, at least lock the street door. Greeks have a habit of walking in without knocking. And if you occupy a bedroom directly on the street don't forget that sound carries. You may find anything taking place inside your room is being followed with lively interest in the street outside. An enthusiastically gregarious English girl I knew, although almost totally uninhibited, found the illuminating comments about her intimate life which followed her down the road next morning disconcerting.

If you do decide to take a house in Lindos you can hire a gas cooker cheaply and Greek gas cylinders are not only efficient—one make has a particularly neat flick-off safety device—but inexpensive. You have to pay a deposit of about a pound on the cylinder and another pound on the balance valve. You get this back when you return the equipment, minus a small charge levied on the balance valve. If you own one of those admirable single-burner Bleuet camping stoves that work off expendable bombs take a good supply of spare bombs with you. They can be got in Athens but are fiendishly expensive. The bigger French gas cylinders can also be got in Athens, at a price, and in Rhodes.

Rents in Lindos are going up all the time but you should still be able to get a house for about £25 to £35 a month. On top of that you will have to pay for the electricity you use and there may be a small charge for water.

The cost of living is what you want to make it. Local food and wine is not expensive and is good. In season, fruit and vegetables are plentiful. But once you start buying imported food, deep frozen or tinned, your costs mount steeply. Greece makes an increasingly wide range of tinned foods herself now. These are cheaper than imported ones but the range is still limited. The quality is good. You can usually get yoghurt. If you are a wine drinker then you can reduce its cost a great deal by buying it in bulk in Rhodes. You have to provide your own receptacles—and it is worth remembering that bottles are valuable things in Greece: they can cost more than their contents. Save bottles. You will need them—olive oil is also cheaper bought in bulk and so is oozo and brandy.

Laundry is as ferociously expensive in Lindos as it is in New York. But why use the services of a laundry woman? Besides paying her a king's ransom you will have to supply her with commercial quantities of soap and detergent. It is simple enough to do one's own washing. And in that sun clothes dry in a flash. And who cares whether clothes are ironed or not? Things like jeans don't need it and a little smoothing down with the hands when articles are wet works wonders.

I said I would take the new house and prepared to move in straight away. The rent was 600 drachmas—just over £8. Getting my mound of luggage from one house to the other presented a problem. The Lindos streets are paved with irregular stones, dark and marble-veined, sometimes touched with a red stain, ankle-turning flags of different sizes that have been polished through the centuries; and they are broken up with gutters, steps down, steps up, drains, pavements of a sort and bodged-up patches of cement and concrete. Carrying loads along them is not easy.

Thanks to a chance meeting the move was unexpectedly easy. Takis, the owner of Zorba, the biggest donkey in Lindos, offered to shift everything in his little three-wheeled Japanese truck. No wheeled traffic, at least none that is mechanically propelled, is officially allowed in the streets of the village. All vehicles must go no further than the Platea. Small handcarts, carrozzi, and wheelbarrows do the transporting. These have now been supplemented by miniature Japanese and German trucks and tractors of great versatility. By convenient administrative connivance the fact that they are not only mechanically driven but insanely noisy is ignored; they negotiate the narrow, steep, broken surfaced streets as nimbly as donkeys and are nearly as go-anywhere.

All my luggage was piled into the truck until the tyres were squashed nearly flat with the weight. Takis settled himself in the driving seat and invited me to clamber on behind. With a great burst of throttle we set off, twisting through the streets and lurching round corners with tremendous panache, Takis driving with enthusiastic and inspired élan as we swept along, greeting friends on the way. In one trip the tractor did what would have taken Savas and his carrozzo many hard, sweating journeys to accomplish.

The state of my two houses was now reversed: the first was now empty and the second a crowded shambles. But the new one was welcoming and would encourage and help settling in. But getting a house in order could wait.

The temperature was still moderate and the weather benign—conditions were as favourable as they would ever be for getting *Aeolus* ready for a maiden sail. There was one difficulty. I had discovered when rigging her that the mainsheet was missing. I would have to make do for a while with jib and mizzen only.

Three friends came with me. Two of them knew nothing about boats but the third had done some sailing. There was a good breeze out of the bay and enough movement of the sea to provide animation, and reflecting facets of water off which the sun struck dazzling flashes of light.

We headed out to sea with *Aeolus* going beautifully under jib and mizzen, so docilely that I soon discovered she would sail well without my touching the tiller. By experimenting with the set of the sails I got her balanced so that we sailed for twenty minutes without once using the rudder. I also discovered that the mizzen could be used effectively for steering.

It was a happy maiden voyage. Some of the aura of contentment it generated I'm sure entered *Aeolus*' timbers, helped to form her steady, agreeable personality.

To cap the quiet pleasure of the day we saw, as we headed back to Lindos bay, the seal. It had its home among the ledges of rock where the Acropolis heights end in a sloping shoulder of land that runs down to the sea. The local fishermen dislike the seal and complain that it takes too much fish, but foreign residents and visitors are on the animal's side. We got so close to it that we could clearly see its sleek brown head, small and round, and its liquid marble eyes watching us. It would dive and then come up for another attentive, intelligent look at us. It appeared to be content and was in beautiful condition but we felt it must be lonely—no one had ever seen another anywhere near Rhodes although its species is indigenous to the Mediterranean.

Seeing the seal was a bonus to a good first day's sailing. My next trip beyond the bay was to be a very different affair. A few days later Boreas, the North Wind, swept over the heights above Lindos and across the bay. The sea rose angrily in response and, beyond the two islands which guard the entrance to the bay, became a heaving turbulence. It was, I judged, disturbed enough to demonstrate *Aeolus'* seaworthiness to the fishermen who had expressed alarm at the 'hole' in her stern—and, for that matter, to myself. What, after all, did I know about her capacities in bad weather? My trust in her qualities was based on confidence in her designer and her builders, and in the look and feel of her.

All the fishing boats were drawn up on the beach, a sure sign that the fishermen took the weather seriously. As I got *Aeolus* ready I was watched with a certain wariness by men working on the path leading down to the beach. I heard my name called and saw a friend waving at me. Hal is a painter and had helped me to get *Aeolus* ready when I first arrived. He had also mended the hole that had been punched in her stern in Yugoslavia, so skilfully that no sign of damage could be seen. He has lived in Lindos for many years, speaks good Greek and is an accomplished cook and dextrous craftsman. I asked him if he would like to come out with me.

'Sure,' he said.

There is something distinctly nautical about Hal. It is to do with the way he walks, a sort of West Point step with the angularity smoothed out of it. But it was only after knowing him some time that I learnt he had been in the American Navy.

As we set off, a fisherman in the group working on the path called out to us.

'They don't seem too happy,' I said to Hal.

'Those guys are always unhappy about something.'

'What did he say?'

'That they don't like the weather: reckon it's too rough to go out.'

I headed for the entrance to the bay and began to have doubts myself as I felt the shift of the sea gathering force as we drew near the two islands at the bay's entrance. But I wanted to find things out about *Aeolus* and the only way to do so was to take her out in a sea.

We drew level with the islands. I eyed the slopes of water ahead with misgiving. *Aeolus* rose to the waves, untroubled. While I assured myself that my doubts were unjustified, we motored on. But the waves were growing bigger, rising higher before us, and our downward plunges grew steeper. Things were rather more than I had bargained for. It was what might happen when I turned to head back that was exercising my mind now. What was Hal thinking, I wondered.

'All right if we go on for a bit?' I asked him.

'You're the boss. If it's OK by you it's OK by me.'

The trouble was that I wasn't really the boss. The sea was the boss. It was all right as long as we were heading into the stuff. But what of the moments when, going about, we would be broadside on to those waves? I was idiotically tempted to tell Hal the story of the two Welsh miners who went to the seaside for the first time in their lives and hired a boat for the day. While they were out, happily paddling about, a storm came up. Religious, like all the Welsh, they fell to their knees in the bottom of the boat. 'Almighty God,' one of them prayed aloud, 'in this our hour of peril we beseech Thee send Thy only begotten Son to succour us.'

'Don't be a ploody fool, Davy bach,' the other miner shouted, 'tell the Old Man to come himself. This is no boy's work, indeed!'

'Going about now, Hal,' I said, recognising the fact that I couldn't just go on steaming ahead forever. 'Hold your hat.'

'OK.'

Aeolus went about smoothly, as steady as a plane banking in the sky. Elated, and relieved, I asked Hal if he minded if we headed out again and tried another turn, a slower one this time.

'OK by me.'

Confident at the way *Aeolus* had behaved the first time, I went about very slowly. *Aeolus'* behaviour was impeccable. On neither occasion did she take any solid water over the side, though we took enough spray in our faces.

We made for home. *Aeolus* slipped the following seas beneath her as calmly as she had breasted them on the way out. And not a drop of water had come aboard through the 'hole' in her stern.

We had been attentively watched from the shore. We got back

to find the reputation of British boatbuilding was high. There was to be no more talk of holes in sterns.

'—and besides,' said a Greek acquaintance who had watched us, after assuring me that the waves had been 5 metres high (my own estimate had been a few centimetres under that), 'she is beautiful and makes our harbour more beautiful.'

Hal was less lyrical. I heard a few days later that he had said when discussing our expedition 'I thought he was going to keep right on going until we got to Turkey. And,' he added, 'there wasn't a Goddam thing I could do about it! It was great!' I only learnt much later that his naval service had been confined to a drawing board in a naval architect's office.

Aeolus had had her first experience of troubled waters. So had I— in a small boat. My next excursion into rough water would be under sail, I resolved. How would she behave then in strong winds and a heavy sea? The opportunity to find out soon came. I decided I would go out on my own. Greeks advised me not to. I assured them I was going to stay in the bay. They pointed to the streamers of spray being whipped off the waves and driving flatly across the surface of the sea, shook their heads in warning and gesticulated to get their meaning home to me. But I was set on going and already having difficulty in handling *Aeolus* at her moorings. I could spare little attention for them. The fool in his folly ... Shades of that destroyer aground off Rhodes harbour, and the resolution I had made about always taking local advice!

Children had been playing with the Wykham-Martin self-furling gear. I found I could neither set the jib properly nor furl it up again. I cursed the mistaken benevolence which had led me into allowing children anywhere near *Aeolus* as she went across the bay like a horse with the bit between its teeth. I cursed my idiocy in not having checked things more carefully before setting off. And I just cursed, pure and simply.

I was in two minds about what to do, floundering—and learning that a boat can behave with all the intransigence of a horse out of control, and that it is even stronger. I was already too close to the rocks near the tourist beach to be happy about cutting the sheet and letting the jib fly and starting the Seagull. If it didn't start straight away I would be in real trouble. At least with the jib pulling, jammed as it was, and however eccentrically, I could turn into the wind and have a chance of gaining some room to manoeuvre and perhaps a little time. Finally, I decided to start the Seagull straight away. If it didn't fire first time then I would think again and turn into the wind. It started first pull and, with that sweet sound obliterating those of wind and waves breaking on the rocks, I headed for the Boat beach like a cur for its kennel—and getting *Aeolus* secured in that wind taught me some lessons. There is no doubt about it, the only way to learn how not to do something is to do it.

10

Willard Manus is a skin diver who brings to his sport an almost fanatical devotion. But it is not just a sport—his catch goes to feed his family and friends, nothing he spears is shot for just the sake of the kill. The next time I went out in *Aeolus* was with him. The sea was calm. There was no wind at all so we motored. In any case, Willard is not the man to allow an interest in sailing to delay him when he has a date with fish. He had lost one the day before, a grouper, and had had to abandon both fish and spear because of failing light. He wanted his spear back and he wanted the fish, and anticipated difficulty. Things would, he felt, be easier if he could work off *Aeolus* instead of having to dive and handle a boat at the same time.

The Seagull pushed *Aeolus* along happily against a hard set. I had replaced the standard tank with a one gallon one to reduce the frequency with which that tiresome chore, refuelling, comes up. But it still did so too often for my taste. Why hasn't someone devised a simple, unmessy way of filling a Seagull outboard's tank? And why don't Seagull make a larger one? Much as I came to admire the sturdy simplicity of that engine, I never failed to curse its primitive filling system—all very well on a river, in a harbour, or in a calm sea. But in any kind of uneasy water it is a messy, awkward operation which should, and could, be avoided. But there is no alternative, in my view, to a Seagull in Greek waters. All its rivals, quieter though they are and with better filling arrangements, are too sophisticated and difficult to maintain. Even a simple operation like clearing the fuel line involves dismantling half the engine on most of them. The Seagull is known in Greece and it is not difficult to get help if you have difficulty in putting something right yourself. Even I, no mechanic, can do most things needed to get one working again. They are good, reliable engines. They are noisy and they are damnably limited. Without sacrificing their great qualities of simplicity and reliability I can see no reason why they shouldn't be improved by having a bigger fuel tank, a better filling system and some means of reversing. The makers maintain that it is not necessary to have a reverse if you know how to handle a boat. The short answer to that is a word of one syllable. As one of the Law Lords interjected during a debate on gaming, when another inadvertently said roulette was a game played with cards, 'balls, my Lord, balls'. There are certain conditions, crowded anchorages, ports and busy rivers, when running with a strong stream, when to be able to reverse is essential. I would recommend anyone who needs an outboard in Greece to go for a Seagull every time—unless one wants an outboard for high speed work—water skiing and so on. But, with just a little extra, what an engine the Seagull could be! As it is, it is pretty remarkable—what other engine would put up with a diet of paraffin and olive oil as some Seagulls in Greece are said to do?

I carry two anchors on *Aeolus*, a CQR and a fisherman, the kind with a collapsible stock. My trip with Willard was to teach me that there was a time and a place for each of them. I was also to learn that there is a time and place for both of them at once—and that a third is useful on occasions, or would be if one had one.

Manoeuvring in accordance with a spear fisherman's requirements I found valuable experience, especially when approaching rock faces—something which my time in the Boat Squadron had taught me about. But in civilian conditions you need a finer touch—the craft you are using is not expendable, a consideration which does much to modify one's approach to certain nautical problems.

Willard, whose tenacity of purpose when hunting fish is remarkable, finally dislodged his grouper from the awkward holes in which it had, wounded, taken refuge. The appearance of a spear fisherman as he goes about his work is dramatic. The black rubber suit, flippers, helmet and goggled mask transform a friend into a sinister aquatic being. The surfacing and dives achieve a ritualistic quality that contain, for me, an element of awe.

Will dived repeatedly, came up to rest, dived again. He would heave himself up out of the water, flop into the boat to rest, say 'son of a bitch' and gasp for breath, bending over. 'Jesus' he would say, shaking his head, and then pull his mask down over his face again and go over the side once more. I would hand him his gun and he would swim until he was once again over the place where the grouper was holed up. A tumble, glisten of wet black rubber in the sun then webbed flippers rise vertically to the sky and sink silently from sight. He broke surface after an impossible time for a man to hold his breath under water. A shake of the head, black and gleaming in its rubber skin, other-worldly, an upraising and sinking of the flippers, and he was gone again.

And then he surfaced. A fish was on his spear. I took it from him and helped him into the boat. He sat bowed and breathing heavily. The fish flopped on the floorboards. It was not the wounded one he had been trying to retrieve but another he had spotted as he went down, also a grouper and one which had recently had a meal. As I watched it agonising it vomited and brought up a whole fish, hardly damaged as yet by digestive processes. The grouper was very beautiful in spite of the large ugly head with its brutal underslung jaw. Its belly was a pale, golden autumn colour, its sides and back pink and green overlaid with russet. As I watched, it died and its eyes filmed over with a pale, milky blue glaze. It weighed $12\frac{1}{2}$ kilos and was the biggest fish Will had caught since he had been in Greece. $12\frac{1}{2}$ kilos is a big fish—for this part of the Aegean anyway.

Greece is a country where the catcher of fish has stature. The catcher of a big fish walks to the acclamation of his fellows. Willard carried the fish over his shoulder and all the way through the village he was stopped, his hand shaken, the fish admired. 'Bravo! Bravo!' people called out, smiling. The streets stirred on our passage. This was an event. A man asked if he could take photographs. He did, shook Will warmly by the hand and congratulated him once more. It was a shock when the photographs arrived accompanied by a hefty bill! There are opportunities everywhere and a certain justice in a hunter being caught. I carried Will's gear for him through the village and so earned a share of the triumph, and *Aeolus* got the reputation of being a lucky boat.

There were things I had to get for *Aeolus* in Rhodes—is there ever a time when there aren't things to be got for a boat? High on my list was something I could use for a mooring. Hal and Will decided to come along. They both, besides being Greek speakers, know Rhodes well. In their company doors would open and I would find it easier to get what I wanted.

The Greek is a friendly man. And the tradition of hospitality to the stranger is very strong among them. At home, Greeks are very different men to Greeks abroad where, often, they are obliged to resort to questionable stratagems in order to make a living. In his own country the Greek, though still avid for a sharp business deal, is ruled by his tradition of hospitality to the stranger. If he considers you his friend he will not do you down. If you are introduced to a Greek by a friend, the man will as like as not forget business and wave aside payment in small transactions. This can at times be embarrassing. Among country people this tradition of hospitality to the stranger often leads to abuses on the part of foreigners. I have heard hippies and flower people boasting of how they have travelled all over Greece at virtually no cost to themselves, relying on Greeks to feed and shelter them. Very often they are the children of well-to-do parents and well able to pay their own way, and the peasants they batten on are often living on a subsistence borderline. How the Greeks remain as tolerant of this kind of sponging as they do is difficult to understand.

I also find it difficult to understand the capricious way in which Greek officials, especially those on Rhodes, sometimes exercise their authority over foreigners. If you are an American you are allowed a residence permit for two months in Greece. If you are British the period is three months. Technically, after that time, a renewal can be refused. This means you have to qualify for another residence permit. You can do this either by applying for an extension or else by visiting Turkey, the nearest foreign territory, for as brief a time as you like—it is sufficient to just stay long enough to get a stamp in your passport to show you have been there. This is a bore but many people don't mind because of the ease with which they can renew their supplies of hash in Turkey—but the Turkish authorities are getting tougher about the sale of drugs. Some enterprising people have been known to grow their own in Lindos, and for them a trip to Turkey is not necessary. My new house was at one time a main source of supply in the village —the weed was grown in the flower beds by some Americans who occupied the house. When I took over all the marijuana plants had been uprooted and only flowers and shrubs of basil remained, that herb which is not only used for cooking but to ward off bad luck. You often see a pot of it in the bows of a caique. Some friends of mine once hired a fisherman to ferry them between a house they had taken on an offshore island and the mainland. One day the boat broke down. Next day there was a pot of basil in the bows. There was no more engine trouble after that. To qualify for a further three months residence in Greece most people from Rhodes go to Marmoris, a small Turkish port only two and a half hours away by tourist boat or four hours by caique.

No one has ever worked out the grounds on which residence permits are granted or refused on Rhodes. Some of the most respectable foreigners in Lindos have been thrown out at a moment's notice; in one case a family with young children to whom great distress was caused by the peremptory expulsion—they had been resident in Lindos for a long time. And yet real scoundrels are allowed to stay, undisturbed, for as long as they like. The orders come from Rhodes, so gossip has it, from someone with a taste for exercising arbitrary power. Whether this is so or not I don't know but whatever the explanation, it is a manifestation of Greek official xenophobia which leaves an unpleasant taste. I cannot understand how a people as kind and hospitable on a personal level as the Greeks can behave with the official churlishness they show at times.

As time went on I began to hope that I would be asked to leave. With a boat of my own a quick trip over to Turkey would, I felt, be no problem. But there is a snag to visiting Turkey. Every time you leave Greece, if you have a car, it has to be put in bond and the fact recorded on your passport, or it has to be transferred to someone else's passport. On each occasion there is a terrible palaver. The Customs officials in Rhodes are pleasant and helpful but the system is ponderous, time-consuming, wildly irritating and out of date in an age of tourism; especially in a country which is coming to depend more and more on tourists.

The junkyard in Rhodes is everything a junkyard should be. It lies off a street that runs at right angles to the road skirting the sea, nearly opposite Petros boatyard—a place well worth visiting to see how caiques are built—and is difficult to find. The street off which it lies is almost entirely given over to workshops, open-fronted, in which oil-blackened Vulcans labour cheerfully over car engines, lathes and Heath Robinson machines whose functions are known only to their servants and, perhaps, Haphaestus, god of craftsmen.

The junkyard is piled high with lengths of chain, sheets of metal, anchors, old lamps, old ovens, iron rods for building, twisted metal frameworks, parts of lorries, bedsteads, wrecked fridges, busts of Italian dignitaries and anything else made of metal which could possibly, sometime, be used by somebody somewhere for something. All this is arranged in mounds. To thread your way through these can be for the unwary hazardous. Nothing is sold as an item, everything by weight.

I found a superb manifold from a large lorry, a thing which, entered as a piece of sculpture, would have won a prize in any Biennile. Filled with cement, and with a good length of chain twisted about it, it would I felt hold *Aeolus* in any weather.

While I was in the yard I took the opportunity of ordering an Italian army beds. These, when the canvas is removed, convert into elegant tables. Hal discovered their conversion possibilities and, as a result, they are now fashionable and hard to find.

Rhodes town is divided into two parts: the old walled city, built by the Knights of St John, and the new one which is largely the creation of the Italians. The Old City is a place of paved squares and narrow cobbled streets, of arched colonnades, and shops nestling within the defences. Access is through gateways in the massive walls. In the complex of alleys, lanes and passageways which make a rabbit warren of the Old City there are mosques and old houses, some with balconies overhanging the streets which bring to mind thoughts of the seraglio —it is not hard to visualise women peering secretly through the wooden lattice-work screens which front them. There are also cafés and tavernas and eating houses where you can still have a meal at reasonable prices —those lining the Mandraki in front of the New Market, built by the Italians, can take the visitor for a ride. But it is so agreeable to sit in the open, sheltered by their coloured umbrellas, and look at the yachts lying in the harbour opposite, that the price of sometimes being cheated is worth paying. And there are others inside the market, where you can eat and drink while enjoying the displays of colour on the fruit and vegetable stalls and watching the jostling, noisy animation of the place.

In the Old City the prices are for the most part still reasonable and the cheating of the tourist not altogether shameless. It is the custom to bargain. If a man pays the first price asked, either through ignorance of custom, diffidence, lack of time or disinclination, then that is his look out and the good fortune of the shopkeeper. To bargain is normal —a hangover from the days of barter economy when haggling was the only way to establish the value of articles.

Much of what is offered to tourists in these shops is specially made for the tourist trade, but there are interesting genuine articles to be found, many of them from Turkey—where the value of local objects as articles for sale to visitors has only just begun to be realised.

Tourists' time is usually limited. They are guided round the sights by guides who take them to the most important places, and on the whole do it well. If you want to see what is of most historical importance without wasting time this is probably the best way. Whatever else you may be taken to see, you will certainly be shown the Museum, once the hospital of the Knights, the Grand Master's residence, and the narrow upward sloping cobbled street in which were the various 'Inns' of the Order.

The Knights of the Order of St John of Jerusalem were divided into eight 'tongues' corresponding to their nationality: France, Spain,

Italy, Provence, Auvergne, Aragon, Germany and England. Germany and England several centuries later were to give birth to protestant branches of the Order. That of England survives to this day in the form of the St John's Ambulance Brigade, ubiquitous at all sporting events, of which HM the Queen is Patron—and which continues the Order's ennobling tradition of helping the sick and injured. It would be interesting to take one of those terrible warrior knights to a football match and point out to him the flat-capped men with first aid bags slung over their shoulders as comrades in arms. The knight would probably burst his armour with rage—they were very proud and patrician knights who only gained admittance to the Order if they could prove at least four generations of nobility (six for the Germans). Their dress would add a lively note to an English winter's day: in armour, a red surcoat with a white cross on the back and front: in undress, militarily speaking, a black robe with a white cross on the breast, like the men on the football field.

There is too much to see in Rhodes in one day, let alone a few brief hours, even with the help of a professional guide. My own feeling is that it is more satisfactory, and a better way of getting the flavour of the place, to simply stroll around. You can read it all up later at your leisure and enliven the pages of the book with the help of your stored impressions. In any case if you are unlucky you may get a lamentably pedestrian, bowdlerised version of history from your guide; and you will be unlikely to be shown much of what has been left behind by the Turks. And they left a lot, including the library of Rhodes which was established by a rich Turkish merchant. The Sultan of Turkey, so the story goes, on learning that the merchant Ahmet-Aga had started the library with 150 books ordered that a further 800 books from the Sultan's personal library should be added to it. The Turks were not always the mere ravagers they are so commonly held to be.

One of the features of the Old City no visitor can fail to notice is the piles of large stone cannon balls lying around. These litter the moats, are strewn about the ramparts, and are embedded in the walls. He will be assured that they were used in the siege of Rhodes. This is almost certainly not so. Most of them were probably made for export. Rhodes was once the centre of the Mediterranean arms industry.

But Rhodes is not just an island containing areas of architectural interest and sites from the days of antiquity, although it has these in plenty. In Rhodes city there are night clubs and grand hotels—which look like grand hotels pretty well anywhere. They are all sited on the west coast of the island, the side most disadvantaged by nature, though more highly developed by man. During the summer months the prevailing winds are generally north-westerly and raise a sea which surges against the west coast's beaches. The east coast is mostly calm in summer and has sandy, sheltered beaches, many of them deserted or nearly so.

During the Italian occupation Rhodes was given certain advantages and some of these have been continued since the island's return to Greece. As a result, some goods are a bit cheaper on Rhodes than on the mainland of Greece or the other islands. Another legacy left by the Italians is a number of municipal buildings including the Governor's Palace, a building in the manner of the Knights of St John, but with its proportions inflated by the vanity of the Mussolini epoch. Seen against the panorama of the town, in a framework softened by clumps of bougainvillaea, strands of palm trees and the soft greenery of the island, so unlike most islands in Greece, it is not too synthetically obtrusive. And it is no more spurious than the three windmills which stand on the mole across the harbour at Mandraki, their sails turning merrily only to catch the tourist's eye.

A special attraction for tourists are two camels upon which they can sit for a fee and have their photographs taken. They are placid beasts and as supercilious as the rest of their kind—but who wouldn't be if he belonged to an order which, alone among living creatures, is the only one that knows the hundredth name of Allah. Even man himself, self-styled Lord of all creation, knows only ninety-nine. Though why the camel of all living creatures should be so honoured I cannot for the life of me understand. It is a beast of admittedly great qualities, ones notable enough to balance its atrocious disposition. Man could not survive in the desert without its help, but there is nothing lovable about the beast. Its breath is corrosively offensive, its teeth filthy and its temper uncertain. It bites and has the distinction of being incapable of mating without human intervention, which is perhaps why it is forever complaining. But with all its faults it has inspired a magnificent piece of verse—one which begins:

> The sexual life of the camel
> is stronger than anyone thinks
> For in moments of sexual excitement
> it frequently ... and so on

and ends:

> Which accounts for the gloom of the camel
> and the sphinx's inscrutable smile.

No animal can be wholly bad which has inspired so distinguished a piece of poetic ribaldry. Before finishing with the subject it should be said, for the benefit of camel lovers, that all this applies to the common or garden camel and not to those altogether superior beasts, the noble racing camel. They are, so to speak, a different kettle of fish altogether.

With our purchases in the car, manifold and chain for me, groceries and milk for Willard's children—why do Americans have an almost religious appreciation for this tedious fluid? something to do with being hung up on the American Mother, I suppose—we were ready to go back to Lindos. Hal, a man who likes his food, was still in some restaurant in the town. Will and I waited for him with growing impatience. Already Rhodes had palled on us and we wanted to get back to Lindos. There is something about the place which draws one even after only a short absence. Besides, it was the first time I had left *Aeolus* for any length of time and I was becoming anxious. What if the wind had got up while we had been away? What if it had veered so that, should *Aeolus* drag her anchor, she would be swept onto the rocks?

When we got to the crest of the hill overlooking Lindos my heart missed a beat. There was a high wind blowing. All the way from Rhodes I had been conscious of it buffeting the trees and bending the grass over the verges of the road, but I only now realised its full strength. *Aeolus* wasn't at her moorings. I restrained an incipient wail of alarm. And then I saw her. She was further out from the shore, moved there by fishermen and secured by three anchors, one of them from Willard's boat, *Maritsa*. But what of her? She had been hauled ashore—there is a fraternity about boats which is universal.

11

There is an Indian saying: 'when the chela is ready the guru will come'. In other words when a man has made his effort and advanced in his Yogic studies, is ready for a further stage, he will find someone to teach him more. I had a number of problems on my hands. When rigging *Aeolus* one of the jaws of the gaff broke. These are laminated and the break was across the laminations. Polly Hope mended the break beautifully for me with Araldite and transfixed the join with a couple of brass screws just to make sure. Then, out sailing one day, the other jaw went. Coming in I lost my balance and came down heavily on the tiller, breaking it at the point where two rivets had been driven horizontally through the laminations. As a result of these mishaps I conceived a suspicion of laminations which was only dispersed later by the assurances of experts that they are, when properly done, stronger than ordinary timber. Subsequent experience has confirmed this for me. There had been some mistake in the way those in *Aeolus* had been glued together. But, thanks to Araldite and Polly, all was well. The tiller was repaired by sandwiching the break between two brass plates riveted together. It was not very elegant but it served and gave *Aeolus* a certain character—and modified her pristine look.

I was still making do with a mainsheet I had rigged myself. It worked but it was a poor substitute for the proper one, which had still not arrived, and tiring to hang onto—I couldn't use the horse, and the ends of sheets and lengths of line were still unspliced and untidy because the fusing had come unstuck. They had frayed and unravelled and had had to be stopped with a knot. They looked slovenly and they worried me. There were also, I had learnt as I handled *Aeolus* and became more familiar with her, certain modifications that needed to be done: the position of cleats to be changed, new ones to be fitted. And the fenders I had, a patent sort one had to inflate, proved to be useless so I bought some scooter tyres to replace them. I wanted the lines suspending them spliced round each tyre and to have the free ends neatly whipped. I also wanted to fix brass eyelets along *Aeolus*' upper strake so that the line from the Wykham-Martin furling gear could run more smoothly than it did—it had a tendency to snarl and get stuck at the wrong moments even without benefit of childish fingers. In short, there was a lot to do and I had little idea of how to set about it. I also needed various bits and pieces, things which can be bought anywhere at home without difficulty but which are unobtainable in Rhodes. Anyone taking a boat out to Greece should stock up with a supply of cleats, brass eyes, hooks and, above all, tools: in fact furnish themselves with a really well garnished come-in-handy bag.

My guru appeared—appropriately enough wading purposefully towards me from the sea. Bill Trower had served in the Royal Navy in both world wars. He was a professional sailor and a man of great resource—a man who liked teaching and was prepared to convey some of his knowledge even to a neophyte as awkward and unknowledgeable as myself. With extraordinary patience, he showed me how to splice, serve and make a whipping. It now seems to me strange that a man can go through life for so long in complete ignorance of these satisfying skills. And how vital they are to anyone who sails boats! I realised this when I examined the main anchor warp one day and found it had chafed badly against rocks. It needed immediate attention. Being able to splice it and then finish the splice off with a reasonable whipping gave me immense satisfaction, as did being able to put *Aeolus* to bed after a sail with all cordage neatly coiled and everything snugged down in workmanlike fashion. This not only added to her appearance but gave her a satisfying air of competence and experience.

Under Bill Trower's instruction, sheets and lines acquired neatness, lost the unfinished and unsatisfying look a rope has whose ends have been merely fused with heat to prevent it unravelling—all *Aeolus*' cordage is Terylene. He also showed me how to make a rope ladder, a 'green stick' ladder, using olive wood which he cut from a tree on the slope above the bay.

I had had a tent made for *Aeolus* in England but it had been made of canvas that was too heavy. We decided to cut it up and make an awning out of it, an essential for anyone sailing in Greek waters. You simply must have some protection from the sun at times. The rope ladder was less of a success than we had hoped, only the most athletic could use it because it had a habit of clinging to *Aeolus*' hull as soon as one put a foot on it. It just didn't do, but it looked well.

Bill Trower and I used to sit on board *Aeolus* in the sun and gossip as we worked. He in his Panama hat and I, when I wore one, in a wide-brimmed local straw affair. They were both admirably unsuitable types of headgear for wear on a boat.

As we worked Bill would occasionally come out with a phrase that caught my attention. And when he brought one of these out he would fix me with his eyes, made more startlingly blue by the white of his pointed beard. 'Always cut towards your friend' he said on one occasion as he sliced through a rope with a razor sharp clasp knife. On thinking it over, I realised there was a good deal of practical wisdom contained in his delinquent advice, however questionable its morality. He would show me knots. I could see perfectly well how they were done—but I just couldn't do them. He remained endlessly patient. I took to walking about with a length of rope, practising—my admiration growing for all those amateur sailors who muck about in boats: what skills they so nonchalantly deploy, whether they sail dinghies or grand yachts.

They say that if you educate a man you educate an individual, but if you educate a woman you educate a family. By the same token, if you own a boat—female most certainly—you find yourself being educated in all sorts of new skills by her. It is, to me, one of the fascinations of sailing—the endless number of things to be learnt.

Lindos bay is always full of action. Bill and I as we worked always kept an eye cocked on the Tourist beach to see what was going on. Nearby, at the end of the beach near a spur of rock, was the preferred place of a little in-group of Lindos habitues who had come up with a strange perversion: they spent long hours every day playing bridge in the boiling sun. Why go to Greece to do something you can do perfectly happily in any back room in London? But, then, I am no card addict. Playing bridge the long day through on a golden stretch of sand under a cloudless sky, and with a glory of sea at one's feet, seemed to me as determinedly perverse as one can get. Better by far to wait for the dark of the night and play the game others favour in that corner of the beach. Walking along by the water's edge there one moonless night a voice came from under my feet. 'I say, watch out where you're going,' it said, 'we're making love.'

Further up that beach, inland near a vineyard, is a low wall. This is a favourite spot for people camping out or, rather, sleeping out. During the day they leave their rucksacks ranged along the foot of the wall. At night they lay out their sleeping bags close to the edge of the water. In the morning, when the sun rises, their flat sausage shapes lying in a line of the stretch of empty beach look lonely and discarded, sad. They live on bread and grapes and what they can scrounge. It is an idyllic life. Years hence they will grow paunchy and have accounts in the bank and form the backbone of the tourist trade. The Greeks are endlessly indulgent to them—and with no thought that they will one day provide a valued contribution to Greece's balance of payments. They keep to themselves. There is always someone with a guitar among them and at night they sing beside a fire of driftwood, drink and smoke a joint or two. They go swimming naked. The occasional indignation expressed at this habit in Lindos seems to me uncalled for. What if they are seen? Most of them have good shapes. The only offensive nudity I know is that of some Scandinavians and Germans. Elderly ladies of these races seem especially unable to keep towels and bathrobes in place. These slip and expose expanses of dead white flesh, pale flub that droops and cascades and lies in folds. Their performance is often made more conspicuous by the efforts of an equally elderly male companion to screen them with his towel. I have never heard anyone voice objections to these grisly performances, displeasing by any standards.

The taverna hard by the rocks in the far corner of the beach serves food as well as drink. Sometimes the waiters are disposed to bring imported beer if you don't specify the kind you want. But if you ask for Fix, the local brew, they will bring it. Here, as everywhere else in Greece, fish is the most expensive thing on the menu. But a good salad can be got at a reasonable price. This, with a lump of Greek bread and a bottle of retsina, can make a very good and inexpensive lunch, especially if you have the salad which includes olives and fetta, the white, soft local cheese.

And, while you watch the life of the beach and the people disposed about the ledges of rock flanking both sides of Lindos bay, a yacht may slip silently in and let go her anchor with a rattle of chain and a splash. Some send their passengers ashore in power boats or hurtle them about the bay on water skis. It is a curious fact of life that no water skier ever pursues his sport out at sea where he has all the room in the world: water skiers always stay in the bay where there are spectators. Is there such a thing as a water skier who isn't an exhibitionist? Or a sponge fishing boat may come in, its approach heralded by the slow plop plop of its diesel engine. As soon as it drops anchor the men on board busy themselves with work. Some, bare footed, tread sponges laid out on the deck. One man leaves the boat to beat an octopus against a rock until foam appears on the creature's body, indicating that it is now tender enough to cook. Beating, according to local fishermen, is not effective during the animals' mating season, when no amount of pounding will make them tender. They lead hard lives, these sponge fishermen, a life which gives diminishing returns—competition from plastic sponges is taking away their livelihood. The boats they use are beautiful, rising high at the bows and stern but dipping amidships to a low freeboard to make it easier for a diver to come aboard or haul a catch in. The sponge boats, like all working caiques, are painted with cheap paints whose blues, reds and oranges are soon faded to lovely washed out shades by the sun. The custom of painting eyes in the bows, oculi, an ancient Mediterranean tradition, is dying out. But an occasional boat still has them—and blocks carved in the shape of fish.

The sponge divers use both hard helmet equipment and sub-aqua gear for their work but there are also men who still dive in the ancient manner, naked and holding a stone, attached to a rope in their arms—the stone is usually tucked under one arm. They fill their mouths with olive oil which they spit out when they get to the bed of the sea. I have never seen this done but I am told the method has not been altogether abandoned. When a diver detaches a sponge before taking it to the surface he squeezes it to express a milky fluid and so ensures next season's crop. Sponges when first brought to the surface are black and viscous, their pores clogged with bits of stone and shell sticking to them. They are trampled under foot to clean them roughly—the real cleaning takes place ashore in depots. This trampling releases an odour to which, it is said, divers can become addicted.

Sponge divers live hazardous lives and make a poor living, but they are independent, brave and self-reliant men. Many of them get the bends—nitrogen in the blood caused by a too rapid ascent—and sustain injuries which can cripple them for life. The gear they use is usually so old and patched that it is hard not to feel pity for a man when one sees him preparing to dive. Yet they are cheerful men and show no sign of being dissatisfied with their lot—at least they do not have to earn their living cooped up in factories, as do large numbers of the Swedish tourists who flood into Lindos each summer, people who get out of coaches to wait, lost, until instructed what to do by their tour guides.

It is dispiriting to see their lack of animation. They seem incapable of independent action, filled with numb docility. If the Swedish welfare state is at all reflected in the thousands of Swedish nationals one sees on Rhodes, then God save mankind from the Swedish welfare state. But some of the younger women show more vitality and, immediately they get to the tourist beach, fling themselves on their backs in the sand and give themselves to the sun with an orgasmic pleasure that is wholehearted.

Rhodes is Apollo's, the sun god's, island. These women's enthusiastic worship must warm the cockles of his neglected heart, and stir hope in him that, one day, he will make a comeback. Indeed, it is hard to live in Greece for any length of time and believe that the old gods have died forever: sleeping, yes: dead, no. One day I believe the sight of one of those offered Swedish girls will prove too much for Apollo. But, until then, they will have to content themselves with mortal Greeks—and they don't have to wait long. The Swedish women seem more desperate in their search for men than the visiting women of any other nationality. It is, a Swedish woman told me, because Swedish men are turning more and more to their own sex.

Working on *Aeolus*, the animated life of the beach and the sea acquired the detachment of a film. Our lives were committed to the service of a boat, the rest was a show to be followed with detachment—something seen in a mirror darkly, more often than not. And the result of our efforts was that *Aeolus* was being worked up to a pitch of readiness that cried out for a long and hard test.

12

When Zeus divided the world among the gods Apollo was left out. He arrived just as the last piece was being allotted. Not in the least put out he told Zeus that, while on his way to the meeting, he had seen an island emerging from the sea, and would be content with that for his share. Rhodes was a nymph and from her union with Apollo seven sons were born. One of these had three sons of his own whose names were Ialysos, Lindos, and Kamiros. They all founded towns named after themselves and one of these, Lindos, flourishes today like a green bay tree. I have not visited Ialysos but I have been to Kamiros and it is well worth a visit. All three towns are mentioned in Homer's 'catalogue of ships' as having between them sent nine vessels to the siege of Troy.

Kamiros is as self-contained a site as any in Greece, as self-contained as Tyrins, but very different. Tyrins is grim and evokes memories of danger and violence. Its great walls are enclosing bastions that rise like a stranded ship of war out of a plain from which the sea has retreated. But Kamiros is a gentle site, domestic, a place of residence and worship displayed upon an open slope of hill steep enough to present the ruined houses and temples in plan. The houses have lost their roofs and only waist-high walls remain standing. There are a few temple columns still upright and statues, rescued by archaeologists, stand about haphazardly arranged. The bright sun of Rhodes chisels the inscription on their bases deep in the marble, drawing attention to the whiteness of the stone, dazzling in that splendid light. The green scrub and groves of pine trees which surround Kamiros, framing it, heighten the site's unity by throwing into relief the subdued colours and restraint of the stone walls and marble monuments. The streets and clearly seen lines of the town's water system lead the eye upward to where a row of giant underground cisterns are ranged in line along a flat terrace running the breadth of the site. As an example of a place made for the use and enjoyment of man Kamiros is splendid, appealing in its cosy smallness. It is compact, constructed with a harmony and grace which must at all times have increased its inhabitants' humanity—no one living in Kamiros could ever have felt overwhelmed or that he was trapped in masonry. But then Kamiros was built by men who could speak with their gods on terms of equality: they were very human deities and much given to the same faults, sins and aspirations as the men who raised them up. The result was that temples and domestic installations fuse together in towns like Kamiros—and the effect is one of light and balanced freedom which fills one with envy. Life in the Greece of those days —Kamiros is a Dorian foundation—could be short and its end violent, but men could breathe while they lived. And they could hope—and what hope is there for the enclosed millions struggling in our modern cities?

Legend peoples the island of Rhodes in prehistoric times with men skilled in the working of metals and with others, 'children of the sun', who were great sailors and navigators. Between them, they provided the skills which built and maintained the ancient cities of the island, whose remains can be found and traced by anyone with a taste to explore away from the beaten track. And what things there are to find!

Bill Trower, I discovered very soon after we got to know each other, was an amateur archaeologist. *Aeolus*, thanks largely to him, was now trim and workmanlike: her jib sheets no longer secured by being wrapped round the stay but passed through a ring on the foredeck, round the samson post and neatly bowsed down. And the mizzen sheet now ran through a newly fitted fairlead, which took it clear of the Seagull's petrol tank instead of catching on it as it came inboard from the end of the bumpkin. We could take time off from our pleasurable work. Bill wanted to see the sites of three of the island's ancient ports. I offered to take him in the VW.

We set off in the early morning. Anne Trower, Bill's wife, came with us. One of the sites was on the western side of the island, the other right at its southern tip, near Cape Praso Nisi, a place of ill repute and wild waters. I was to get to know it much better later on. Bill was uncertain where the third site was but we hoped to work out its position in relation to the other two.

The bare tops of the ridge of mountains that divides Rhodes along its length rise from a covering of maquis and stands of pine. The slopes of these mountains descend in a series of ranges to valleys and amphitheatres, and then run on down to the seaboard or peter out in plains that stretch to the sea. Once covered with trees, these ranges were denuded by the Turks during their occupation of the island. The Greek government is now engaged in reforestation and, slowly, the island is becoming bright with the tender flush of young trees. The varied conformation of Rhodes offers a prospect which constantly presents one with new discoveries. One never has the feeling of being enclosed: the eye is almost everywhere led onto a sea whose spaces are sewn with islands, and whose horizon is bounded to the north by the coast of Asia Minor. To the south-east there is nothing but an expanse of water that stretches, unbroken, to the coast of North Africa.

Bill Trower is a man whose enthusiasm is always on the bubble, eager to communicate his knowledge—a great asset to anyone too idle to stop at frequent intervals to consult a map, as I am. The one we were using was not very good and we were unsure of the best way to get to our first site. As we drove towards a village I spotted a track leading off the road. It appeared to be going in the general direction we were making for. There is something irresistible to me about tracks going off at a tangent. I asked Bill and Anne Trower if they minded if we drove along it a little way.

The track climbed gently away from the road, turned a sharp bend and then straightened out. We had only driven a short way along it when I spotted, spread out below us, a number of circular clearings in the scrub. They were obviously man made. Some had a pole sticking up in the centre, and where the ground sloped downhill, it was retained by a wall of stones. They were, at first sight, obviously threshing grounds. But why so many? There was no community that we knew of nearby large enough to use all of them, or to provide the labour necessary to build them. We parked the car and went to look more closely. The retaining walls had niches in them, places which could have held a lamp or an urn. They were evidently ancient burial places some of which, as the straw strewn about indicated, were used as threshing grounds. But where were the ruins of the considerable settlement their presence implied? Looking around, my attention was caught by the enormous mass of a great rock, a great bare boulder, grey and elephantine in its bulk. There were symmetrical rectangular openings in the side facing us which, even at a distance, seemed certainly man made. But their axis was tilted over at a steep angle. It just didn't make sense.

We clambered towards the primordial stone, stumbling across scree and loose stones, forcing our way through the low growing, dense maquis, and over shallow erosion runnels. When we got to the rock we saw that it had at some time been hurled over onto its side by an earthquake. Rhodes, like virtually the whole of Greece, is seismic. A dark line along the face of the rocks of Lindos bay shows clearly how the sea level has been changed in the recent past by some convulsion of the earth.

What we had stumbled on were rock tombs, three of them carved in the boulder and progressing from a first, tentative abandoned attempt to one that had been completed, but still with traces of clumsy uncertainty in its workmanship, and a third in which the craftsmen had mastered their medium and done their work with confidence. Looking at the record of that early struggle with intractable material was very moving. How many thousand years ago had the people who had made these tombs struggled towards the triumph of providing their dead with suitable resting places, towards giving them a worthy shell in which to affront the infinite?

We crawled into the best of the tombs, whose floor was covered in sheep and goat droppings, and began to scrape away the silted mud which had gathered in the lower part of the canted over tomb. Each burial place had a platform carved out of the living rock on its higher side, presumably upon which to lay the body. Carefully digging in the soft earth with sticks, we turned up bits of bone and potsherds. The tombs appeared not to have ever been disturbed. We decided to leave well alone and report our find to the archaeological authorities. We only noticed when we got out a purple, insect eating lily, sinisterly exuberant, growing at the side of the tomb.

We took a different route back to the road and on our way found a Cyclopean wall and, above it, a flat space with more circular burying places. We drove on to see if we could find any traces of a settlement large enough to account for the number of round burying places and the rock tombs. We came to two clearings just off the side of the road. In each of them was a beehive shaped, partly ruined, kiln. There were also bee skeps painted bright indigo and a few that were just small logs hollowed out, whose bee population seemed no less industrious and content than those housed in the more sophisticated hives.

The discovery of the kilns was exciting. It meant that somewhere not far away was a good supply of easily accessible marble, and probably marble that had been quarried and worked. In fact, somewhere near, it seemed safe to assume, would be an ancient town of some size.

Much has been said and written about the removal to foreign museums of the treasures of Greek antiquity. Lord Elgin has been greatly abused and so have, with more reason, the Turks. But were it not for Lord Elgin the controversial marbles would probably not exist today. And, even if by some miracle they had survived, they would be more threatened with destruction now than ever before—the Acropolis is being inexorably eaten away by the fumes given off by Athenian factories. The metal ties which bind the great blocks of marble together are being consumed and so is the marble itself. Against this insidious attack there is as yet no known defence. So a time may come before long when Lord Elgin will be blessed—and not least fervently by the Greeks themselves.

The destruction of Greece's treasures has been remorseless. But far more have been lost through being fed into kilns, such as the ones we had found, to make lime for building than were ever removed by conquerors or collectors.

Not far from the kilns we found what we were looking for, and which we would not have spotted but for their discovery, which had alerted us and made us keep a sharp lookout. We saw, dispersed over a wide area near the road, white rocks. They were half covered by vegetation and at first sight no different to others strewn about every hillside. Was there a pattern in the way they were disposed about? Or were they just broken off outcrops of raw marble? It was hard to decide. I pulled off the road. There was no shelter from the sun here and the heat struck fiercely up at us from the rocks. There was a murmur of bees in the air and the fricative sound of cicadas. Bill Trower moved off like a casting hound. I struck out on my own.

There was no doubt about it. We were walking over the ruins of what must at one time have been a considerable city. There were great rectangular blocks of marble lying concealed in the vegetation, some skilfully incised. These were not fashioned by fumbling, uncertain craftsmen feeling their way but had been worked by inheritors of a civilisation in flower. We found a marble bowl with a lipped rim, presumably so that the sacrificial blood could run tidily away into the runnel cut in the pedestal to receive it. We discovered lengths of half-section marble pipes. Guttering? Part of a drainage system? We came upon marble steps and a marble floor with square holes in it to key columns into position. Wherever we walked we found pieces of worked marble.

And in this forgotten place were rocks so worked upon by wind and weather that only close examination could establish that men had not had a hand in their fashioning. Some had certainly been worked upon by craftsmen. I had seen similar examples of the way men had learnt from, and exploited, the work of natural forces in the Nabatean city of Petra, in Jordan—that 'rose red city half as old as time'. And, as at

Petra, the surface of the ruined Rhodian city was strewn with potsherds. Bill, assiduous in collecting as a magpie, picked up pieces, rubbed them clear of dirt with his fingers, and dated them with what accuracy I wasn't competent to judge.

A russet accent in the undergrowth attracted our attention. We climbed over fallen walls and the foundations of buildings, their crumbled walls cascades of rubble. What had caught our attention turned out to be a roofing of dead branches and leaves laid across sheep byres built out of great marble blocks from the ruined city by shepherds. In just such fashion had the barbarians built beneath the walls of fallen Rome. There was an elemental, dignified quality about these simple structures, whose construction had contributed to the destruction of what must once have been a place of importance in the early Hellenic world. Their building had involved much hard labour, but men never willingly occupy places greater in scale than those they are accustomed to. I once saw a labour camp in the rain forest of French Equatorial Africa. Large wooden barracks had been built by the French in clearings in the forest to house labourers from the interior of the Gaboon. They were long rectangular buildings, these barracks, with high gabled roofs. The African labourers refused to live in them. They were eventually persuaded to do so—and promptly built a little conical hut of palm leaves in the middle of the floor of each of them, with an entrance so ignobly small that a man could only enter the hut by crawling flat on his belly and wriggling himself inside. In these leafy huts, dark and filled with the smoke of their cooking fires, they lived contentedly surrounded by empty, unoccupied space.

A little way down the road from the ruined city was a flat place where I could draw the car off the road. From here, spread out before us was a panoramic view of the Aegean of the tourist poster, a flat shimmering expanse of blue watered silk out of which rose arid islands garlanded with a rim of foam and, beyond them, the backdrop of Asia Minor. Marking the surface of the still sea were slicks of different textures—places where the waters moved in channels under the influence of obscure forces. Toy-like boats lay far below us, embedded in a sheet of glass, their movement through the water betrayed only by a broadening arrowhead in their wake.

I got out the Admiralty chart of Rhodes and from it identified the islands of Khalki and Alimnia, both places I wanted to visit, and stages in the journey I hoped to do before long to the island of Symi, which lies hard off the Turkish coast, whose headlands point at it like threatening fingers.

Something puzzled me as I looked to the southwest. There was a spur of land projecting north beyond the southern tip of Rhodes, where Cape Praso Nisi lay hidden by a spine of mountains. The out-thrust land had no right to be there. And then I realised what it was. I was looking at Sarta, an island off Scarpanto (Carpathos), some forty miles away. I believe that on a clear day it is possible to see Mount Ida on Crete from Rhodes. With such visibility navigation was going to be a good deal easier than I had anticipated. But I carefully studied the view spread out before us, memorising features which I felt might help me when I came to sail for Khalki, Alimnia and Symi. But when would that be? Not yet, and not as soon as I had hoped, I was soon to discover.

We moved on. We were hot and tired and glad to be back in the car, to feel fresh air from the open windows being scooped at our faces. The road plunged down in steep curves. We came to a hairpin bend and found a place of shade and running water by the roadside. It was in just such a spot that nymphs used to get laid by shepherds, or lusty gods pretending to be shepherds—and I daresay many a shepherd soothed a nymph's conscience by claiming to be a god.

Water flowed in a filigree of rivulets, lace-like, over the face of mossy rocks at whose base grew delicate ferns. Butterflies hovered, fluttering, over a pool of water captive in a cement basin upon whose wall we sat and ate our lunch. Bread, brown and filling, cut from a flat, cartwheel loaf. Olives, cheese and tomatoes. We drank retsina, but not before we had quenched our thirst with the cool, delicious water of the pool and washed our faces—how good that water was, chilled, refreshing and splendid to taste. It was a place filled with dark shade broken into patches by dappled sunlight, of tangled softly moving branches.

A workman arrived on a motor scooter. He was covered in cement dust and sweat had traced runnels in his face. He was dark brown from the sun and leathery, lean as men are in these climates who work with their hands. We greeted each other. Bill Trower speaks Greek, wildly anglicised. He gesticulates and moves his small body about restlessly to make his meaning clear. I have only enough Greek for simple courtesies. We offered the man food and drink. He refused drink but, out of politeness, accepted a token of food and offered us flakes of an orange in return. Yes, he knew the town on the hill, he replied to Bill's question. It had been a place of importance long ago, so it was said. Were we scholars, archaeologists? There was much on the island that was still unknown, he said. The conversation turned to the Italian occupation of Rhodes. For my benefit he elaborated what he was saying in Greek with simple sentences in Italian. He had been a boy in those days. He had little with which to reproach Italians. Only one thing they had done was bad, in his opinion, and he had suffered as a result: they had forbidden Greek to be spoken in the schools and all teaching was done in Italian. This, he felt, was wrong. I heard this complaint often on Rhodes, though most Rhodians willingly concede that the Italian occupation of the island had on the whole been beneficent, and had left behind many things for which they had reason to be grateful.

We had spent too long over our exploring and our lunch and we had to go if we were to see our ports. We said goodbye to our friend and got into the car. A tractor pulling a trailer came up the hill and stopped. Tractor and trailer were festooned with people singing and talking animatedly. There was a gay and festive air about them. They called out greetings to us and waved. I backed the VW to let them pass and they smiled their thanks. There was an arcadian spirit about them, a freshness and vigour emanated from the men and vitality from the pretty girls. An elderly man climbed down from the tractor and came towards us. He thanked us in English for having made way for them. No, he said in reply to our question, they were not working. It was a picnic. They were out for the day and enjoying themselves. No, there was no special reason. They had just felt like it. Lucky people! They lived in a different world from all those tourists and people like ourselves who come to Greece, when they can, for a breath of unconfined air and space.

We started off down the hill, looping and swinging down curves, towards the sea. The road ran for a stretch beside a dry watercourse whose bed was gouged out so deeply in places that it must, during the season of rains, contain a great violence of water. The road levelled off and became a diminishing track which led us towards a tower and a couple of houses close to the shore. A woman was working in a field close to one of the houses, the only person in sight. The track divided, one branch leading to the houses and the other in the opposite direction, towards a solitary shack at the edge of the sea. We took this one. The shack was empty but showed signs of occupation. It was occupied, we learnt later, by an old and solitary man. Lying in the shade of some scrub near the ramshackle wooden building was a dying ginger cat, skeletally thin and very young. We should have put it out of its misery but hesitated to do so, inhibited by a misplaced respect for someone else's creature. I found an old tin, filled it with water and placed it beside the animal. Only a slight movement of its flanks showed that it was still alive. We left it. But we felt troubled and not even the finding of two old kilns could dissipate the sadness brought on by the sight of the cat's silent agonising.

I made no record of the ancient port's name. It was near Glyphada, I believe, on the west coast and must once have been a place of great commercial importance; a centre for the manufacture and export of amphorae—judging by the quantities of potsherds exposed in layers where the sea had cut away the shore. The day was spending and there would only be enough daylight left to visit one of the remaining two places Bill Trower wanted to see. We agreed that it should be the one near Cape Praso Nisi. We were glad to leave. What had once been a bustling commercial centre was now reduced to a place lived in by a solitary old man and a dying cat hardly out of its kittenhood. The moral was too gloomily and oppressively evident to need expression.

The southern end of Rhodes' west coast has nothing to commend it. The last feature of interest is the Knights of St John's keep of Monolithos, a fortified eyrie set upon a crag which towers giddily above the sea. After this, the highlands fall away to a plain beside the sea. The earth here is dry, a clogged grey clay, dead and matt, deeply fissured and inert, covered with sparse tall grass and reeds—a sterile moon landscape on a small scale.

We never got to Cape Praso Nisi. The road became a track and then a trail used only by goats. Even this petered out. We drove on up a stony hillside, treating the VW like a jeep. The light was dying. We acknowledged defeat and turned back, tired but elated by the discoveries of the day. When, later, I again saw Cape Praso Nisi I was once more tired—and far from elated.

13

Days became weeks, hurrying on with disquieting speed. The sun was getting hotter but, one day, a rainstorm of tropical intensity burst over Lindos to remind us that the time had not yet quite come when the sun would shine out of a cloudless sky for months on end.

My trip across the island with the Trowers had given me food for thought. Excursions of the kind were something I had to resist. They were a distraction. The sea was what I had to concentrate upon—and it was high time I spent more time on it. I was getting drawn away from the intention I had of sailing *Aeolus* more and more, further and further. A boat can isolate you from people but it can also, very effectively, introduce you to them—and to a host of new interests. I kept assuring myself there was plenty of time and a great deal still to do in the way of getting things absolutely shipshape on *Aeolus*. I found myself nevertheless being drawn into things. It was so easy on the way to and from the Boat beach to stop at Costa's and join friends sitting on the benches outside. Or to squat on the cement platform at the front of the shop. At most times of the day there would be a group of people drinking and gossiping there. Costa speaks English, helps visitors with their problems, interprets, gives credit and acts as a liaison officer between foreigners and Lindians. His shop is a meeting place and minor forum. You pass it going to and coming from the Platea. He sells cold drinks, groceries, bread, yoghurt, cigarettes, tinned food and odds and ends. And he has a heavy hand with drinks. There is no need when ordering at Costa's to ask for a double—you get it, doubled. It is a good place to find out what is going on, hear the latest scandal or wait for someone you want to see. Sooner or later they are bound to pass. Opposite is a shop run by the Looms of Lindos, a weaving concern started by an American to boost local crafts. The road from Costa's to the Platea is lined on both sides with tourist shops selling dresses, hats, souvenirs, sheepskin rugs and bric-à-brac. As tourists pass, the shopkeepers murmur invitations to 'Just look, madam. Come in: just look. No buy!' And many do come in—and stay to buy. Going into the village from Costa's you pass a church on your left, distinguished by a graceful campanile, partly whitewashed but with its upper part left its natural tawny stone. You turn sharp right here and are then in Lindos proper. If you look up to your right you will see in the rocks above a necropolis, and to your left, a blazon against the clear blue sky, the Acropolis.

Few tourists stray from the route leading up to the Acropolis. It is worth doing so. And to just stroll aimlessly through this lovely village is rewarding. Throw away your guide book and just look. This is a place made for the eye's delight. Every wall and angle, the relationship between street, sky and surrounding country, the irregularities of house and lane and stuccoed wall offer rich satisfactions. The sky is a flat, even blue, the stone of the houses (when they are not whitewashed) light biscuit colour which absorbs the sun, mirrors its golden rising and setting. As you walk along the twisting, narrow lanes you will perhaps get a glimpse of inner courtyards where much of the domestic life of Lindos takes place. Vines grow in them, a canopy of shade suspended on wires. There are fig trees and beds of flowers. You will even see in some the broad, polished leaves of banana trees. These garths usually have a well which the household at one time depended upon for most of its water for domestic purposes. Now that Lindos has a piped water supply these wells are largely disused and the water in them, undisturbed, provides a breeding ground for mosquitoes. Now that water is no longer precious, taps are left profligately open and the water runs away from stagnant pools for mosquitoes to use as breeding grounds. The mosquitoes are not malarial but they are still a nuisance—and one which could be easily avoided. Paradise had the snake. Lindos has mosquitoes and the cinema.

On cinema nights Lindos is bedlam. I know people who, on cinema nights, leave the village. The cinema, a touring one, sets up its equipment near the church. The film is projected on to the side wall of a building opposite. The sound is turned up so full that it is distorted. The result is a diabolical possession by sound. And it goes on for hours —an unbearable Chinese torture from which there is no escape except flight. As an experiment I have tried to see how long I could endure it at close quarters. I have never been able to do so for more than a few minutes. Consequently, I have never seen a film in Lindos— nor have most of the other foreigners.

A curious feature of Greek life is that noise is not only tolerated but positively welcomed. A jukebox will play at full volume in a taverna and the patrons will continue their conversations, apparently oblivious to a noise level that strains the ear drums and the larynx of foreigners. I have heard that tolerance of noise is in inverse ratio to intelligence. In which case.... But, of all the sources of noise in Greece, pride of place goes to that ubiquitous curse, the transistor radio. Other noises, curiously enough, are less tolerated. An American yacht, charging its batteries one day, was peremptorily ordered to stop doing so because an important Greek visitor was disturbed by the noise. And yet the sound was a pretty unobtrusive purr. Odd. Even odder, a shotgun was fired to attract the yacht's attention when they failed to respond to shouts. It was probably just a piece of officiousness; something the visitor to Greece must learn to put up with at times from police and officials.

I found dropping in at Costa's was becoming a habit. It is temptingly pleasant to sit on the cement stoep, and pleasant to feel the sun's heat through the seat of one's pants. A seat at Costa's is better than the cinema any day. Almost all the life of the town has to pass his shop and almost the full weight of tourist traffic. Only those who go up to the Acropolis by donkey avoid it, taking the other, lower road out of the Platea, the one that forks left and leads to the Boat beach.

When tourist buses are in, the street passing Costa's is jammed with jostle and bustle. People wearing every kind of undress that the mind of man can conceive or misconceive crowd along it, clog together in knots, kibitzing at the shops and each other, strolling and making loud comments. The most incontinent undressers are without doubt the Germans and Americans. The women are given to shorts too tight about the bottom and crutch, the men to infelicities of shirt and hat. For some obscure reason men of both nationalities buy high-crowned embroidered women's hats sold in the tourist shops and wear them with every sign of serenity. The occasional Englishman adds his bit to the passing theatre of the absurd by wearing a pair of those extraordinary baggy shorts which come down well below the knees. Combined with an earnest diffidence of manner, the effect is arresting.

The resident foreign community of Lindos has its own fashions, as have the semi-residents like myself, the long term visitors, so to speak. My fancy is a pair of very tired bathing pants and a shirt worn tails flying. Willard Manus, on the whole a sober dresser in jeans and sweat shirt, achieves distinction by crowning himself with a WREN officer's hat which he picked up off a stall in the Portobello Road. Jeans are the most common wear for both men and women. But the really exotic note is struck by the odd Flower person: painted symbols on the face and hands, a loose-flowing Russian style smock, heavily embroidered, for a man: a long loose robe embroidered round the square yoke of the neck and hair braided in thin rats tails, to which small bells are tied, for the woman. Very attractive. Sandals or bare feet are usual for all groups.

Tourists find endless entertainment looking at the residents' clothes and the residents enjoy studying that of the tourists—both groups find each other very peculiar, both entertain the other; and the Lindians find all of them incomprehensible.

And there are the Beats and the Hippies whose dress is international —though Beats will soon be a forgotten group: jeans and long hair for the men, jeans and long hair for the women. Jeans and long hair are de rigeur and fashionably unkempt. The men are usually bearded and the women have a tendency to big bottoms which they have difficulty in containing within their shrunken denims. The Beats are very tribal and keep to themselves except when there is an open party, but there are exceptions who fraternise. The totem of the Beats is a guitar. The Flower People, of whom there are few, are distinguished by a striking cleanliness. Their clothes, for the most part white, are usually spotless and crisply laundered. They are undoubtedly the most decorative of all the people who throng Lindos. The sharpest dressers are easily the Italians, men and women, but they are prone to wearing clothes whose excess originates in incoherent fantasy rather than originality.

Lindos is by now used to most things. It took an Italian woman to demonstrate that they hadn't yet seen everything. She appeared in a flesh coloured jump suit so tight that it clung to every bump and crevice. She was very beautiful. Seeing her reminded me of an occasion when I was walking along a bush path in West Africa. I saw approaching in the distance what appeared to be a completely naked white woman. As there were to the best of my knowledge none within a hundred miles or so seeing her gave me a bit of a shock. The woman turned out to be an Albino African. The effect of seeing what at first sight seemed to be a naked woman walking across the Platea at high noon was rather similar—incredulous surprise.

There is in Lindos a summer colony of Italians, most of them from Milan. Many of them own houses in the village or are friends of people who do. Their numbers increase every year. The women are often beautiful, sometimes elegant and usually not only intelligent but well educated. Both men and women are usually multilingual. But, whereas the women give the impression of being supercharged, the men convey a feeling of not quite firing on all cylinders, of lacking the vital quality so evident in the women. They fish enthusiastically and eat every sea thing in sight down to the humblest shellfish. They have a taste for speedboats. They are a coterie, keeping very much to themselves and only mixing with certain other foreigners in Lindos. They convey an impression of having hereditary squirearchical rights in the village; and the behaviour of the Lindians towards them reminds one that, once, the Italians were masters of Rhodes. They usually return to Milan in a state of exhaustion after their holiday in the sun. Their going leaves a gap, a hollow that nothing fills.

Polly Hope passed and wrenched me out of my Lotus eating by suggesting a sail to Rhodes in *Aeolus*. The suggestion fell in very well with my plans. A longish run in *Aeolus* was in my mind as part of the working up towards an extended cruise. We agreed we would set off next day very early. And the Hopes when they say very early mean very early—not, as is generally meant in Lindos, somewhere round 10.30 or so.

As I brushed the dust of the stoep off the seat of my pants I was told there was to be a party that night. Would I come? Parties in Lindos start by a sort of spontaneous combustion. After some discussion, and a few more oozos, the gathering at Costa's began to disperse; some to drink elsewhere, some to lunch and others to an immediate siesta.

The siesta is a Lindos custom which is very easy to get into. Between 1 and 4 in the afternoon the village dies. The whole island of Rhodes between these hours is somnolent except for tourists charging about like mad dogs and Englishmen. The siesta is a custom which gives the impression to foreigners that Greeks are lazy. They are far from so. Most tourists get up in the morning at an hour when many Greeks have already done hours of work, taking advantage of the cool of the early morning. During the hottest hours of the day they rest, sleep or sit about in tavernas drinking coffee, gossiping, dozing, playing cards, or engaged in a game of tric-trac, played with dice and counters like those used in draughts. The visitor, envious, dubs them idle. When the sun begins to lose its heat Greeks start work again, and certainly do no less than people in more temperate climates. As a largely peasant people they probably in fact do a great deal more work than the urban inhabitants of industrial countries.

I am uncertain of the value of the siesta. It is sometimes refreshing but, more often than not, I find myself waking up feeling much the worse for wear. A swim is the only cure. The ideal is to live somewhere where you can flop straight from bed into the sea. But in Lindos this is not possible—there are no houses with their feet in the water, more's the pity. Wherever you live in the village, you have a walk to the sea.

This is good for the tavernas.

There were things to do on *Aeolus* if we were to get off early the next day. I bestirred myself. Others in the village were doing the same. The butcher's shop on the corner was open and so was the saddler's where the donkeys' saddles are made—wooden frameworks padded with straw and covered with cloth decorated with beads. The saddler is about the only man in Lindos who knows how to splice. Dimitri's taverna had a few Beats sitting gloomily over glasses of oozo as I walked past. The greengrocer's was open and the 'Turk' was sitting outside the door eyeing passersby with a stern look. He is a man who must have been very big in his day but has been crippled with an affliction that has bent him nearly double. From this penitential posture he studies the world with alert eyes over a nobly hawked nose and fiercely brushed up whiskers. He wears jackboots, breeches and dun coloured felt hat of the kind much favoured in Yugoslavia. He is a man cast in a heroic mould, blood brother to those heroes of the War of Independence who, armed to the teeth with knife and gun, stare out at you from patriotic posters. We exchanged greetings.

The Boat beach was busy. Fishermen were working on their boats and others, sitting in the shade of the caves above the beach, were repairing their nets, the bright yellow nylon meshes held firmly in their toes as they worked.

A sponge fishing vessel came in and tied up at the jetty—an indication of how shallow the draft of these boats is. That is why they roll so much, a tendency which is increased by the top hamper they carry. One of the crew stepped ashore and started beating an octopus against the concrete of the path leading to the landing stage, using a stiff overarm swing like a bowler delivering a cricket ball.

Octopus and squid (which is better eating, in my view) are prized delicacies in Greece. They are usually fished with tridents but there are men who haul them out of their lairs, using only their bare hands. At night bright lights are used and I have seen a small boy tempting an octopus with a white plastic sandal as bait. I have not yet brought myself to have a shot at catching them. I find the thought of handling those slimy tentacles with their rows of cup-like suckers, white rimmed against the brown flesh, unpleasant. I will get around to it sometime. But I have acquired a taste for eating them, seduced by Mavis Manus' preparation of the beasts—she is as persuasive a cook as Willard is a determined fisherman. But it took me a long time before I tried them: we all have our blind spots. I found a similar difficulty in Corsica about bringing myself to eat sea urchins. These are not much fished in Lindos—and there is none of the enthusiastic enjoyment of them one finds in Corsica, where their eating is a ritual. A fruit box piled high with them is placed on the table, flanked by bottles of wine and large lumps of bread. Empty fruit boxes stand on the floor at the foot of the table to receive the debris. You are encouraged to the feast by your hosts' exhortations to 'eat! Eat!' And your gormandising is made easier by a special instrument used to open the sea fruit, making their preparation not only simple but quick. I have never seen these instruments anywhere else.

The method of fishing the urchins is as simple and effective as is the method of opening them. A long bamboo pole, split at one end, is used. This is thrust down into the water and the spring, made by splitting the cane, grips the sea urchin sufficiently firmly to detach it from its resting place. While in Corsica I learnt to distinguish male from female sea urchin. This, far from being a useless bit of knowledge, is important because it is only the female which is edible. The male is black and round, the female flatter in shape. She ranges in colour from a purple so deep as to be almost black to a light, slightly greenish brown. Some are positively ginger. It is not always easy to distinguish male from female when the creatures are in deep water. But there is one infallible way. If you see a sea urchin with a pebble balanced on its spikes or a piece of seaweed draped over it you know it is a female. 'You must understand, monsieur,' my teacher explained, 'elles sont comme les femmes, pudiques.' That's as may be. Modesty may well be a female characteristic in sea urchins but it is not always very evident in women in Lindos, foreign women. I confess that, sometimes, walking along Lindos beach I find myself wishing for the days when there was more reticence about displaying human flesh. The sight of some women lying sun bathing, seen from certain angles, is not particularly conducive to a belief in their modesty—nor is it particularly conducive to arousing interest in them, and this could be a matter for concern in an age of Unisex. And without interest where are we in our relations between the sexes? At sixes and sevens— mostly sevens. I saw a signal example of this when I first went to Lindos. A female sergeant in the Israeli army appeared in a taverna with a woman companion. A donkey boy made a pass at the companion and was promptly laid out by the sergeant. How was the donkey boy to know they were married? Had the Egyptians seen that incident they would have realised what they were up against in tackling Israel.

It must all be very puzzling for the Greeks at times but they are learning fast—affairs between men, of course, are an old Greek custom which has never died out. All things considered, it is admirable the way the Lindos people manage to keep their feet pretty firmly on the ground. God knows, the pressures on them, and the temptations, are becoming great enough to send anyone round the bend. But it is the foreigners who go round the bend.

14

Polly Hope had rescued me from slipping in to a *dolce vita* phase—something very easy to do if one gets into the habit of drinking a few oozos round about lunch time when the sun is bright overhead, the shade tempting, the passing show beguiling and the conversation it inspires sometimes takes wing. The party the evening before had gone on very late. I was slightly hung over and not very inclined to go to Rhodes. I pottered about getting things ready on *Aeolus*. From the path high above me a voice called out. Polly waved an expansive arm and, laden, started down the track, followed by John. Between them they were carrying enough food and drink to sustain twice our number to Rhodes and back—and beyond. They were punctual. It is a rare quality in Greece. The Greek is no respecter of time and it is as well when invited anywhere to ask if the time appointed is 'Greek' time or not. If it is, any time an hour or two after the set one is all right. To my sorrow, Polly was not wearing The Hat. The Hat is a confection of note—a fertile straw bonnet lush with a growth of plastic leaves and enormous daisies. It is a sublimely fantastical hat for sea excursions. In a boat, crowning Polly's long, straight strawberry blonde hair and Valkyrie body, in a bikini whose adequacy depends upon posture, The Hat has the attention attracting force of a French horn suddenly blasting out in an orchestra of tin whistles.

There was a slight breeze. Hopefully, we set sail and prepared for an agreeable day of sailing silently in the sun. But the winds of Greece are uncertain and variable. I have known a wind come plunging down from the high land NW of Lindos bay and then, in some extraordinary way, veer right round and come hustling back from the opposite direction, whirled about by the cliffs as though gyrated in a washing machine. And I have sat outside the bay with the wind coming every which way—boxing the compass so that I sat, helpless, sails flapping and with every appearance of distinguished ineptitude. Once, sailing beautifully towards Lindos before a steady, driving wind I was suddenly becalmed. Yet all around there was wind enough. A friend standing on the Acropolis said there was a great circle of absolute calm about me—everywhere outside the circle there was a fresh, whipping wind. The formation of the islands in these seas, especially when their coasts drop from a height sheer to the water, affects the wind at sea level in curious and puzzling ways. There are times when, if the wind is fresh, you can find yourself in sudden hazard—for the wind dives off the land and at sea level strikes across the water with vicious gusts that buffet you angrily. You either have to stand in very close to avoid these, and get blanketed, or else keep well out to sea.

The wind soon died on us. We started the Seagull—so much for our hopes of sailing to Rhodes with only the wind whispering in the rigging and the music of water against the hull. We would have instead the noise of the engine, which soon becomes tiresome and makes conversation a strain. But, still, I would be able to familiarise myself with the coast and find out how the engine would behave on a long run.

The morning was fresh and it was pleasant to know that ahead of us was a long run with the sea to ourselves. We drank coffee and stretched out on the cushions the Hopes had brought. Crossing Malona bay as we headed for Rhodes we saw two dolphins. They were some distance away and in a sober mood. We were, I suppose, not going fast enough to attract their attention or stir their playful spirits. Often, they love to race beside a boat, forge ahead and dive deep to emerge again far behind, then surge forward with a powerful, slicing rush and overtake, to start criss-cross leaps and dives inches in front of the bows. Their delight in the sport is evident and the joy in the fluent ease of their movements infectious. But these two just moved steadily along, glistening polished backs emerging from the water at intervals with a slow, oily movement. Squares. But even this staid progress was stirring—it is always exciting to get a glimpse of these appealing charmers of the sea.

The Seagull stuttered, hesitated and died. I had deliberately let it run dry to see how long it would run, and how far *Aeolus* would go, on a gallon of fuel. It had run nearly two hours and done, I estimated, ten miles. I used these figures from then on as a basis for working out what quantities of petrol and oil to carry—supplies in Greece can be uncertain. I filled the tank and pulled the starting cord. Nothing. I pulled again. Still nothing. Once more. I swore. I took the plug out and cleaned it. Pulled the starting cord. Nothing. I pulled it again. Nothing. Pulled again. Still nothing. There was no point in swearing again.

John Hope was trained as an engineer. The two of us settled down to find the fault. After attending to each item we thought might be the cause of the trouble we had a shot at starting the engine. Nothing. We all went for a swim—delicious so far out, the water cold and invigorating.

The sun was hot by now. We ate, had a drink and lazed for a bit. Then, confident and fortified, we set about the engine once more. Nothing. We then did what, according to that insufferably pie instruction book of Seagull's, we shouldn't do—kept pulling that damnable starting cord.

This is the whole crux of the matter '... if the engine won't start (always supposing that there is fuel in the carburettor, and that it hasn't run out of fuel) and shows no sign of life after three or four pulls of the starting cord, and ONLY three or four, WHIP OUT THE PLUG AT ONCE ... don't go on pulling the cord.' And so on. Then ... 'if the plug is removed at once, and the points cleaned, on replacing the plug the engine will start immediately.'

But will people do this? ... No, they won't ... instead they go on pulling the starting cord for twenty minutes or so, pumping more and more fuel into the engine, and filling the plug with oil, and then have to row home, and sometimes (if they've got the strength) write a furious letter to the manufacturers.

'We have no sympathy with these people at all.'

In defiance of everything its makers said, the engine capitulated in the face of our importunate pulling and started. We smiled at each other, exchanging looks of mystified triumph diluted with apprehension. The engine didn't sound very healthy but we decided to go on—neither of us was keen on tempting fortune by stopping it and trying to get it to run more smoothly. Better an engine running roughly than one not running at all, we felt.

John was doubtful about the wisdom of going in to Mandraki. None of us had our passports with us and I had left the AA carnet for *Aeolus* behind. In the circumstances he thought it might be better if we didn't go there. The port authorities, he felt, might be difficult. Surely, I said, no one would behave towards us as though we should have proper ship's papers? I was later to find out that indeed they would.

Anyway, we needed petrol so we decided to put in near Petros boatyard, close by Bamboula's, a restaurant built over the sea on stilts, and where until the Greek government stopped it as undesirable, one could watch men happily engaged in the eccentrically agreeable Greek custom of breaking plates. I can't think why this innocent diversion has been banned. It must, surely, be one of the most effective and harmless ways there are of getting rid of tensions. It is also a very effective way of giving *stimmung* to a party. There used to be a client at Bamboula's who used to smash plates over his head with every sign of satisfaction, sitting with broken china piled round his chair and gazing about him with amiable self-approbation. We shall not see his like again—presumably.

We filled our petrol containers at the petrol station opposite Bamboula's and then, tempted in spite of the generous quantities of wine we had on board, decided to have a drink in the taverna. Fatal decision. Having decided to drink we were tempted to eat as well. There is nothing more lotus eating agreeable than to sit in a taverna with a bottle on the table and a spread of meze before one: tomatoes, olives, peppers, bread and cheese. We dawdled, reluctant to leave, but conscious at the back of our minds of the mechanical question mark hanging over us. Would the engine get us back to Lindos? We decided we had better find out before any more of the day slid past, settled our modest bill—the prices in Bamboula's go up like a fever patient's temperature chart in the evening when there is a band and dancing.

The engine loafed into activity after some persuasion, emitting a ragged and unhealthy sound which made us anxious. But there was nothing for it but to go on. If the worst came to the worst perhaps evening might bring a wind that would help us back to Lindos. I let in the clutch and we moved off to the waved farewells of the taverna people and a cluster of small boys. These, like flies, are ubiquitous in Greece. The early afternoon sun beat down on us and, working on the wine, made us soporific. We made no attempt at conversation, absorbed in the effort of staying awake. I thought about the party last night.

I had arrived late—reasoning from past experience that things would be just warming up if I got there at about eleven. There was no sign of life in the lower room of the two-storeyed house but a shambles of used plates, cutlery and empty bottles indicated that there were people about and something was going on. I called out. There was no answer. I called out again and then once more. While I was standing, uncertain what to do next, my host appeared, heavy-eyed and with a steep list. He greeted me amiably, with evident unrecognition and total vagueness, swept a hospitable arm round the room, said 'help yourself, everybody's somewhere' and staggered back into the room from which he'd emerged. As he closed the door he said in confidential, discreet tones: 'got company'. I don't think he recognised me, even after our conversation, although we knew each other quite well.

There was a loft ladder leading to the room above. Following the sound of music, I climbed it. A few heads turned slowly in my direction as I got to floor level, studied me with total disinterest, and looked blankly to their front once more. It was a disconcerting reception. I knew everyone in the room at least by sight and to say hullo to. The room was thick with smoke and the clinging smell of burning joss sticks. I tiptoed across the room towards a vacant space on the floor. Everyone was barefooted so I slipped my shoes off. There was nothing that looked like alcohol to be seen so I tiptoed back across the room to the stairs. A few eyes opened heavily and followed my movements with stupefied torpor. I felt like a man who has without thinking whistled a few bars of a ditty in the hush of a cathedral—although the room was by no means quiet, but filled with low background music, a composition of silences, drum beats and whistles, what sounded like the scuffing of shoes, the rattle of bones. Now and then a hoarse voice sounded. I clearly heard the word 'man' once, so the music wasn't as far out as all that.

I rescued the bottle I had brought with me from the table downstairs. Holding its enticing coolness gratefully I slid reverently back into the room. Africa had taught me to respect the devotions of others. I settled myself with my back against a wall, beside a camp bed, only vaguely aware in the dim light that it was occupied, and poured myself a drink. At the liquid sound a girl turned over and rescued a glass from the floor. She held it out. I filled it. She smiled her thanks, took a sip, placed the drink on the floor, and rolled back, adjusting her partner to her liking before settling once more into immobility.

A man sat propped against the wall opposite me, his head bent towards one shoulder and his mouth slackly open. A girl slumped beside him, eyes closed and with her chin pointing at the ceiling. The naked electric light bulb overhead filled her eye sockets and the hollows under her cheekbones with shadows. Her face looked like a death mask, a macabre adjunct set upon a body whose slack contours were moulded attractively by the same light which pared her face down to a skull.

I finished the bottle and waited a bit in the hope that something might break the funereal wake. Nothing did. I crept away. The record player clicked as I left and shifted a new disc into position. It was the only sign of life stirred by my subdued departure. I walked soberly out into the night. I had never before seen so turned-off a collection of turned-on people—the lot of them stoned out of their senses.

The engine stuttered bringing me back to the present. John and I made a simultaneous movement towards it. But all was well and it resumed its ragged beat and kept it up until we got back to Lindos.

I spent a lot of time after that trip having the Seagull looked at by self-styled experts in Rhodes or in having it seen to by local ones. It would run like an angel in their workshops, start at once when I got it back and once more attached to *Aeolus*, and then for no discernible reason refuse to function. It became the most diagnosed and treated engine in Greece.

The sun was setting as we entered Lindos bay, turning the Acropolis rock and the fortifications which crown it to gold gradually enriched to bronze and deepening to red as the sun died. The columns of the Hellenic ruins stood out against a sky streaked with tumescent crimson. A few lingering tourists stared down at us from the ramparts high above us. On the flat rocks to the left of the entrance to the bay the last obstinate sunbathers were reluctantly gathering up their things. We moored *Aeolus*, relieved at having got back so easily, but with regret that we had done no sailing.

Social activity in a place like Lindos goes in spurts. There is, all at once, a clutch of dinners, parties, picnics and other occasions—a visit to the cinema in Rhodes or to one of the Turkish restaurants there. Then there is a lull, an absence of organised occasions which is total.

That evening marked the beginning of a round of events. Greek friends, Betty and Michael, were giving a dinner and there was a bottle party later in the evening at another house, which, undoubtedly, would go on all night.

Mavis, Willard and I were the only foreigners at the dinner party. Greek hospitality is always overwhelmingly generous. The wise man, or the experienced one, fasts before going to a meal in a Greek house.

A long table was laid in the courtyard and we sat about drinking as Betty, whose given name in Greek is Paraskivi—Friday—and women guests carried out a stream of dishes from the kitchen and placed them on the table's white length until it was covered with food: large bowls of tomato and cucumber salad, meat balls, dolmades—minced meat and rice wrapped in vine leaves—kefthedes—sausage shaped rissoles of chopped meat—and souvlaki. Souvlaki in Greece is usually what is called kebab in the Middle East—pieces of meat on a skewer and cooked over a grill. What the Turks and some Greeks call kebab, donner kebab, is lean meat pressed into a cone. This is cooked by revolving it in front of a panel of heat. Thin slices are then cut off the outside, exposing uncooked meat, and served rolled up in a peta, a pancake made of brown meal which is very similar to the Indian chuppati, but greasy, smaller and thicker—about the size of that other Indian bread, the parata, a flaky chuppati about as big as a large saucer. The meat laid on the peta is garnished with tomatoes, peppers and onions. Seasoning is added and a topping of yoghurt. It is delicious and a meal in itself. Very good ones are made by a man I was for a long time convinced was the head of the Jewish community in Rhodes, served from his miniscule shop in an old archway that stands on the left of the square at the bottom of Socrates street, looking up the street. He only opens at three in the afternoon. His name is Kirie (Mr) Cohen —a gratifyingly recognisable name in such exotic surroundings. After the conquest of Rhodes by the Turks the Jewish community was left undisturbed in the Old City, the Turks confining their enthusiastic slaughter to Christians. Those who survived were driven out beyond the walls of the Old City. It is curious that a people who spent so much time massacring Greeks, Armenians, Christians and Arabs in commercial quantities should have laid off the Jews, the accepted Aunt Sallys of so much of the world's violence for so long—a creditable restraint which makes the usual Turkish blood lust more puzzling.

There were also bowls of that delicious food Tzadsiki on the table, a dish made with yoghurt and garlic. You scoop it up with bread in the same way you do with that over-rated Swiss dish, fondu. There was also that other excellent dish, a spread, taramasalata, a compost of fish roes, garlic and lemon leavened sometimes by the addition of bread crumbs to make it go further. And there were fried potatoes and chipped, slices of egg plant in batter, olives, nuts, green peppers, sections of cheese—all the different kinds of meze to support the staples of the meal.

When a guest showed signs of flagging he was urged to new efforts by Betty in her Australian English and in Greek, her brown eyes bright with pleasure and generosity. More quietly, her schoolmaster husband seconded her efforts.

After dinner there was dancing. Greek mixed dancing has some resemblance to Scottish—a resemblance that brought honking Highland hoots from Mavis who, for so small a woman is capable of surprisingly loud noises—but it is less boisterous than Scottish dancing. The measures are sedate and the only physical contact between you and your partner is a holding of hands—there is not even the innocent abandon of an arm about the waist.

The simplicity of a Greek party is pleasant, a relaxed and homely feeling in contrast to the tautness one feels in the background of even the most sedate of foreign parties.

We left Betty and Michael's house at one in the morning and took a back way through the village. The lanes and alleys were deserted, tranquil under the light of a nearly full moon. Our footsteps echoed sharply in the stillness of the night. The party we were going on to was at a house close to my new one. Its previous tenant had been an American school teacher, a thin blonde refugee from New York schools. The experience of teaching in them had bitten deeply into her —her stories of near rape at the hands of her pupils, muggings and rackets, were told to the accompaniment of expressions of her relief at having escaped from that life. 'Brother!' she would exclaim, 'I'm telling you and I'm not kidding,' or 'that kid was stoned right out of his skull. Was I glad when ...'

The interior of the house had been transformed by its new tenants. When the school teacher had it there had been mobiles hanging from the ceilings, objects found on the beach, pieces of twisted wood and pebbles on every mantelpiece and shelf: and a display of dildos carved in wood which she claimed to have found when clearing rubbish away from under the sleeping platforms. There had been children's drawings everywhere. Now, the house was stark and empty, a shell which proclaimed impermanence. Even the people and the music failed to dispense its feeling of stark emptiness. The atmosphere was thick.

Our host unstuck himself from an anaemic girl he was dancing with, waved to us and said 'Hi!' as we deposited our contribution of bottles. The usual policeman attendant upon foreign parties gave us an uneasy smile, a death's head of an unwanted guest always inflicted by the authorities if they get wind of a party. No one could ever explain what purpose these guardians served—but it was a good way for the police force to get free drinks and to pick up girls: perhaps it was a welfare measure for them, a sort of comforts for the troops, Greek style.

I quickly grew tired of the party and left, walking down to the Platea through the deserted village. *Aeolus* lay quietly in a spectral sea. Three parties in two days. It was time I took her to look at Symi and the Turkish coast. Tomorrow I would take the Seagull into Rhodes once again, and then set off. So much for plans made at the blossoming of a new day. Tomorrow had already arrived—and the day brought an imperative instruction from solicitors to return at once to England and attend to matters connected with a threatened libel action against me.

I flew home. The plane crossed the sea I had hoped soon to sail more widely. Islands lay spread out below us—some lapped with a fringe of surf, others high peaked and with traces of ancient occupation clearly visible upon their dun, primaeval, desolate slopes. And, in places, there were irruptions of land just breaking the sea's surface—mere outlines, crescent shaped broken saucers, jag toothed, that showed where a range of volcanic mountains had, in past ages, sunk. It was a sea of infinite temptation—an expanse peopled with islands of legend. Come hell, high water and all the fustian acrobatic tricks of esurient lawyers in array I would be back to sail among them before long.

15

Helen was the first among women. Her beauty launched a thousand ships and caused a major war. Lindos, because of its beauty is the first among the lovely towns and villages of Greece, and the sanctuary built in the tenth century BC on the great rock which dominates the village was dedicated to the first among goddesses, Athena—Athena Lindia.

Aeolus, lying watched over by friends in Lindos bay, was the first of her kind to be built. In common with Helen, Athena and Lindos she has beauty. What more compelling reason could I have for escaping from London and the legal business which had wrenched me away from Greece.

I had flown from Athens to London. My air fare should have bought me a share in the airline. I decided to return by train and economise by doing without a couchette, hoping the train would be empty enough to allow me to stretch out on a seat for the night.

The Acropolis Express leaves Ostend daily for Athens, an enormous improvement over the old train which used to lurch across Europe, gathering passengers at every stop on the way. It was usually overcrowded, the water ran out and, in Yugoslavia, the soldiery occupied it and conducted military exercises upon the persons of female tourists. You had to make changes en route and suffer painful incertitudes as a result of the misinformation you were fed about when and where these should, or would, occur. The whole business of travelling by the old train called for endurance and courage beyond the normal call of duty—and a degree of Oriental resignation beyond the capacity of most.

The Acropolis Express has a direct connexion with London and is a fine train, one which moves with decision, knows where it is going and how it proposes to get there. It doesn't run out of water and you can get food on board, though it is more satisfactory and a great deal cheaper to take one's own.

You meet people on trains. It is one of the interests of travelling, and on expresses particularly you meet people who have a right to claim your attention. I did. For the first few stops in Belgium there was a quick turnover of passengers—the Acropolis Express gets off to a slowish start. They were for the most part office workers, I judged. And then we stopped being a suburban commuters' train. I found myself alone in the compartment with a single other passenger. He was a Turk and he sat opposite me. I like Turks, the few I have met. This one obviously wanted to talk. He was nervous and kept glancing at the corridor outside, getting up and going to the door, sitting down again. Finally pulling a very long nail file out of the inside pocket of his jacket, he wagged it at me and said 'It is not right.'

'Oh?'
'Yes.'
'Really?'
'He should have killed me.'
'Oh?'
'Yes.'
'Really?'

I cleared my throat. The conversation appeared to die. But I wanted more. Who should have killed him? And why?

The Turk shook his head like a man in pain and unable to understand the strange impositions of fate, a man overwhelmed by recollection.

He had done this several times. It was what had first stirred my interest in him, marked him as a man with a story to tell.

During the next several hours I heard what was on his mind. I heard it again and again, interrupted by long silences, accompanied by disapproving clucks of the tongue, head shaking, self-deprecation and admonition, triumphant sly grins and pauses.

He had had an affair with a Belgian woman. Her husband, an army officer, had surprised them at what according to my sorrowing Turk was not the most convenient of moments. The husband was armed but had not fired. This seemed to rile the Turk. Any man, he said, should kill in the circumstances—but an officer, armed, who failed to do so ...

'Look,' he said, spreading his arms wide again, 'here I am.' This proving his continued existence was not a figment of my imagination, brought the outsize nail file to within a hairsbreadth of my face.

He felt deeply for the honour of the Belgian Army, for himself— a man insulted by not being killed: indeed, for all men—one of whose inalienable rights, he appeared to think, was the right to die at the hands of the man he had cuckolded.

'I am very wicked' he muttered at intervals with every sign of satisfaction. He fixed me with bright, deeply shadowed brown eyes. 'I am married.' He sighed. 'Imagine such a man. In uniform and armed. Me, with his wife! And here I am. An officer, too.'

He smiled a smile of gaiety and innocence. 'When he came in I was frightened,' he went on. 'I had no knife. But I had this.' He shook the nail file at me. 'Get quickly from clothes.' He accompanied the words by a lightning plunge of his hand into the inside pocket of his jacket. He shrugged his shoulders and slumped despondently. 'Perhaps I should go back to Turkey. You think?'

I was, as a matter of fact, thinking very hard. But his question was purely rhetorical. He shrugged again, sighed, and started to clean his nails with the file. He put the file away, said he was tired, and suggested sleep. I wondered about the wisdom of going to sleep in the same compartment, and thought of moving to another. He stretched himself out on the seat. I did the same on the other. He got up. I watched him warily. He put out the lights and settled himself again, giving me a slight smile. I wondered if he had guessed my thoughts. Just before he fell asleep—I made sure I had stayed awake until he did—he said: 'Me, I would have killed him, in Turkey: and I am not an officer.'

I was grateful to the Turk. He had helped to pass the time. He had also made me resolve that, should I ever feel tempted to stray from the paths of rectitude in Turkey, I wouldn't. This is the kind of knowledge no traveller can afford to ignore. I had, years ago, learned that Mediterranean man has a lower flash point than the Anglo-Saxon. It was as well to be reminded that this was still so—even if I was engaged in a protracted affair with a boat. The Turk left the train in Germany, shook me by the hand and gave a reminiscent shake of the head as he closed the compartment door behind him.

I left for Rhodes on board *Miaoulis*—the boat that had taken *Aeolus* to Rhodes. This time I travelled deck. I met Charlie on *Miaoulis*.

Wherever you go in Greece, however small the place, you are likely to find a Greek home from America or Australia—from everywhere on earth, for that matter. But Greek-Australians and Greek-Americans predominate. They are usually elderly men who have spent from thirty to fifty years away from Greece. They are nostalgic. When they are abroad they dreamt of coming back to Greece one day, of dying there. Having returned, they find much not to their taste—are torn between love of Greece and dissatisfaction. When they find an Englishman or an American they like to talk to him, recall their days in the States or

Australia. They are sometimes a bore and difficult to escape from, sometimes interesting. But whatever else they may or may not be, they are always helpful, always willing to oblige and to go to endless trouble to be of service to the traveller. The Greek tradition of hospitality, with them, is able to express itself to the full because there is no language difficulty—though they often speak surprisingly bad Anglo-American or Anglo-Australian considering the years they have spent in those countries.

Charlie had been in Australia for some fifty years and spoke fluent, wildly fragmented Australian. I once saw an enraged British sailor cursing a French port official, 'Frogs. Frogs. Frogs. Bloody something frogs.' He thrust his head forward. 'Tie your something hands behind your something backs and you couldn't something well talk!'

Anyone who served in the Forces during the Second World War may remember a circular about the Free French, instructing all ranks that the first F in the abbreviation FF stood for the word Free. Good soldiers, denied their expletive crutch, but trying to comply, found themselves linguistically confused. Charlie, denied the expletive bloody, which he pronounced 'pleddie' would have been similarly confused, and seriously handicapped conversationally. He came from Castelorizzo, that Greek possession which is the furthest east of all Greece's islands. It lies close to Turkey and some eighty miles from Rhodes. Like most Greeks, especially expatriate ones, he was a patriot. Castellorizo, to him, was the jewel of the Mediterranean, the crown of Greece, the pearl of the world. The fact that today it is an island of only about 400 inhabitants weighed not at all with him. Let him who would ignore Castellorizo! He would be the poorer for it, Charlie thought. He described his island's beauties to me with fervour and recounted its past glories. When he learnt that I had a boat he pressed Castellorizo's claims to a visit on me with passion. When another Greek tried to extol the glories of his own birthplace Charlie swept him aside with a contemptuous 'don't talk pleddie nonsense'. That fixed him. As a result of that meeting I know that one day I shall sail to Castellorizo, where there is a sea cave claimed to be more beautiful than the Blue Grotto at Capri, and where one can base oneself to explore the coast of Asia Minor.

The bus cleared the last rise. And there was Lindos below. For the first time, I failed to take in the sweep of the bay, the great rise of the Acropolis rock out of the sea, the luminous white of the houses bright against the incredible blues of water and sky. My eye went straight to the spot where I had left *Aeolus*. And there she was, lying as I had left her. Only then I allowed myself the pleasure of looking at the most beautiful sea-place on earth.

Lindos in ancient times was renowned for its shipbuilding and was sited further to the N-W than the present village, in the neighbouring Viglika bay. Today the site has only a few vegetable garden plots and single-roomed huts on it, occupying a plain which stretches back from the sea to the rising land below the coast road.

Ancient Lindos' power was based on a standing force of 10,000 men, it is claimed—like Sparta it relied on men and not walls: the site had no natural defences. There is an area still known as Miriandri—10,000 men, presumably the place where they had their barracks or training ground. Nothing now remains to mark the spot where there must once have been great commercial and shipbuilding activity, with all the attendant installations needed for their support: and, as yet, no excavations have been made to uncover what the centuries have destroyed and covered over. So the increasing thousands of tourists continue to pass on their way to the present Lindos without a glance at the ancient site.

One's instinct is to treat with reserve the story of Lindos' standing force of 10,000 men, in spite of the name Miriandri—there is a suspicious coincidence about the figure 10,000, the number of men Xenophon led in the great march from Persia. Xenophon promised a tenth of the spoils taken by the 10,000 to Apollo and Artemis. Rhodes is Apollo's island and Lindos a religious focal point of the island. By association, in the garbling process of history—? And Artemis was widely venerated across the way in Asia Minor. But there is a curious story told in Lindos by the old people which supports, in a tenuously indirect way, the claim that Lindos' main centre of power used to be located at Viglika.

After the siege of Troy, so the story goes, Helen visited Lindos and stayed with the widow of King Tlepolemos, King of Lindos, who was killed at Troy. At night, while Helen slept, the bereaved Queen overpowered her and, in revenge for her husband's death at Troy, the blame for which she laid at Helen's door, executed Helen by hanging her from an olive tree at Viglika.

When asked, Lindians deny that Viglika was more important in antiquity than the present village of Lindos—and yet the story told by Lindians names Viglika as the place of Helen's execution. It is hardly likely that the King would live in the lesser part of a settlement, or that the Queen would drag her victim over rough country all the way to Viglika from Lindos. Helen's fate, according to this Lindos legend, is startlingly different from Homer's version of what happened to her after Troy: first to Egypt with Menelaus, and then to Sparta: Queen again.

I started at once putting *Aeolus* into commission again. Most of her gear had been housed in a boathouse shared by Polly and John Hope and Willard Manus. She had ridden to her moorings quietly and without trouble while I had been away, I was assured by everyone. Nothing had been touched and she had suffered no harm.

During the journey back to Greece I had, I thought, solved the reason why I had had so much trouble with the Seagull—I had simply forgotten to make the proper libations to the gods. In the part of Africa in which I had served no right thinking man would dream of doing anything of importance without making an offering to the gods first—and always, before drinking, a man would pour a measure upon the ground for the spirits of the ancestors. I had at one time been meticulous about libations. But I had grown slack and then forgotten to perform them at all. The fault was mine and I had been warned. It was not as though I didn't know that Greece was a magic land.

I needed crew for my trip to Symi. My intention was to sail south round the tip of Rhodes, rounding Cape Praso Nisi, and then head north, and make for Symi via Khalki and Alimnia, the main islands off the west coast of Rhodes which I had seen from the heights when visiting the burial grounds and lost city. My interest in Symi had first been roused because it was the island where the Knights of St John used to build the frigates with which they harried the Turks. They also drew their crews from Symi, and from Kalymnos, another sponge fishing and caique building island. Both islands still build boats to this day and are still engaged in sponge fishing. I had heard there was a new and interesting boat building venture on Symi—and I have long had an ambition to own a caique.

The people of Lindos maintain that no yacht has left Lindos and made the passage round Cape Praso Nisi. I don't know if this is true: I doubt it. It may have been said to discourage me because they thought *Aeolus* too small to make the passage. Certainly, later, when I sailed past the Cape as crew of a yacht, I got a very disquieting view of its turbulent waters as we kept well clear of it on our way to Carpathos and Crete. The Lindians were positive. You must not, they said, try to round Cape Praso Nisi. I took their advice, especially as David Helton, a writer who lives in Lindos, and who had offered to come with me to Symi, had had almost no dealings with boats at all. Praso Nisi would have to wait until another occasion. David is a Texan. He is tall and slim and slight, with a drooping moustache and leisurely manner, a civilised man and very pleasant companion but not a sea dog.

We made our preparations and assembled our gear. I noticed with alarm that David's included a crate of beer. Normally the most accommodating of men, he would, I realised, be adamantly opposed to any suggestion that it should be left behind. Besides, I had my retsina and oozo. He was a beer and brandy man. So be it.

We set off, heading north for Rhodes. This meant that we should not, this trip, go anywhere near the islands of Khalki and Alimnia. The sea was calm and the sky cloudless. There was no wind. In this flat calm sea we could have loaded ourselves to the gunnels with bulky crates of beer and they would not have hampered our handling of *Aeolus*. We were seen off by friends, all irreverently sceptical about our prospects of getting anywhere near Symi, or anywhere much at all for that matter.

At David's suggestion we decided to make our first stop at an inlet near Cape Vudhi, not far from Rhodes, a place where the actor Anthony Quinn owns land. We thought we might spend the night there, get things straight on board, and make for Rhodes the next day, sample its fleshpots, and head for the Turkish coast and Symi the following day: a nice leisurely bummel in a boat.

The inlet was a deep fiord-like cut in the rocky coast. We nosed our way in and let go our anchor in deep water some distance from the shore, keeping well out so as not to disturb a couple sunbathing on the beach at the end of the fiord. We opened a bottle of beer and a bottle of retsina and started to prepare some food. The man on the beach got up, entered the water gingerly and began to swim towards us, using a laboured breast stroke. We greeted him politely as he came alongside.

'You know this bay is private property?' he stated, ignoring our invitation to climb aboard and have a drink.

'Oh, really?'

'Yeah. Belongs to Anthony Quinn.'

'Oh? Who's he?'

He took that one between the eyes.

'You ever heard of the picher, *The Guns of Navarone*?'

'As a matter of fact I haven't.'

David, prepared to be more amiable than I was, said 'Sure, I've heard of it: yeah.'

The man looked as though he had had a profound faith restored to him. 'Well,' he said, 'they shot that picher right here.'

To my certain knowledge there are at least two other places claimed to be where *The Guns of Navarone* was shot. It was a good film but where it was shot was a matter of profound indifference to me.

'Really?' I said, not prepared to forget that he had opened the engagement. I have always found the word 'really' one that is calculated, in the right circumstances, to give the maximum offence with the minimum effort. I appeared to be right, as far as our gamekeeper was concerned, anyway.

'Well.' He began to make an authoritative gesture with his arm, lost his grip of *Aeolus*' gunnel, went under, and swallowed water. He came up flurried and sputtering, regained his hold and said '—all this belongs to him, he bought it.'

'Not the sea, surely?'

He thought about that. I could see him doing it. The travail reminded me of a journalist interviewing a visiting American wrestler.

'And I understand, Mr Katzenellenbogen, that you are a college graduate?'

'Sure. Yeah. Yeah, dat's right.'

'What may I ask did you major in?'

'Wrasslin' and clog dancin'.'

It was clear that our visitor's IQ was about the same as the wrestler's.

'Maybe you never heard of Anthony Quinn either?' he asked me, trying to be offensive.

'As a matter of fact I haven't,' I said, being both offensive and untruthful.

He beamed. 'Say, what you two guys doing here, anyways?' He looked at David. 'You American?'

'Yeah.'

'Say, that's a nice boat you got here.'

'Would you like to come aboard?' I asked, always ready to grasp an olive branch when it is proffered.

He jerked his head in the direction of the beach. 'Nah, got a dame wid me' and added with sublime inconsequence 'we got fried chicken for lunch.' He raised a hand in salute and ploughed his way back to the beach.

Of such encounters is the stuff of travel made, and it had demonstrated *Aeolus*' capacities as a peacemaker.

David looked at me thoughtfully. 'Maybe we ought to get out of here.'

'Right.'

Two speedboats came skidding into the fiord and nosed towards the beach. They were full of Frenchmen and girls in bikinis on a trip from Rhodes. The place resounded with animated talk and laughter. They landed on the beach and our friend immediately walked over to them. There was a brief discussion, a great deal of protesting talk, arm waving and indignant female exclamations, then the French party settled down on the beach and busied themselves with preparations for a picnic. Our friend hung about uncertainly.

As we heaved up the anchor his girl friend set out towards us, topless, on a Li-Lo. We waited for her. 'Have you,' she called out when she got within range, 'seen the amphorae lying on the bottom on the other side?'

The surrealist note set by this encounter was maintained throughout our trip which lasted a week.

As we drew near Rhodes the weather turned ugly and the wind quickly freshened to a driving assault which whipped tops off the waves and flung stinging spray at us. Until then we had been going happily under sail at a nice, steady wind.

We decided to make for shelter. The place we eventually found to give us a lee was close to a naval establishment. We were soaking wet and very relieved at having found shelter of a sort from what was by now a very agitated sea. David had suffered more from the squall than I had because, when the weather looked as though it was turning, I had put on some lightweight oilies. We got out the brandy bottle. A sailor hailed us from the shore, a naval rating. Through an interpreter, and with much difficulty against the sound of the wind, he informed us that it was too rough for a boat to be out. It struck us both that we were at least as well qualified as he was to know this. We must, he went on, put in to Mandraki for shelter. But that is precisely what we've put in here for, I pointed out.

'Everyone must go to Mandraki. All yachts have been ordered to put in there.'

I pointed out that making for Mandraki would mean putting out into what he was telling us were conditions too bad to remain out at sea in. This cut no ice with him. We must go to Mandraki, he insisted. Conditions were too bad for boats to be out. Rather than risk being blown out of the water by the Greek Navy or, a more fearsome prospect, getting involved in a protracted argument with officialdom, we decided to take the easy way out and chance it with the seas.

Bedraggled, wet and frightened, we made it into Rhodes harbour, got a line ashore and, stern to as is usual in Greek ports, made fast.

'Have you,' asked a spectator standing on the quayside looking down at us, 'come all the way from England in that little boat?'

Had we hell. We had come a mere 25 miles. My tyro status as a sailor had been exposed in one innocent, lancing question. But the fact of its having been asked at all made us feel a bit doggish. I noticed when we got ashore that David's normal stiff legged Texan saunter had a roll to it. Still, the question did indicate that we had come in and secured in a reasonably competent fashion: Rhodians know about boats—this was, after all, the capital of an island whose traffic with the sea had been so important at one time that the Romans adopted the Rhodian system of maritime law for the whole of their empire.

It was the first time I had stepped on to the Mandraki from a boat and it gave a more particular savour to the occasion than did landing in Rhodes harbour from a ship. Coming ashore here enrolled one in the ranks of all those who had during the course of ages visited this staging post between east and west. And who hadn't been here?

Rhodes, the city founded by Lindos, Ialysos and Kamiros in 480 BC, had seen the march of conquerors, received the visits of kings, opened her doors to scholars, artists and traders through the centuries. It had been the Clapham junction of the Mediterranean, and a springboard for some of man's most seminal endeavours: Cadmus, according to legend, dedicated a bronze vessel here when he founded a temple to Poseidon. He was at the time searching for his sister, Europa, who had been carried off by Zeus. This was how the Phoenician alphabet came to Greece.

Peoples of myth and legend: Myceneans, Cretans, Acheans, Dorians and Phoenicians among others, came to Rhodes, Persians, Macedonians, Spartans, Egyptians, Romans, Saracens, Crusaders, Genoese, Venetians, the Knights of St John, who were a Russian salad of nationalities, Turks and Italians all held Rhodes at one time or another, if not by physical occupation then by political influence. The Germans held it in World War II, the last to do so by force of arms. The British then held it after them—but only as stewards—between 1945 and 1947, when the island once more became part of Greece.

Alexander the Great came to Rhodes and so did St Paul. A bay near Lindos is said to be where he landed. It is, reasonably enough, called St Paul's bay. There is a little chapel there which is the scene of an annual, mildly Dionysic, panegyry—a religious festival which provides an occasion for secular jollity without diminishing its sacerdotal character. It takes place once a year. Panegyries, all varying in nature, are held all over Greece on saints' days.

Haroun al Raschid knew Rhodes, and Cassius stripped the city of its works of art—at any rate of all those he could lay his hands on: and, remembering what rapacious fellows the Romans were, that must have meant pretty well the lot. Pliny reports that he counted 3,000 statues in the Rhodes of his time, a hundred of them of colossal proportions— an output by native craftsmen which makes credible the gigantic task of fashioning the Colossus of Rhodes, once one of the seven wonders of the world: and which Chares of Lindos, its sculptor, took twelve years to cast and raise. The traditional stance of the Colossus, legs astride, is rejected by some authorities in favour of one in which stability was achieved by placing one leg in front of the other and adding a staff. This would have given a triangular base, a shape which would have simplified the enormous problems involved in erecting the statue in a legs astride position. The Laocoon, that serpentine group of statuary, once as lauded as it is now vilified, was also a Rhodian work— Michaelangelo himself was present when it was excavated from ruins in Rome.

Caesar visited Rhodes and so, according to an inscription in the public lavatory beside the Shell petrol station, did Kilroy—that most ubiquitous of travellers.

One famous visitor to Rhodes has, undeservedly, been almost forgotten—Dieudonné de Gozon, a Knight of St John, to whom goes the honour of slaying the last dragon to have been killed in christendom. Dieudonné was accused by the Grand Master of the Order of setting the whole thing up as a publicity stunt designed to get the job of Grand Master for himself. The Grand Master may well have been right. Dieudonné did get his job. And so deserves to be remembered, if only for being among the earliest to appreciate and exploit the value of publicity. There is an account of how Dieudonné went into training for the event which is a fascinating record of his dedicated professionalism and a monument to partisan writing.

I don't suppose, as his bid for power was successful, that anyone paid much attention when Dieudonné's enemies spread malicious rumours that what in fact he'd killed was probably some old crocodile bought cheap in the bazaar in Alexandria, and smuggled into Rhodes for him by a wily Levantine white hunter of the day.

David and I had our own dragon to slay—the problem of what to do about getting to Symi in the prevailing conditions. We decided to stroll over to one of the cafés facing the yacht harbour and talk about it over a drink.

16

The resemblance was strong enough to get me out of my seat. Surely the coincidence was too great? I must be mistaken. I muttered an apology to David and left, followed by his expression of politely tolerant surprise. I overtook her—not difficult, as she was handicapped by her too high, pointed heels. When I had out distanced her enough for my interest not to be too obvious I turned and walked back towards her. But I didn't really need additional confirmation. My short walk behind her had confirmed my opinion—nowhere else had I seen a woman with quite that same metronomic swing and surge and tumble to her haunches, such generosity of flesh contained in shiny black, or such ritual a pile of black hair.

> De ses cheveux élastiques et lourds,
> Vivant sachet, encensoir de l'alcôve,
> Une senteur montait, sauvage et fauve,

'But what is she doing here in Rhodes?' I asked David when I rejoined him and explained the reason for my sudden departure, satisfying his eyebrow raised enquiry.

'Working,' he replied laconically. He pointed with his head at groups of American sailors walking down the road. 'Sixth Fleet.'

The woman was a whore whose Byzantine opulence had struck me when I had spotted her once in the Piraeus. In the darkening streets she had stood out like a queen among her sisters as she prowled the broken down quarter.

Whenever units of the American Sixth Fleet put into Rhodes some enterprising entrepreneur flies doxies in from Athens—an undertaking of such logistic complexity that it must involve some pretty shrewd and streamlined staff work. The intelligence side alone of the operation can't be simple to set up—and the casting of bread upon the waters to oil the operation must add up to real money.

I should have realised at once, without needing even the sight of the busy liberty boats shuttling between shore and the grey ships to make it clear to me that the American fleet was in: but only now did I realise how many of the women passing by were camp followers. Lucky the sailor to whom fate assigned my Pirean Gaea—no sailor would find, however long he searched, a more opulently curved Earth Mother to satisfy his yearning for the comforts of land.

This venerean traffic is an interesting example of the commercial enterprise the Rhodians have shown throughout history—the result of being fought over through the centuries, so invaded, sacked, used as a pawn in the struggles between peoples and nations, so often becoming a battlefield and the cockpit for fierce ambitions on the part of rulers and states, so exploited, swapped and generally mucked about—without so much as a by your leave from anyone—that they have developed in self defence an opportunist commercial sense only exceeded in sharpness by the Lebanese.

The Rhodians speak Greek. Whether they are Greek in their hearts is a matter for conjecture. Greece since the War of Independence has been strongly nationalist in spirit—and it would be strange if this were not so. She has had the task of creating a state, in modern terms, out of a conglomerate of islands and peoples whose traditional inheritance as Hellenes is a cast of thought dominated by the concept of the independent city-state, the polis, and who were subject to the repressive rule of the Turks for centuries—whose authoritarian rule, if it did not actively, as a matter of policy, attempt to extirpate the Greek idea, was so harsh that it made it almost impossible to sustain even as a romantic abstraction. The people of Rhodes, more than anywhere else in Greece, were caught up in a succession of violent upheavals each of which helped to tear up the people's roots and confuse their loyalties—to such a point that they have lost identity, become an amalgam, a sort of human *tarama salata*. However, one value has remained constant with the Rhodians, whoever held the island and whatever religious or political ideas were imposed on the population: money. And money is what the Rhodians understand—it is something that, however transient anything else may prove, is always with them: the diversity of form it may take makes no difference.

There is an Arab story about three blind beggars whose habit it was to beg for alms beside a bridge. A rich man crossed the bridge one day and gave them alms. When he returned later he found the three beggars fighting. Angry, he stopped and asked them the reason for their quarrel. 'This fool,' the first beggar said pointing to one of the others, 'wants to buy khubes with the money you gave us. And this one wants to buy aish, but I, I want to buy samoun to satisfy my hunger.'

'Fools!' the rich man said, 'those are the three Arabic names for bread—you all want the same thing and you are fighting about it!'

The story is told to illustrate the futility of the quarrel between Islam, Judaism and Christianity—the three great monotheistic religions which have come out of the desert countries of the Mediterranean.

Had the three beggars been Rhodians they would have, quick as a flash, calculated the correct rate of exchange, split the take, and been off like arrows to invest their share in some tourist enterprise.

Money to the Rhodians is the one stable element in an uncertain world—something, whatever its current name may be, which represents a pole—a constant and a lodestone which attracts their attention like a lamp shining in the dark of a stormy night.

An American sailor, discussing the imported whores, said: 'Those broads got dollar signs in their eyes.' He must have hit on a Rhodian one. And yet the Rhodians are soft and welcoming; and their devotion to money never expresses itself with the rancorous greed one finds among French people connected with the tourist industry, a savage hunger for the visitors' money, accompanied by a contempt which is chilling. Though the Rhodians may not have strong political or sentimental attachments to the Greek state, they are still Greek enough in spirit to temper their commercialism with hospitable generosity to the stranger: and they offer their friendship with an easy warmth.

The Mandraki was gradually filling with people. Soon the road in front of the New Market and the yacht harbour would be closed to traffic and given over entirely to pedestrians. The evening promenade is a pleasant custom, a mass stroll in the street to see and be seen: an occasion when man banishes the motor car and asserts his right not to be pushed around by the mechanical Frankenstein. To sit peacefully at one of the cafés on Mandraki during this period and watch people, unharried by cars, enjoying the evening is worth every penny you may be overcharged by the café you have chosen—and the reason why these places will never lose their position as the most popular catering establishments on Rhodes. As a bonus there is the life of the yachts to watch, and the groups of spectators on the quayside enjoying the show the boats offer make an added attraction.

The diversity of people who pass is a constant fascination. To look and be looked at is the main sport of an evening out on Mandraki. The Rhodians turn out in force to see the tourists, the middle-aged and elderly among them to marvel; the young, if they are men, to see if they can find a foreign girl to get off with. The female Rhodians, if they are young, are accompanied by their family or at least by a duenna, and mask with discretion their curiosity. One of the marvels of the modern world is how, except for unimportant and limited exceptions in places like Athens, Greek women are kept from contact with male foreigners—from women foreigners too, for that matter—except for restricted contacts as domestic servants. In spite of this, young Rhodian women are feeling the effects of tourism and becoming its victims. Marriage in Rhodes, as in all Greece, is a matter of arrangement between families. The commercial element is very strong. The prika, a girl's dowry, forms the basis of the marriage contract and is the subject of hard bargaining into which a variety of elements enter: education of the girl, social position, looks. The system is very similar to that prevailing among certain people in parts of Africa south of the Sahara —more supporting evidence for the belief that there was a massive Greek colonisation of some areas of this region of Africa in antiquity.

A substantial part of the dowry, the cash part, may be paid in advance, perhaps all of it—the intention being to improve the future groom's capacity to support a wife. So far so good. But a new element has entered into things. Occasionally, now, a prospective bridegroom, money in his pocket from an advance prika payment, and tempted by the bright lights of Rhodes, falls in with a foreign girl and starts living it up. The dowry money soon disappears and so may the man— as far as the Greek girl is concerned. The next step is for him to begin to depend on foreign girls for a living—there is no shortage of ones prepared to foot the bill for a personable companion. Or he may find himself in demand by foreign men. Whatever way of life he chooses, the position of the abandoned girl is desperate. Without a dowry her chances of marrying are virtually nil. The number of Greek men prepared to marry a girl without one is negligible, especially in agricultural communities, or urban ones like Rhodes town where ties with the land are still strong. There always has been, of course, the hazard that a scoundrel with sisters of marriageable age—a man may not marry until he has seen his sisters settled—will devote the dowry money he has received to providing a dowry for a sister. In some cases this is done by arrangement: a certain proportion of the dowry money, it is agreed beforehand, may be used for this purpose. A girl also used to, and in general customarily still does, bring a house with her to the marriage. This is now on occasions replaced by a taxi or, if the favoured vehicle is a large American one, the price of half a taxi. Whether house or taxi, this constitutes a property which it is difficult for a man to make away with—and, like the returnable dowry in Africa, represents a safeguard for the stability of the marriage.

We lounged in our chairs, drinking and grateful for the feel of stable earth beneath us while we discussed our plans, keeping an eye on

Aeolus and the people passing at the same time. David doubted the wisdom of trying to make for Symi. Apart from the weather, about which we were both doubtful, he was finding his tight jeans a difficulty on board and his hands were giving him trouble. They were already beginning to blister. We were both reluctant to abandon the attempt, influenced, at the back of our minds, by the thought of the leg pulling we would have to put up with on our return to Lindos.

As we discussed things I became conscious of the behaviour of a sailor standing on the quayside among a group of people looking down at *Aeolus*. He was showing all the signs of a man who was there for a purpose; questioning people, looking about him and other signs of impatience.

I walked over. As I approached, a man pointed to me. The sailor turned. 'You the captain?' he asked politely.

'Yes.' I have never got used to being addressed as captain—a title Greeks readily bestow on anyone in charge of boats above a certain size; and it's not a very big size. The sailor asked for the ship's papers. I handed him the AA carnet which was all the 'ship's papers' I had. He looked at it with mistrust. It took me some time to convince him that that was all he was going to get. He eventually accepted it. In spite of his misgivings he was amiable and went off with a rueful grin after sketching a salute. I could get the carnet back in the morning, he informed me as he went off, from the Port Office.

David came over and we went on board *Aeolus* to tidy things up. Every move we made was attentively watched by the people standing above us on the quay. I suggested we put the awning up. It would, if we slung it low enough, screen us from the kibitzers when we went to bed, which we proposed to do lying one on either side of the centreboard casing. When the time came David chose to lie on a side thwart and the after deck instead. Though I have now slept often enough in both places, I am still not sure which is the more comfortable.

When we had finished tidying up, and had got the awning slung between the masts, we decided we couldn't face cooking in front of an audience so we went back to the café. We were finishing our meal when we were joined by Manolis, the Greek captain of a German yacht, *Cormoran*, which had taken part in the 1955 transatlantic race. We asked him what he thought of the prospects of our making Symi the next day. He was non-committal. 'The weather is not sure,' he said. Best to see what the Port Captain had to say in the morning. He looked up at the sky, turning his head one way and then the other. The movement gave his lean body and long featured face an immemorial look. So had sailors looked at the sky ever since man had first ventured on the sea—but in this quickly angered sea the movement is sharper, more immediately alert, than it is among men used to the more ponderously moved waters of the northern countries. He shook his head doubtfully. 'You know. The sea ... You never know.'

We decided to have an early night. By lowering the awning almost to the level of the gunnels we got enough privacy to undress and get into our sleeping bags without offending any susceptibilities. But it was an athletic performance. Just before falling asleep I realised that Manolis was the first person who had not expressed doubts about the wisdom of going to Symi in a boat of *Aeolus*' size. It was a tribute to his eye for a boat, I assured myself.

David and I agreed next morning that neither of us felt much inclined to hang about Rhodes. The lights had remained lit on Mandraki all through the night and there had been a steady trickle of visitors to peer down at us—not that they could see much, but it was still like living in a goldfish bowl and made sleeping no easier.

I had taken the trouble to get the carnet back the previous evening, so we were able to slip out of Mandraki before life in Rhodes began again. The wind was in the north west and I didn't particularly like the look of things. Yesterday's bulletin had still to be posted at the Port Office when I looked. We set the sails and headed north east. My intention was to sail wide of the northern tip of Rhodes and take a look at what things looked like in the direction of Symi. There was broken water over in the direction of the Turkish coast and we ourselves were already feeling the movement of the sea. We decided to turn more to the west and take a closer look. In the distance we spotted two yachts heading towards Rhodes from the direction of Turkey, both motoring. Ignoring this warning we kept going.

A flurrying squall hit us and before we knew what was happening we found ourselves in broken water—the yachts had distracted our attention long enough to let things sneak up on us. I held the course but soon after thought it prudent to haul down the sails and start the Seagull—and realised that going overboard would not be any more difficult than falling off a log. Conditions were exhilarating and made it tempting to go on. But Symi was a long way away. We cleared the tip of Rhodes and turned almost due west, heading straight into the worsening weather. It was cold.

I have never yet met anyone who has believed that the Mediterranean even in summer can be cold enough to make you long for warm clothing. Nor have I ever, in spite of uncomfortable evidence to the contrary, ever quite brought myself to believe it. When the weather is fine conditions can be so beguiling that one forgets. But in an open boat at sea in a turmoil of wind and water you can be very cold, while on land, or in a bigger boat with shelter the temperature is still comfortable. And in a small boat space is cramped. One is fully occupied handling the boat. There is very little chance to get warm clothing out and get dressed up. But Mr Metaxas' brandy is always easy to stow and have ready to hand.

A blister had broken on one of David's hands in spite of the protection of a pair of nylon mittens I had dug out of one of the lockers for him. They were a relic of winter sailing at home which I had magpied aboard 'just in case they would come in useful'.

We decided that, all things considered, there was little point in persisting in our attempt to make Symi. But, still reluctant to abandon our bid, we held our course. *Aeolus* was taking things beautifully, rising easily to the waves and moving ahead confidently but I had a niggling, persistent worry about the Seagull at the back of my thoughts. I remembered only too clearly its temperamental behaviour on the trip to Rhodes with the Hopes. But it was running staunchly and had never faltered on this trip. I was to learn by experience that it only became temperamental when the weather was perfect and conditions ideal. It obviously got bored when things were easy. This may seem too anthropomorphic to swallow. But I have known other machines which have behaved unaccountably.

Some years ago I attended the wedding of Miss Hope Cook, of New York, to the Prince of Sikkim, that enchanting and tiny Himalayan kingdom—and learned on that occasion how inanimate things can respond to forces outside the natural law.

I was to make a film of the wedding. I was late getting to Sikkim and had to start work almost immediately, my interest instantaneously triggered off by a pre-wedding ceremony in which an astrologer inscribed symbols on the bride's hands with a gold stylo. The wedding ceremony itself was followed by seven days of celebration and entertainment in and around the Palace. There were shows given by drummers, dancers and mummers, raptly watched by the polyglot crowds that had poured into Sikkim's capital, Gangtok, for the occasion: pigtailed Tibetans, refugees from the Chinese occupation of Tibet, who had found sanctuary in tiny Sikkim, big men and solid women, smiling and assured, who looked even larger than they were in contrast to the small cocky Nepalese who form a large proportion of the Kingdom's inhabitants; gentle, lovely women from Sikkim itself, and people from all over India, who strolled about and talked and looked at the carnival of events provided for them.

Among the attractions was a Punch and Judy show and, the only incongruous note throughout the whole proceedings, two male prostitutes from India, one a female impersonator riding a gaily panoplied hobby horse, who gave a show in mime and dance. There was such a morbid fascination for me in their corrupt performance against the setting of snow-covered mountains and fluttering prayer flags that I shot more film on them than I should have.

The Buddhist marriage ceremony was to take place in the Royal Temple, which stood in a large open space by the Palace. An American TV company was shooting the wedding in black and white. I was using colour. When the American chief cameraman heard this he laughed. They were using fast black and white film rated at 500 Weston, he told me. And even then he had his doubts about whether it would be fast enough. I hadn't a hope was what he clearly thought. And then he dispelled my gloom. 'Tell you what,' he generously suggested, 'give me a hand setting up the lights and we'll fix them so maybe you'll get something.'

He had been told he could use six lights, he said. More and the town's electric supply would probably blow up. I thought about the telegram I had sent to Sikkim after being invited, at impossibly short notice, to make the film: 'WHAT LIGHT AVAILABLE?' I had got back the illuminating reply 'SOME LIGHT AVAILABLE.' With the thought of flickering torches wavering in the shadowed darkness of a temple, I had armed myself with colour stock normally used for scientific purposes. It had the advantage of being faster in tungsten light than in daylight—but, I knew, would still be too fast for the bright clarity of the Himalayas. I had not had time before leaving England to get the proper neutral density filters which would have corrected this. So I knew that, however much I stopped the lenses down, I would have to accept a degree of over-exposure in the outside shots, especially the long ones.

When I returned from India I saw a film of the Dalai Lama taking his theological examinations. It had been taken by a member of his entourage with a superb eye for a picture. The film was over-exposed, grossly over-exposed in some passages, and was quite the most beautiful film I have ever seen—the pale washed out colours of the film conveyed the ethereal, spiritual quality of the proceedings, and also captured the same good humoured robustness which one found among the Tibetan refugees in Sikkim. A more sophisticated cameraman would never have had the boldness or imagination to do what that amateur one achieved by accident and ignorance—combined with a natural gift for composing his shots. I wish I had seen that film before leaving for the wedding—I would have deliberately gone for extreme over-exposure. As it was, I did everything I could to reduce this as much as I could.

We fixed the lamps to beams high above the thrones to be occupied during the ceremony by the groom's father, the Maharajah, the groom and the bride. Lighting the Maharajah was simple: the throne he was to occupy was high. Those of the bride and bridegroom were much lower, his a fraction higher than hers.

The next day I suggested to my benefactor that we go back and check the lights. 'Relax,' he said, 'nobody can do anything, not with the lights the height they are.' I urged a precautionary look. He laughed good humouredly. 'O.K. let's go take a look.' We found that during the night the monks had moved the position of every single light because, they said, the positions in which they had been installed were 'not propitious'. When a Buddhist monk says something is not propitious its no use arguing. Give up. Give in. We chose our moment and discreetly shifted the lights back to their original positions, ones more propitious for us.

The interior of the temple was rich with colour. Walls, ceilings and supporting columns merged into one, united by a complexity of intricate, cursive designs covering them. Long pendant sleeves of bright materials hung from the ceiling. Writhing dragons, fanged and sinuous tongued, intertwined with floral motifs in solid colours, greens, reds, golds, silver. Tankas, religious paintings on scrolls, hung on the walls, flanking altars upon which silver vessels piled high with heaped rice and twisted rolls of bread—symbols of fertility and longevity—gleamed in the light of candles. And in glass fronted recesses life-sized figures, legs crossed in the lotus position, sat with calm majesty. Lustrous, glowing, fashioned in gold and silver the Lord Buddha himself and the saint who first brought Buddhism to Sikkim, contemplated the infinite and by their presence proclaimed the triumph of reason over the demons of Tibet—those implacably savage spirits which were before the triumph of Buddhism, the spiritual rulers of the high Himalayan places.

Monks busied themselves about their offices—some of them gigantic men, shaven headed, and built like international rugby football forwards, their dignity of bearing exalted by a genial simplicity of manner.

The body of the temple was crowded with guests: ambassadors from all over the world and their staffs, sombre in black coats and grey spongebag trousers, envoys, representatives of the Indian Army in khaki, bemedalled reminders that the Chinese invaders of Sikkim's north border were stirring menacingly; dark robed Bhutanese from the neighbouring kingdom to the east of Sikkim, conspicuous by their independent bearing, people from a country which had made no bones about throwing down a defiant challenge to China that they would fight on India's side; delicate Indian women in bright gossamer saris, bearded Sikhs, soberly dressed American friends and relations of the bride, richly gowned relatives of the groom. And there were also Lepchas there—those strange, endearing people who practise polyandry with a twist: a woman will marry brothers, up to three of them. And the ménage lives happily. When I asked a Lepcha woman if there were not problems connected with such a marriage she looked at me with clear calm eyes and said: 'Why should there be problems?' And when I asked how one knew who was the father of a child she replied 'What does it matter who is the father of a child? It is the mother that matters.' The Lepchas are a dying people. The Himalayas will be very much poorer for the loss of them.

The bright pools of light from the lamps above focussed attention on the Maharajah, the bride and the groom: the bride in a heavy white gown in the Lepcha fashion down to her ankles, the Maharajah in glowing brocades whose stiff richly embroidered folds caught the light and became lambent. The groom also in brocades and, like the Maharajah, wearing a round Tartar hat.

Bells tinkled. Monks intoned. An abbot sprinkled water from an aspergillum dipped in a silver bowl of water held by an acolyte, and tossed handfuls of rice in the air which he took from a salver held by another. Tall crested helmets of felt, bright yellow, as imperious as those worn by Ulysses and Hector at Troy, rose from among the deep red of the press of monkish robes—the Buddhists of Sikkim belong to the red, unreformed sect and look with suspicion upon the yellow, reformed sect to which the Dalai Lama belongs. But they tolerate them—unlike the Bhutanese who will have nothing to do with them.

The wedding ceremony was a ritual full of beauty, mysterious but lucent in its purity, the product of a civilisation that was gentle, one in process of being eclipsed by the rivalries of India and China. At its conclusion everybody joined in by ceremonially offering scarves to the Maharajah, the bride and the groom, one to each, until the heaps of material growing before them threatened to overwhelm them. Attendants took them away and new piles grew. The scarves offered could be made of the cheapest cotton or the most expensive silk but they had to be white. In the old days—when noble ladies in these parts, on a journey, still carried both a dagger and a phial of poison to ensure death before dishonour at the hands of bandits—the scarves had a more functional use and were used to strangle people.

No cameraman has ever had more exciting targets. Immediately I started shooting my camera began to give trouble. And yet, outside, it had worked perfectly. The TV company's hand camera broke down. They had never had this happen before. Later they were to find that a good part of the material they had shot was out of focus. This is something that just doesn't happen to professionals. A pirate Indian cameraman who had gate-crashed the ceremony had his camera die on him.

I got some good footage, in spite of camera trouble, but I spent a lot of time on my knees fiddling with it to make it work. What I said ill-accorded with my devotional posture. I suppose my camera didn't break down completely because I was, after all, making the film at the invitation of the Prince—but I was clearly being given a warning. After the ceremony, when I started shooting the guests drinking and feasting under marquees set up in the space before the palace and the Temple, my camera worked perfectly.

I offer no explanation. Van der Post tells of a similar experience with a camera when filming in a place particularly sacred to the Bushmen of the Kalahari.

Cameras broke down for reasons that I can't explain in a temple in the Himalayas. For reasons that I can't explain an outboard engine broke down when it shouldn't and ran like a bird when it had every reason not to. But then Greece is a country where the gods are as close to the affairs of men at sea level as they are on the mountains of the roof of the world.

No, I need not have worried about the Seagull. I had more reason to worry about David and myself. Neither of us, I felt, was in control of events to the degree we should have been. If this weather lasted we would before long both be feeling, and probably looking, like pieces of sea-wrack.

We decided it would be wiser to head back for Rhodes, not stopping there, but making our way to Lindos—and taking our time about it. David was becoming anxious about the supply of beer. We would have to keep our eyes open for a taverna where we could replenish supplies.

As we got under the lee of Rhodes things became quieter. We began to relax in the warm sun and calming seas. We were at last able to give Mr Metaxas a rest—not that there was much of him left.

17

The weather was improving and, as we got further under the lee of Rhodes, the sea grew quieter. But we still had our problems. The wind had come round and we were exposed to its intermittent waywardness. Occasional flurries whipped a trouble of shallow waves up and then died away. It moved like a will-o'-the-wisp. One moment it was there, the next it had died away. It would breathe like a zephyr, fade and then pulse up in a series of sharp puffs. It moved about the sea like a boxer in the ring, feinting and weaving, keeping us guessing, never settling in one quarter long enough to let us get its measure. To hoist sails or not? Like a judo black belt fighting a novice, the wind's changes of direction and strength bewildered us. We tried sailing and sat becalmed. We started the Seagull and a fine steady wind sprang up from just the right quarter to help us on our way under sail. But we had been fooled before and ignored its courting. It blew steadily and was not to be denied. We gave up, hoisted sail and listened, content, to the sweet, pleasured sound of water against *Aeolus*' hull. We exchanged gratified looks and a moment later our sails flapped slackly. The only thing to do was start the engine again. I pulled the starting cord. Nothing happened. I pulled again. Still nothing. Another pull. No. One more. We decided to pretend we had all the time in the world and didn't much care anyway if the thing started or not. We had a drink, pumped some water out of the bilges and started clearing up the shambles in the bottom of the boat. What was badly needed were lockers under the side thwarts to stow all the bits and pieces one needed to have ready to hand, I decided, and resolved to have them put in as soon as we got back to Lindos.

While we were playing our petulant game of pretending that we didn't much care if the engine started or not, *Aeolus*, the custodian of the winds, whom I had been at so much pains to ingratiate myself with, unleashed one of his more wayward charges. It sneaked up and swept a jumble of water at us, lifted articles of clothing from where they were hanging to dry, and wrapped them about us and every available projection. By singular dispensation nothing went overboard. It then gave a dazzling display of how to be everywhere at once and nowhere in particular as it dervished around, at one moment blowing steadily and the next slapping us with quick, veering buffets that sent spray flying off the waves and over us.

When we had the last sail tie snugly fastened and the last sheet and bit of cordage untangled, I decided to try and start the engine again. It started at once. The wind died—with such suddenness that it seemed as though someone had closed a door—and a short time afterwards, as we motored steadily along, got up again nice and steady and from exactly the right quarter.

David had found his nylon mittens hampered him and he had taken them off. Handling wet Terylene lines had opened up more blisters on his hands and he was in great discomfort. We regretted our decision not to stop at Rhodes. We were already opposite Anthony Quinn's inhospitable fiord but felt disinclined to put in there for a rest, and kept going. What we wanted was somewhere that would give us shelter when the weather came up again, and where there was a taverna.

'There' David said, pointing.

I thought I had studied the coast fairly attentively when going to Rhodes with the Hopes but I hadn't noticed any tavernas.

But David was right. And he continued to be right. The house which he claimed was a taverna looked to me just like a house and nothing more. It stood close by a small beach in a miniature cove at the end of a bay. Two large rocks flanked the entrance to the cove. I proposed to go in on a stern anchor but, if it didn't hold, there would be a danger of the wind swinging *Aeolus* against the rocks.

Three men, who had been mending a fishing net on the verandah of the house, walked down to the beach when they saw we were going to come in. I ran *Aeolus* at speed in to the cove and they lent a hand hauling her bow up on the beach. I got lines ashore to prevent her swinging against the rocks and the men insisted on adding a couple more of their own. She now lay in a spider's web of rope which, I felt, in a way trapped us as much as it secured her.

I asked the men what the weather was going to do. They looked up at the sky, shook their heads doubtfully, and made uncertain gestures with their hands. They knew as little as we did. We walked up to the taverna together and ordered drinks. An old man offered us a bit of meze; an olive and a piece of tomato he carefully speared with his fork and held out to us with a beaming smile and encouraging nods. One of the fishermen was the owner of the taverna. His wife assured us there was food. Ordering food in a Greek taverna always has an element of adventure about it, of uncertainty. This has nothing to do with language. However fluently you may speak Greek this is no insurance that what you order is what you'll get. Only in the more sophisticated places will you get the 'it's off' with which a British waiter rancorously gets a bit of his own back. Not so the Greek. There is always an element of your being the guest even in a restaurant. A guest has to be pleased. Only a churl would disappoint a guest. So, whatever order, you smile, say 'malista' and go off and get whatever you happen to have.

While we waited for the food to arrive we talked with the men, drank and shared meze. The taverna had only recently been built in the hope of getting custom from the activity anticipated as a result of Anthony Quinn's acquisition of the neighbouring bay, we were told. But, so far, there had been no trade from this source—virtually no activity. A shrug. Never mind—*Dhembirazi*. Later, perhaps. There is a strong element of fatalism in the inhabitants of these islands, a resignation to what circumstances may or may not bring that is oriental.

A bare-bottomed child played at our feet, crawling and sprawling uncertainly on the concrete, as it chewed at titbits handed down to it from the fishermen's table. Greek indulgence towards children is endless and is more often than not expressed by stuffing them with food. The result can be unfortunate: flesh mottled with fat and limbs swollen so that they walk spread-legged like stuffed manikins. It is a way of proclaiming your prosperity—just as, until Ataturk stopped it, the Turks used to favour very fat women: and the Egyptian officer, once he reached the rank of major, saw to it that he attained an impressive corpulence. The Ibos of West Africa for the same reason put their women into fatting houses until they become like balloons. This was before they got married. Once married, they saw to it that hard work quickly reduced the women to proper proportions.

Our food arrived and was what we had ordered. But then that was all they told us they had: fish. Fish in a simple Greek taverna is served either fried or grilled over a charcoal fire. Too often it is served burnt. But this is to be expected. Just as one must expect food to be served either lukewarm or cold. The Greek in general mistrusts hot food and, however piping hot it may have been when you saw it on the stove, will arrange for a decent interval to elapse before serving it to you. Hot food is unhealthy, he believes, an opinion he shares with believers in

Yoga. On the other hand he likes serving drinks very cold—so cold sometimes that you have to wait for the ice in your bottle of beer to melt before you can have a badly needed drink. And wherever you may be in Greece you can get cold drinks—one of the results of a governmental law fairly recently introduced which compels anyone dealing in food to have refrigerators and deep freezes.

The sun was warm and we were sheltered from the wind. Only an occasional flurry of blown sand reminded us of its strength, which would make it impossible to get away for a while yet. We gossiped, discussing who was doing what with who and when. In a community as small as Lindos everybody's business is everybody else's: and it's no use trying to keep anything quiet. But, as we talked, I realised how my concern with *Aeolus* insulated me from much of what was going on, and that there were gaps in David's knowledge of current affairs. We brought each other up to date, exchanging our scandalmongering in the interests of accuracy—each as anxious as the other not to misjudge or reach conclusions based on inexact or insufficient information.

Gossip is in the air of Lindos, you absorb it with the hothouse air you breathe, try as you may to avoid doing so. What started us off was the mention one of us made of the name of a peculiarly unpleasant recent arrival in the village, a large man, slackly fat, bearded and with a mop of uncombed hair. English and a poet, he was loud mouthed, foul mouthed and dirty. He insulted elderly women, sponged on anyone he could and scooped food off tourists' plates with his bare hands, stuffing it into his mouth and shouting obscenities as he lurched about with bits of their meal sticking to his beard. Only Greeks would have the kindness and patience shown by the people of Lindos towards him. He was eventually shunted out of the village by foreigners having a whip round for money to present to him—making it a condition of the gift that he left Lindos. His departure was greeted with universal relief—no longer would his shouted invitations to anyone he saw to 'come on and turn on' make everyone with a joint on him quiver with apprehension that police attention might be attracted. We found even talking about him repulsive and turned to the subject of a girl who had caused some amusement, when she first arrived with her husband, by saying to a predatory man at a party that, though she had often thought about adultery, she would never commit it 'like physically, I mean.' 'Like physically, I mean' became something of a catchphrase —a reply made jokingly by a woman in answer to a man's joking proposition—'Why not?' she would say, 'but not, like physically, I mean.'

The phrase would soon have been forgotten had the girl not started an affair with a donkey boy. Its progress was followed with sporting interest. A husband about was a hazard. Perhaps it was the challenge this offered which inspired her to take the plunge—like physically. The lovers eventually found a beach on the other side of the bay, the only place secluded enough for their purpose. The trouble was the girl could barely swim. But, with astonishing recklessness, tackling a swim a good swimmer would have thought twice about, she set off for her tryst and made it. She soon became a very good swimmer.

She was more fortunate than another woman, much older, who announced on her arrival in Lindos that she was looking for the primitive—and lost no time in making her choice among the donkey boys. The experience was a disaster. 'Boy, was he a flop!' she reported. Disillusioned, but undeterred, she went to the opposite extreme and found a Greek poet. 'Love with these guys is for the birds,' she announced after this experience and took up astrology, with the help of which she was able to advise on the conduct of several love affairs in accordance with the best zodiacal auspices. She sublimated her own yearnings by turning to the modelling of priapic painted ornaments in terra cotta.

The frenzy with which foreign women in Rhodes conduct their sexual lives is sobering. Perhaps it would be a good thing if practical steps could be taken to make things easier for them. The Yoruba, a West African people, have a custom which might well be adopted elsewhere: its adoption by the Greek Tourist Board might afford some protection to Greek women whose husbands get involved with foreigners. For one week every year Yoruba women are given complete licence. During that time they may do and say what they please. They take full advantage of their liberty and roam the streets in bands, dancing, singing and shouting Bachae whose ribald obscenities are often the prelude to physical assaults upon men. They will surround a man, taunting and throwing jibes at him while they circle round clapping their hands, hips and breasts tumultuous, as they close in to overwhelm him. When the week is over the lusting furies once again become demure and obedient, conforming to the seemly pattern all societies like to pretend reflects the true nature of women.

From discussing what a week of licence would do to people in Lindos we went on to talk of this and that, and returned briefly to the subject of the swimming girl. The small beach where she and her lover used to meet was near a place I had visited when I first came to Lindos. While swimming around close to the rocks that line the shore, diving with a snorkel to inspect them, I found a few pieces of shell-encrusted pottery. I began casting around, swimming out and then back in a line to the shore, quartering the area, and came upon a sandy hollow in the sea bed that was littered with the broken bits of amphorae. A ship must have gone down there. Scattered among thickly strewn small shards were larger pieces, mostly the necks and handles of jars. And there was a length of anchor chain so encrusted with sea growths that for some time I thought it was a strangely shaped stone formation. There was also the outline of a wall. I dived and brought up some pieces of pottery and then came upon what at first sight looked like a complete amphora, a very large one. I managed to get my hands on it but it was too heavy to lift. I went and got Willard and between us we got it up to the surface but only after he had secured a line to it. When we got the massive bit of pottery into the dinghy we found it to be a number of broken amphorae fused together into a large single one. You cannot be too careful in Greece about anything you may find so, when we had looked at it enough, we let it sink back down to the hollow from where we had raised it.

The Greek government is now very alive to the value of objects from Greece's past and clamps down with draconian severity on anyone taking them—quite rightly. But they have swung from one extreme to the other: from past indifference to neuresthenic alertness. Officials now treat any found object, however trivial, as though it were archaeological treasure. And in doing so tend to view anyone reporting a find to them with unconcealed suspicion, assuming felonious intent in even the most innocent. It is better to leave anything you may come across where it is, especially anything in the sea. Don't even bring up an old bottle unless it is clearly stamped HP sauce or Guinness.

It is a great pity that this is so and that Greece vigorously discourages archaeological discovery on the part of visitors—and is not more encouraging towards finds and the exploration which leads to them. As Israel has shown, even amateurs, controlled and directed by an expert, can produce valuable results. In a place like Lindos where so much of the past lies undisturbed and unseen—a site potentially of the first importance—virtually nothing has been done. But some work has been carried out on the Acropolis by Danes—in the 1920s. Today, in place of a constructive approach, the easy way is taken and, at best, conservation is the cry—a policy which leads to silly regulations like the one about painting all doors and windows brown while allowing hideous anachronisms to be built. 'You foreigners like the old, we Greeks like the beautiful,' said a Lindian who had just completed gutting one of the old houses and modernising it with chrome and plastic amenities.

Tourism is bringing wealth to Lindos but none of it is being used to ensure the future or to uncover the past. There is a real danger that Lindos may be destroyed in the process of becoming just another resort. Already, a new taverna, a cubic concrete block, has broken the line of the beach when seen from above, spoiling its sweep. Other buildings are planned.

And the much needed and welcomed amenities being brought to the village are being allowed to get out of control through lack of imagination. Heavy black electric cables, slung between the buildings and across streets, have spoiled many of the lovely glimpses one gets when walking through the village, of sea and sky and rock framed in the curve of a lane or the geometric lines of space between buildings. The cables could at very little extra cost have been put underground where they cross streets. When they run along the sides of houses it doesn't much matter because they can be whitewashed over. But the bars of ungiving and rigid black across scenes of sea and sky are a crime which has destroyed a beauty of dreams. They are perhaps a fitting symbol of vandalism in a village which is in danger of becoming a microcosm of the disorientation of our times, a place where dropouts can hole up, turn on, freak out and poison themselves and their surroundings with the effects of their, for the most part, self-induced, distraught unhappiness. And most of them are lost because they are without a cause, without purpose, products of an age of liberty without responsibility. They have nowhere to go and nothing real to fight so they set up Aunt Sallys of their own making whose putting down at best gives them only a sour satisfaction. Their generosity is not engaged, their strength not challenged and their curiosity unsatisfied. A Pied Piper could lead them anywhere. Give them a job and the tools and they could work wonders—it only needs someone to set the ball rolling and there could be a chain of projects under way in Greece, with their help, every bit as exciting as the marvellous archaeological enterprise of Israel's Masada.

The sun moved behind a shoulder of hill and a wash of evening shadow filled the hollows in the rocks. We had loafed the day away and now it was dying around us. The taverna owner's wife brought a pressure lamp and its glare of light killed what remained of the day, isolating us in a pool of harsh light.

When we stood up and said goodnight there was consternation. 'But where would we sleep?'

Where we would sleep was on board *Aeolus*. They tried to dissuade us. I wish they had succeeded.

I woke slowly, aware that something had disturbed me, but only half registering. There was a movement on my head. I was slow to realise it was not just part of the sailing bag I was using as a pillow touching me. I sat up. Fuddled with sleep, I became half aware that a weight had left my head. I got the torch clipped to the mizzen mast. David sat up and asked what was going on. I switched the torch on and the beam, unerringly directed by chance, fell square on the bunched body of a plumply big and alarmed rat.

We spent the rest of the night chasing it. Where in such a small boat could such a big rat hide? In the morning there was no sign of it on board, of that we were certain—but to make sure we practically took *Aeolus* to pieces. As we worked we cursed the two fishing boats moored near us. They were the cause of our disturbance. The rat, accustomed to going aboard them for fish snacks, had treated us as another source of supply. What we needed were some of those big metal discs ships attach to their shore lines to prevent such visits. The short answer, we resolved, was no lines ashore anywhere near inhabited places where there were fishing boats moored, and a departure from our present mooring just as soon as we could get everything back in place, whatever the wind and weather.

18

The tourist beach was a stretch of almost deserted sand. We could slip in and get to our moorings unobserved, but it would have been more fitting had we crept back into Lindos bay under cover of darkness. We set out to accomplish something, failed miserably and returned after what had become a pub crawl down the coast. Yes, we should have chosen the dark. But circumstances brought us in at the end of the day, the time when the hills around the bay are already in shadow and the columns of Apollo's temple on the Acropolis are touched with the sun's last rays, a golden tribute before it dies.

> Tlepolemus Heraclides, right strong and highly made,
>   Brought nine tall ships of war from Rhodes, which
>   haughty Rhodians manned,
> Who dwelt in three dissever'd parts of that most
>   pleasant land,
>   which Lindus and Ialysus were, and bright Camirus
>   call'd
> Tlepolemus commanded these, in battle unapall'd.

Those ships had set out with high purpose, Troy their destination. We, too, had set out with purpose in a mini way. Tlepolemus had not come back and no more ships had sailed from Lindos to Troy. We had come back and *Aeolus* would try again for Symi. But when? And after Symi ... ?

We plodded up the steep path from the Boat beach with as much as we could carry. The rest of the gear would have to wait until tomorrow. We had been away a week. What had happened since we had been away? Who was here and who had left? A week? In that week there had obviously been a great turnover of people—we saw no one we knew. We might even make it to my house and get our breath back before facing the raillery which, deservedly, we would sooner or later have to face. We could have slipped through side streets but decided to see who was about in Lindos by Night; we might as well get the leg-pulling over.

We were drawn by the sound of music in the air. Early as it was, Lindos by Night was jumping. We passed a man and a woman, strangers and foreign, zonked out. Still on their feet, but only just. We were home! The jukebox was belting it out at full volume. No wonder we had heard music! The small platform at the top of the front entrance steps was already full with the overflow from inside the taverna—no one we knew except for a few donkey boys prospecting the new talent. Inside, there was no room to move. We walked past the front entrance and glanced in at the side door. Hands waved and faces mouthed cheerful enquiries. We could hear nothing and waved jovially back, indicating in mime that we would be back presently; and went on our way.

I only realised when we got to the door of my house that it was the night of my Greek lesson—and there would barely be time to get ready before my teacher, Giorgio Kharalambos, arrived. My inability to speak Greek worried me but I had never done much about it—there always seemed to be too many other things to be done.

There was almost always an elderly man, lean and tanned to the colour of leather, down at the Boat beach when I was there, busying himself with a small boat. I gave him a hand turning it upside down one day so that he could paint the bottom. He spoke to me in Greek with such clarity of diction that I felt I ought to understand every word. On the spur of the moment I asked him if he would give me lessons. He asked me if I spoke French and inclined his head with satisfaction when I replied yes. He switched to French and we quickly made our arrangements. He had, ever since then, taught me with patience and a persistence undaunted by my stupidity. To my alarm, he insisted that I should learn to read and write before trying to speak. Not satisfied with having me learn to read and write print, he insisted gently, but with absolute pedagogic firmness, that I learn to read and write script as well. 'Siga, siga,' he would say, 'slowly, slowly. Read and write first, then speak. It will be quicker that way.' And so he guided me like an infant through a children's book and set me simple sentences to copy.

There is really nothing in learning to read and write Greek, apart from a few pitfalls unknown to other languages. For instance, you must remember that a B in Greek is really a V. When you see the word *Tabepna* you know it is taverna: the P is of course Greek for R—and an R is a sort of squarer than usual N. So far so good. Fairly simple. Just remember that H is I. All this applies to capitals only, of course. When you get to the small letters it is a different kettle of fish; and, talking of fish, there is no difficulty in remembering that ψ is ps as in psaria—fish, and for catching fish, particularly octopus, you often use a trident. It's nice to have things simplified by the occasional use of a pictogram. Before leaving capitals, one must remember that Y stands for another I sound—it also serves when used with O to make the OO sound. Now for the small letters: n with the right leg a bit longer than the left is of course an i: u with a long left leg is m: v is n and p is r, the same as in capitals: w is o, u is i. And, to avoid getting confused, it should be remembered that an o with a right handed tick on the top is an s. You will not forget that w is o. When you come to script all you have to do is remember that, as with print, things are not what they appear to be. Don't go by familiar shapes—they almost never mean what they should. However, don't be discouraged by apparent difficulties. You will feel it has all been well worth the trouble the first time you manage to decipher the inscription on the base of a statue. It won't help you to order a glass of water but it will make you feel good. That I haven't learned to speak much Greek was not my teacher's fault.

David had just dumped the gear and gone when my teacher arrived. I apologised for still being so scruffy and had my apologies courteously brushed aside as we settled at a table. But I was too recently returned to concentrate, and my teacher with his usual perceptive courtesy did not insist. Instead, we drank a glass of oozo together and he smoked a cigarette as he replied to my questions about Lindos and its past.

How much did he know, I sometimes wondered, about what went on in the Lindos of today? He never gave the slightest indication of wanting to know anything about what foreigners got up to—a subject which could lead to long interrogations from Lindos people unless one took evasive action. He was a man who fished and read and led a busy life, ignoring what went on in the town, standing apart from it—always greeting foreigners with unfailing courtesy, as did most Lindians even when they knew the people as thorough-going scoundrels. But then, to the average Lindian, the life a foreigner led was something so outside their experience that they made no attempt to understand. Foreigners were different. Foreigners were 'them'. Lindians were 'us'. And what 'they' did had absolutely nothing to do with what 'us' did, not that 'us' did too badly in the way of deviating from the straight and narrow. But that was different. The people of Lindos have a built-in cut-out as far as foreigners are concerned. Take their money and put up with their habits. And when they bilk us by doing a moonlight flit, leaving rent and grocer's bills unpaid, accept it with vociferous resignation. Others will be along to make it up on. But how the French would scream and rage and curse all foreigners in similar circumstances! On the face of it the Lindians resignation is puzzling—and yet, when one thinks about it, is it? Since pre-history the Lindians have seen foreigners come and go—wave after wave has swept over them: conquerors, raiders, colonisers, corsairs, imperialists. And all of them had to be paid either in cash or kind, and what you didn't offer with as good grace as you could they took and you were lucky if it wasn't taken with violence. But the tourists, far from robbing you (except for the occasional maverick) give you good cash and put up with your mild robbing of them. They even make you free of their women and leave yours alone. And when has that happened in history before? But then the Lindian women of today have, presumably as the result of centuries of depradations, developed a natural defence which effectively protects their virtue—so not too much credit can be given to foreigners on this score. No one who has heard a Lindos woman's voice would ever voluntarily get within range of it for more than the strict minimum of time. To hear a Lindos woman calling her child is to experience a torture the Chinese couldn't better. To do so she uses her loud voice. She has two kinds; her loud voice and her very loud voice. The very loud one is reserved for times of anger, times when she has to fling her vituperation, hurl it, anything up to six feet away. Her loud voice, the children calling one, is used when her young are somewhere over on the other side of the village, a mile or more away. This is her ordinary conversational voice and is quite sufficient to bring them to her side—after they have carried out a conversation with their mother in similar, if more childish, tones.

The tearing sound of calico, acid screech of virago, rasping of nails on sandpaper, grinding of teeth, scrape of a file on steel, the hoarse breath of steam under pressure and the moaning dirge of a dying air raid siren, whistle of steam kettle, clash of old tin cans tied to a cur's tail, whine of high speed generator, grinding of dentist's drill, the shriek of a diving fighter plane. Jumble all their sounds up and put them in a mixer. Give them a whirl until well blended. Feed them onto a tape and play at full volume until distorted. Do that and you will get something like a Lindos woman's voice. And the young females begin to acquire it very early. The insane high-pitched yell with which a drill sergeant of the Brigade of Guards delivers his orders is, in comparison to the conversational tones of a Lindos woman exchanging the time of day with her neighbour, the warble of a little songster courting its mate in the next hedge.

No, the ladies of Lindos need never fear, ever, for their virtue. But they take no chances. Besides having cultivated larynxes of best quality asbestos they are particular in their dress. And disapproving of others' dress. Surprisingly, they take in their stride the near nudity which is common among foreigners; most bathing costumes worn by visitors are far from reticent, and some of the girls' dresses are as revealing as they can possibly be. No, this the Lindos ladies accept as part of the price they have to pay for the prosperity being brought to the village by tourism. What rouses their resentful disapproval is ankle length skirts and tight waisted, high collared Victorian blouses. The maxi, in whatever form, is for them, out. And a head scarf sends them into clucking disapproval. They also are not at all for mini skirts. And yet they themselves wear a skirt which comes only just below the knee. When they bend about their chores—many of which, such as scrubbing steps, take place in public—they show an extraordinary expanse of considerable leg, cut below the knee by rolled stockings and, higher, by drooping folds of bloomers. It is a spectacle which makes the miniest mini-skirted dolly girl a paragon of modesty by contrast.

I have never yet seen a Lindos lady swimming. But if they did go into the water they would, I imagine, wear a sort of Mother Hubbard such as I have seen other village women wearing: an enveloping garment of great decorum which, when immersed, rises in billowing jellyfish folds that balloon up around its wearer and, below water, reveals all. When a woman makes for the shore it clings to her shape, outlining every fold, cleft, roll of fat and quaking expanse. But the intention is there—and it is intention which counts. When the garment is dry it is of convential modesty.

The other item of dress Lindos women object to is the headscarf. These offend them. And they object to them for the same reason that dresses longer than the ones they themselves customarily wear offend them—because they are different and remind them of what the 'peasants' wear, for the Lindians consider themselves to be several cuts above the other villages. The others are 'backward'. Their women still wear long skirts and headscarves. But the Lindians are modern and progressive, and no one who is modern and progressive wears either long skirts or headscarves. On the other hand, Lindians also are modest so they wear skirts designed to combine an awareness of fashion with the modesty becoming a respectable woman. When you present vistas of your person to the world as you bend over about your chores that is not immodest. Immodest is what the foreign hussies are. But they bring money to the village and they are 'they' and nothing to do with women like us. Respectable women are women who wear clothes like us and do everything in a manner similar to ours. Anything different is wrong—and nothing to do with a woman who has a husband to look after and children to bring up: or a husband to catch and children to look forward to. And what if the men do go to the tavernas and spend their time with foreign women? It doesn't make much difference to us—in winter they go off hunting or sit in the tavernas playing tric-trac most of the day. So we women live in our woman's world and continue to marvel at the way foreigners dress and behave. The men are so different, too. They even carry things for their women and take them to tavernas, let them drink in public. It is all very puzzling. Nothing to do with us but interesting to gossip about. And one never knows if they are married or not to the women they live with. And there are foreign men who live together like husband and wife, they say. Our own men too, after all ... But they don't set up house together. Still, what men do is their affair. With women it's different. A woman should stay at home and see to the children and her house, not walk about with nothing on—or too much on—and drink and smoke and behave like a man. And she should go to church. We do.

The Greeks are a religious people. They are also a superstitious people who have never forgotten the old gods. The Greek Orthodox church, like the Catholic, is founded on beliefs that go back to the dawn of time—beliefs which are still alive in Greece. The Orthodox church has adapted and canalized these ancient beliefs, made them sacerdotally acceptable and monotheistic—officially. But it has left, within its framework of ritual, room to accommodate more ancient beliefs: and who knows what came from where and which from when, anyway? The saints are there and they sit in majesty, enshrined in icons and frescoes, stiff and remote in their rich, Byzantine fashion: suitably magistral to receive as God's surrogates, and the surrogates of the gods, the pleadings of suffering men. And the church which houses them is a blaze of gold and silver, candles and the coloured glow of images on walls and ceilings. Incense fills the nostrils with its penetrating, sensual appeal; benign and pervasive—as far removed from the smell of goats and cooking and kitchen as anything can be.

Jesus Christ, the Virgin Mary, the apostles and all the saints are invested with reality, are made present. Contained in heavy, ornamented frames of gold or gilt or silver they are charged with an aura of sanctity. Often, only their faces and hands are visible. The rest is covered with beaten metal, worked and shaped around the head and hands and set in an exuberant baroque frame. In the more modest churches the exposed head and hands of the figure are, instead of being painted, mere cheap coloured prints.

There are churches everywhere. Even in remote places you will see these whitewashed, Byzantine buildings with tiled domes. In the humbler ones the dome is untiled, but often painted red instead. The proportions of these little churches and chapels are always perfect and they stand out with radiance from their surroundings. They are never locked. At the most, the door will be tied with string or latched with a bit of wire to keep it shut against marauding goats. Inside, it will be scrupulously clean and a lamp will be burning more often than not. There will be flowers and votive offerings hung before an icon or an image; small metal plaques showing a leg or a head or an arm, sometimes the whole body of a man or woman: whatever part of the body for which relief is sought is represented. These votive images are a way of making quite sure there is no misunderstanding. God is busy and so are the saints, his helpers. Give them something to help them avoid mistakes and to jog their memory. Shrines in Africa often have rattle sticks for the same purpose. These are hollowed out rods containing seeds. When a suppliant has a request to make to the god he takes one of these and bangs it on the ground as he makes his request. 'Do you hear me, God?' the man says. 'I want a bicycle for Christmas.' He bangs with the stick. 'A bicycle. You hear? A bicycle. And I want it this year.' Bang bang bang. Each time he pounds the carved staff on the ground the seeds rattle and make sure the god hears his request.

Man is weak and alone. He needs all the help he can get. So hang a little plaque beneath your favourite saint's icon. That way he has under his nose all the time a reminder of your affliction. He may get around to you in time. But if there is nothing to remind him he may just forget you. And then where will you be? Suffering and without hope. No, the older cults are not dead. The Greek Orthodox church has spread its mantle over them, enfolded them in one compendious faith. And it has done it more pervasively than even the Catholics.

I visited an old African chief once who was a Catholic. On either side of the entrance to his compound were ju-jus. 'Father,' I said to him, 'I thought you were a Catholic.'

'Yes, I am.'

'Then why have you got ju-jus in your compound?'

He smiled.

'Na, be same like insurance for white man, sah,' he said.

Greeks have more than a touch of his realism in their approach to religion.

The Catholic Father in the area in Africa where I was had the good sense never to make an issue of the old household gods' presence. Given time, they would, he knew, reassert their dominion without a doubt. All he could do at best was stave the time off a little. When the Portuguese missionaries left the extraordinary African kingdom of Benin, in West Africa, all that remained there of Christianity, when the British arrived, was the cross—used as an instrument of torture and a pectoral ornament to symbolise authority in rulers and deities.

In Greece one constantly feels the presence of the old beliefs. In some of the churches there are painted figures gazing blindly from walls, their eyes gouged out—the eyes of a saint will cure barrenness. Perched on an abruptly steep sugar loaf hill on the road to Lindos is the monastery of Tsampika. If, after some years of marriage, you are still childless, take a barefoot walk up to the monastery and you will conceive. To make it a certainty you should tie something round your waist: a piece of string, a scarf—anything will serve to represent Aphrodite's girdle. This place was once a shrine to the goddess. When the child is born you must call it Tsampiko, or Tsampika if it is a girl.

Is there some connexion between the gouging out of painted saints' eyes and the Arab custom of offering a guest the sheep's eye to eat? Both customs have the same element of sympathetic magic about them —as does the Yoruba one of a new chief having to eat the heart of his predecessor. The modern way to accomplish this duty is to first let the heart dry, grind it to a powder and then drink the dust down in a beverage—presumably this is how you consume a saint's eyes. Beer is usually used for the purpose in Africa. But Greek women are abstemious and probably content themselves with a glass of water with which to wash down the productive charge.

If you are a Lindian, once the generative process has been started, an interesting custom ensures the future wellbeing of the child. If a pregnant woman walking through the village smells cooking she must go into the house where the food is being prepared and ask for some. It is the baby asking for the food, not the woman—and if she fails to enter and ask she will lose the child. This possibility of losing a child is very much to the fore in people's minds, so much so that as soon as a child is born they hang a little silver medallion round its neck. On one side is the Madonna or a saint and on the other the words 'may it live'. A pessimistic approach, but a step or two better than the gloomy custom of the Trausi, a Thracian people, who, according to Herodotus, howl with grief when a baby is born—this is presumably to scare off the evil spirits lying in wait to do the child harm.

David arrived. My teacher immediately prepared to take his leave, refusing to stay and have a drink with the two of us. We accompanied him down the street. David left us when we got to Lindos by Night and I walked on with my teacher until we came to the Church of the Panaghia. The church is only a short distance from Lindos by Night, and the sound of the taverna's jukebox surrounds the building with its amplified frenzy. The juxtaposition is not inappropriate for the Greek Orthodox Church has always remained in close contact with popular life, identified itself intimately with people and their pleasures, whose direction it often takes upon itself, instilling a religious element into them.

This identification is personified by the Papas, a priest whose vocation is evident and declared, made plain for all to see by his distinctive dress: tall stovepipe brimless hat, full beard and long hair gathered in a bun at the nape of the neck. He wears a straight black robe down to the ankles. It is a uniform of grace, the habit of a religious. The Papas is a man who is not only the spiritual head of a community but, at the same time, very much a member of that community; and in the fullest sense. He marries and has children. He works. You can see him in the fields, robe tucked into trousers, working like any other man. You can see him sitting at the tiller of a boat and chugging out to sea like any other fisherman—but his beard and hair gathered into a bun mark him out as unlike other men. He is the Papas. You can see him sitting outside a taverna with the boys, glass of oozo in front of him or cup of coffee—one of the boys—but standing out from them in his long black robe and tall hat; and yet not set apart. There is an ease and a naturalness about his mixing. The other villagers accept him as one of themselves—and as a man apart from themselves. He is the Papas. No less God's representative because he works with his hands. He is usually a man of little education who will never rise in the hierarchy of the church, whose higher appointments are drawn mainly from the monastic orders, the celibates. But he is the foundation on which the Church rests. He is the Papas.

19

On our way down the east coast of Rhodes we had uncovered an unexpected number of tavernas, most of them until then undiscovered by anyone we knew. We had stopped at those we were able to stop at, and noted for a future visit those which weather conditions made it impossible for us to inspect at the time. We had idled in the sun. We had fished. I had brought out with me to Greece a rod which was guaranteed to hold anything—even a shark, I had been assured. To date, it had never caught anything of any kind. But at least I had learned how to avoid bringing up a line that was not only catchless but a tangle from which the spoon with which I was trolling hung pathetically: and that was about all I had learned.

I once crewed for a Frenchman in French West Africa, in the Gaboon. He had sailed an elderly trawler out from France and set himself up in business with great success, supplying fish not only to the French community in Libreville but to the Africans as well. There was an old Breton member of his crew who, whenever we went out, set lines and hauled in barracuda on them regularly. When no one else's lines were getting anything his were always busy. I never discovered his secret, and yet I used to watch his preparations closely. He would first tie a piece of red flannel above the hook, high up, where it was attached to the spoon. He would carefully select from a box of them a corn husk, rejecting others after close inspection. I never discovered what made him select one particular husk and reject others to all intents and purposes identical to the one chosen. He shredded the chosen husk on a board bristling with nails like a pincushion and tied it above the piece of red flannel, so that when the line was towed the flannel could only be seen in glimpses through the wavering fronds of corn husk. Other men in the crew used the same technique and yet caught nothing at times when the old man was pulling in barracuda hand over fist. I always hoped to get his secret out of him but I never did before he left the boat. The other Europeans in the crew also left, finding Africa too much for them, until only the owner-captain remained. Faced with the prospect of no more fish, the Governor of the colony offered him a replacement crew of African convicts. The offer was accepted but the captain stipulated that at least one other European should come with him. None of the French were willing to go so I did. We caught no barracuda on our trip but we did catch a giant ray in the trawl—and settled an argument which used to go on among the French about whether these fish were viviparous or not. All over the beaches of Libreville round, dark objects were found which the Africans claimed were the eggs of rays.

The ray we caught was so large that she completely filled the trawl, covering the rest of the catch: an extraordinary sight to see the net come up bulging with the bulk of this giant fish, a sting ray, which the French called a piss ray. I soon found out why. When the trawl was opened the ray slothered out on its back and dribbled a yellow fluid. And then she began to give birth, each of the young coming out of the mother neatly folded like a pancake, unfolding as it came out. Three were born. The captain told me to take one and throw it overboard. I did so and we all watched, fascinated, as the new-born ray, about the size of a soup plate, fluttered the thin borders of its body and made for the deeps—perfectly able to take care of itself only a few minutes after birth.

First cutting out the wicked barb at the base of the tail, the crew tried to force the mother ray through the fish hatch, but she was too big, about the size of a blanket. The only way to get her through the hatch was to hack her to pieces—which the men did, laughing and joking as they struck with their machetes.

It was all very interesting but didn't teach me much about fishing—or how to troll, for that matter: with or without a rod. But it would have been a consolation prize of a sort to have pulled off a brilliant piece of rod and line work on our abortive trip.

It was, I suppose, a fitting end to our inglorious voyage that we should end up celebrating in a taverna. We parried a few amiably offered comments as we pushed our way in—there may have been others less amiable but there was too much noise going on to hear anything very much—and found some seats.

The place was as crammed full as my West African fishing boat's trawl—and the music was African, but adulterated, an anaemic offshoot of Africa. And the dancing was the same—couples jerking in a pallid mime of copulation, separated, a joyless onanistic performance as removed from the vital magic dance-simulations of Africa, which inspired them, as process cheese is from rich, ammoniacal camembert.

Distributed about the tables, the donkey boys of Lindos make hay. But they rarely dance Afro-European in Lindos by Night. They try this at parties only—and even then dance with awkward reticence, unable to shake off the natural reserve with which the Greek of today approaches anything to do with sex: a far cry indeed from those robust pornographic works left by their ancestors, which museums all over the world reserve for contemplation by members of their staff only, and rare scholars. No, there is no suggestion of pagan *lebenslust* in Lindos by Night when there is Afro-European dancing, but echoes of it when there is all-male Greek dancing: then, the miming becomes explicit and frank at times, with the flavour of days when the dances were done for the same reason that dancing is done in African tribal society today—to induce in the forces of life a climate propitious to the propagation and continuation of the race. God knows, whatever kicks visitors get in Lindos by Night from mixed dancing, it is not done with that purpose in mind. What kicks do they get? Their expressions give no indication. Turned on or turned off their faces remain blank, neutral masks—abstract and often sad, self-worshipping.

Outside in the street the older citizens of Lindos pass backwards and forwards in front of the open doors, gaze in and go their way. Perhaps one day an outraged wife will bring herself to burst in and make a scene, protest against her husband spending money on foreign women. But I doubt it—the Greek man sits as firmly in his marital saddle as the American woman does in hers.

Lindos was a dying village until tourism infused new life into it. But it has survived through the centuries, somehow. And its inhabitants will probably survive tourism. At least the exactions of tourism are less peremptory than those of many of the village's masters have been; but, whereas these probably strengthened family ties through necessity, tourism's influence must surely weaken them.

I found that even our not too strenuous last lap down the coast had tired me enough to make me think of bed fairly early, and I didn't feel inclined, after the freedom of the sea, for jollity under the eye of uniformed police. The Lindos police are maddeningly ubiquitous. At a private party you may at least avoid their presence by applying for a permit to play music after eleven at night. There is a charge for this. And the permit does not guarantee that police won't enter your house without so much as a by your leave, but it does offer some chance of immunity from police presence.

I passed Adonis, one of the donkey boys, leaning against a wall and we said goodnight, *kalenichta*. How can one forget the old gods in a place where men and women are called after them? The encounter turned my thoughts to Aeolus. I had used his name in an effort to ingratiate myself with him, but he seemed to me to have been less than kind with his favours. Why, this year of all years, should the weather prove so temperamental? The seasonal winds were just not behaving as they should. The Admiralty *Pilot* was specific on the subject. '... from between NW and NE over the open sea, with remarkable persistence. These are the etesian winds, known to the Turks as "Meltem". Their strength is normally between Beaufort forces 4 and 6, but sometimes reach 7.' *Normally* was the word that mattered. And what was normal about the dancing dervish box-the-compass-stuff we had been meeting? And where was that mirror calm blue sea, between times, blest with a breeze of gentle intention, to fill the quiet sails? *Aeolus*, it seemed to me, had had to endure more than her fair share of windy tantrums. Was it going to continue that way?

I was wrong to think ill of the God. What better way to learn than to have to cope with mettlesome conditions? *Aeolus* had been given the opportunity of showing how she could rise to adverse occasions. And I had learned to handle her more surely and to deal with the problems of lying off a beach in a heavy swell or making the shore through breakers. I should have been grateful. But I only realised this later when an allergy of mysterious origin struck me down and put me out of action.

Italians in Lindos insisted that I must have got it from a caterpillar found on pine trees, a fearsome animal, according to them, which induced symptoms identical to the ones I was suffering from: swelling of the wrists, ankles and eyes, accompanied by a furious itch. I was forbidden alcohol, sun and sea and given pills. My affliction continued. I went to a specialist in Rhodes and he gave me some pills which worked a miracle.

When I was again able to face the sun and the sea the weather was fine and the wind steady from the northwest, and sailing in on it came an old Dutch barge. Her owner was an American, Bill. I never knew his other name. The barge was a wonderful old boat and her owner as hospitable as only an American can be. Immediately you went on board you were handed a glass and shown a demijohn of wine which was, I believe, spiked with brandy. I am not sure if this was so for the wine was sweet. Perhaps the kick it held was an illusion, a product of the euphoria which seemed to possess everyone who set foot on board that boat.

The barge became a focus of activity, the centre of comings and goings, as she lay like a dark Leviathan, immobile, in a bay whose activities her stolid bulk reduced to Lilliputian proportions. The barge was solid and black and gave one the impression that not even the sea in a rage could move her from where she had planted herself. There were steps in her monumental rudder which let you climb easily on board, and on her decks there was room enough to do whatever you would—and that was usually lounging and dancing and drinking.

Her arrival was the signal for a quickening in the tempo of Lindos life, and coincided with the arrival of Jeanne-Françoise who, from the moment she arrived, had Lindos by the ears. She was French, intelligent, beautiful and highly educated—in the illuminating way that Latin women so often are, and she had a talent for wearing next to nothing in a singularly incandescent fashion. She was always fully aware of what she was doing, found entertainment in it and set to work on her admirers with a zest equalled only by the self-awareness with which she twisted them round her little finger.

Her effect on one of a small party of American psychiatrists—they were on a sort of world-bummel convention and were taking time out in Lindos—was remarkable. Until her arrival I had managed to avoid being button-holed by this man as I worked on board *Aeolus*. I had heard him in action. Whenever I spotted him advancing through the water towards me I managed to find something to do on the side opposite to the direction of his approach. He was a conversational bumper and borer, a decorticator of confidences which he was going to get, or else. He should have carried a camp couch about with him.

When I saw him advancing straight at me, and not in his usual elliptical fashion, I knew I was for it. I took my customary evasive action but he followed me. We circled like slowly spinning tops. I did a sudden whip-pan with myself, reversing direction and avoiding his eye as I swept by him at speed. He just reversed his direction too and we started circling again. It was no good.

'Morning' I said as though I had just noticed him.

He wasted no time in niceties.

'You know that dame.' It was a statement rather than a question.

'Which one?'

'You know, the French one.'

'Oh? Yes.'

'You know her.'

'Yes, I do as a matter of fact.'

'You know her well?'—This time there was a touch of enquiry in his voice.

'Not really. Only since she's been here.'

'You know anything about her?'

'Anything about her?'

'Yeah, you know. Where she comes from. Her folks. I heard they got a château.'

'They may have. One of her ancestors has his coat of arms over one of the Inns of the Knights of St John in Rhodes.'

'That right?' A pause. 'That right? I been to France. Been in a château too.'

'Really?'

'Yeah. She's a phoney.'

'Oh?'

'Does she put out?'

'Why don't you go and ask her?'

'You want to know something?'

'What?'

'You're being hostill.'

'Hostile? Dammit, you come and ask me personal questions about a woman I hardly know and then tell me I'm hostile because I tell you to go and ask her yourself. If she'd been someone I did know well and you'd asked that—'

'Now wait a minute. You want to know something?'

'What?'

'You need help.'

'I need what?'

'Help.'

'Hell's bells, I'm sitting quietly mucking about and minding my own business ... You come up and start an interrogation about someone who—'

'You know what your trouble is?'

He didn't wait for an answer.

'You're a regressive.' He embraced *Aeolus*, sky, sea and me in a sweeping gesture. 'All this. You're escaping. You're trying to get back in the womb.'

I dived overboard. I wonder how his clients got away. Once in the water all I could do was keep going. If I went back to *Aeolus* he would be waiting for me. I decided to make for the Dutch barge. I felt I needed a drink.

There was a flowered plastic bathing cap in the water between the barge and myself.

'Hullo' Jeanne-Françoise said.

'I've just been talking to an admirer of yours.'

'Who?'

'The psychiatrist.'

'That is something I would not willingly do.'

'Nor would I. That's why I'm here.'

'It was not an interesting conversation?'

'No.'

'He told you you would like to go back to the womb?'

'Yes.'

'He is a pederast, that man.'

'Judging by the state he was in about you I would have thought that was the last thing he was.'

'You are wrong.'

'How do you know?'

'Because he told me the same thing.'

'That makes him a pederast?'

'Of course, it's obvious.'

'I think I must have a drink.'

'Me too.'

We swam slowly side by side towards the barge.

'Jeanne-Françoise, that bathing cap you're wearing—'

'You do not like it?'

'It isn't altogether you.'

'It is the only one I could get in Rhodes. You are right.' She pulled the cap off, looked at it, grimaced, and tossed it away. Her long, straight blonde hair trailed behind her in the water in darkening strands.

'Jeanne-Françoise?'

She turned her face towards me and laughed. 'Yes, he did ask me.'

'He did?'

'Yes, of course.'

'And?'

'I told him my pet tortoise was too jealous.'

'Is it?'

'Yes.'

There is a madness in the air of Greece. The voice of sanity brought our conversation to an end. 'What you doing talking to that horse's ass?' Bill the Barge shouted to me as he waved his glass in the direction

153

of the psychiatrist standing on the Boat beach watching us.

Tall, hair in locks, and dressed only in a floral print wrapper down to the ankles, bare chested, Bill the Barge looked like a South Seas beachcomber. On a barge, dark hulled against a turquoise sea and background of golden animated beach he symbolised Lindos' role to be as the coming in-place of the Mediterranean. Soon, the pedallos and beach umbrellas would arrive.

Until now the only beach umbrella on the sands was one set up by Willard Manus' mother. Beneath its shade she took on all comers at Scrabble, her victories only helped out when absolutely necessary by a liberal interpretation of the rules, aided by passionate semantic appeals to anyone within earshot, which threatened at times to disrupt the Scrabble sodality she had formed. She sustained her formidable, summer-long stamina for the game by periodic incursions into the sea, where she engaged in a therapy which consisted in marching determinedly in rhythmic cadence in one place, arms held high in front of her like an athlete taking part in a walking race, while waist deep in water. When absorbed in this mantic devotion she assumed a trance-like disregard for her surroundings. In a nylon Bahamian 'straw' hat and sun top, deeply tanned, she achieved an authentic mystic withdrawal from the feverish activity going on around her.

Another sign of the shape of things to come was the girls from English Villas draped about Bill the Barge's boat. They were staff and guests from a place set up by a British Holiday and Travel Agency, the first foreign commercial breach to be made in the up to now purely local, and largely amateur, exploitation of residential possibilities in the village. Their presence gave substance to the persistent rumour of a large hotel to be built in Lindos sometime in the not too distant future.

Presently another sign of the direction things were taking arrived. A large power yacht, its lines drawn with the brashness of a strip cartoon, dropped anchor in the bay. Various speedboats were disposed about it. Soon after the yacht's arrival one of these began to scythe about among the swimmers in the bay while, on board, drinks were set out by white coated stewards.

As the portents of Lindos' future multiplied, the burly figure of the psychiatrist patrolled the Boat beach, glowering at the barge as he kept his self-appointed watch over Jeanne-Françoise.

And then another boat steamed into the bay. The antithesis of the nautical gin palace, *Nyata* was a boat who had to work for a living. Her captain and owner, Jim Slacke, caused as big a stir among the foreign ladies of Lindos as Jeanne-Françoise had among the men—but wholly unconsciously.

That evening, as the sun sank behind the hills, an owl perched on the tip of the Dutch barge's mainmast. From this point of vantage, immobile and inscrutable, it loftily spattered the deck with its droppings. It could have been a portent.

20

The party was for Tsampiko the grocer's daughter. It was to celebrate her engagement. A Greek engagement party is no mere junketing—but an occasion for the meeting of families, the exchange of gifts and the sizing up of one another. It is also a Rubicon. Once it has been crossed a going back is difficult.

Tables were set out in the walled inner courtyard of Tsampiko's house, and there was one up right across the breadth of the house's main room. A harvest festival of food and drink covered them. There were so many guests at the party that some of them had to take to the flat roof of the house to ease the congestion.

Everyone was dressed in their best, the foreigners also in suits and dresses, for once. The noise was deafening as people shouted greetings across space and talked as Greeks love to talk, all at once and at the top of their voices. But a silence fell when the exchange of presents between the families began.

Manolis gave Angelitsa a necklace and a bracelet, a ring and other trinkets. As each was produced there were cries of admiration and approval, admiring comments. Angelitsa glowed. Tsampiko gave Manolis' father and brother suits, shirts, socks and shoes—and presents to Manolis' mother as well. For Tsampiko and his wife there was nothing—all the weight of a wedding in Greece falls on the bride's family. Her father not only has to provide the dowry but has to bear all the other expenses, including those of the engagement party.

When the presents had been exchanged, the drinking and eating, which until then had been desultory, began in earnest. The noise increased. Faces flushed, voices rose, bonhomie grew. But I had a date at the beach to keep early in the morning with a carpenter who was going to fit lockers under *Aeolus*' side thwarts, and left early—before the Cretan dancing began which was to swing the night along until the dawn. Manolis came from Crete.

He and Angelitsa were on the roof talking to friends. I climbed up to say thank you before leaving, slipped on the top step after I had taken my leave and went down the rest like a parcel down a chute, wrenching my arm. I was to have trouble with it for a long time to come. It was not the most convenient of injuries for sailing. I had not poured a single libation during the whole course of the evening—it is unwise to forget the observances due to the gods.

Manolis, the carpenter, and I spent some long hot hours working on board *Aeolus* fitting the lockers. It was thirsty work. When we had finished we walked up the hill together. I left him at his workshop and went on to Costa's. My arm gave me a good excuse for sitting on his stoep, glass in hand, watching the world go by. And it did.

He came free-striding along between the tourist shops, a large man carrying a large walking stick in his hand and wearing one of those round, narrow brimmed hats often worn by small boys at prep schools. He wore precious little else. Beside him, bum boat to a battleship, walked a rachitically thin little man. The two of them stopped at Costa's and ordered beer. The little man introduced me to Jim Slacke, who had come from Cyprus single-handed and was heading for Malta. He had decided to break his journey at Lindos in the hope of picking up someone as crew. I was looking for crew myself. It seemed as good a reason as any for proposing myself to Jim as crew, which I did with some diffidence, explaining my limitations. I considered these handicapped me enough without loading the dice against myself still more by mentioning my injured arm. Jim didn't reject the idea of my joining him as crew out of hand and we had lunch together.

Nyata stayed on in Lindos and became as much the focus of things as Bill the Barge's boat had been until she quietly slipped away one day.

The girls from English Villas now made *Nyata* their headquarters when they had time to spare. But the atmosphere on board *Nyata* had much less of the Youth at the Prow and Pleasure at the Helm élan of Bill the Barge's boat. Most of the activity on board *Nyata* was nautical—a coming and going of dinghies, using a water skiing board towed by Jim's inflatable, and sailing *Aeolus*. It was a relaxed, lazy time. Nothing definite was said about when *Nyata* would leave or about my crewing her to Malta. This vagueness suited me and gave my arm a chance to mend. I justified not telling Jim about my injury by persuading myself that, as *Nyata* was more a motor vessel than a sailing one, my arm wouldn't be too much of a disability.

Nyata was a lady of character and experience who had had her ups and downs. She was a lady with a past, fifty years old, and came from Dumbarton. She was 57 feet overall, with a length on the water line of 52 feet, and was powered by a Perkins main engine of 100 h.p. and a Perkins auxiliary of 40 h.p. Her draught was 7 feet and her beam 15. She had narrow bows and a canoe stern. She had come out to the Mediterranean in 1961 and become derelict in Cannes, where she stayed from 1962 to 1963. Beatniks occupied her, gutted her, and sold all her fittings for what they would fetch. Abandoned, she broke loose from her moorings in a gale, became waterlogged and played havoc while adrift, damaging a number of other boats.

She was refitted at great cost at St Marguerite, an island off Cannes. Jim Slacke collected her there for her owner and took her to Malta via Majorca, Ibiza, Algeria and Tunisia in 1965. She broke down in a SW gale between Pantellaria and Malta and was towed to within a few miles of Malta by a Danish freighter which refused any payment. She had at that time no sails or auxiliary engine. A tug towed her into Malta harbour and charged £40 for the service.

Jim Slacke bought her in 1966, refitted and altered her, installed an auxiliary engine and gave her a suit of sails. Since then she has travelled the Mediterranean with him on charter work, surveying and taking on anything that comes along: leading a tumbled about life and gaining attraction in the process. She was a lady well qualified to take the education of an inexperienced sailor in hand.

The man who had convoyed Jim to Costa's, and introduced us to each other, asked Jim if he could come with *Nyata* to Malta. After much hesitation Jim agreed. We were to regret the decision and learn that the sea isn't the only place in which there are queer fish.

The idea was to sail southwest from Lindos, round Cape Praso Nisi, the island's southern tip, and then head northeast up the Carpathos Strait between Rhodes and Scarpanto, making for the island of Santorini—whose seismic convulsion sometime in the past is thought to have destroyed the Minoan civilisation of Crete, overwhelmed by the earthquake's tidal wave. After Santorini we planned to thread our way through the islands, calling in at one or two, and then turn southwest and head for Kythera. We then proposed to make for the Peloponnese and turn north up the west coast of Greece. That was the plan.

After a flurry of last minute preparations we set off from Lindos. Hands waved and handkerchiefs fluttered from the shore. The weather forecast promised northwesterly winds of force 1 to 4 and calm seas. We ran into heavy weather as we got near Cape Praso Nisi—the Cape, it seemed, was jealous of its evil reputation and intended to see that it kept it. The wind increased rapidly to force 8—we had an anemometer on board. Giving Praso Nisi a wide berth, we turned north to head up the Carpathos Strait.

Nyata had been pounding heavily for some time and shipping water over her bows. Conditions worsened as we drew level with the Cape. *Nyata* has a quick, sharp roll and we had to hang on hard as she beat like a metronome from side to side. I had already developed a technique to avoid using my injured arm and, at the cost of various bruises, had quickly mastered it. Our companion began to feel unwell. We did what we could to make him comfortable and gave him our sympathy, but there were things to do. *Nyata* was taking a hammering —the going was not the kind a lady who was, after all, getting on should have to put up with. Jim decided to turn back for Lindos. The world was a desolation of howling wind, grey sea in turmoil, spume-swept, and a menacing coast glimpsed through a lather of water.

We reached Lindos in the dark and abandoned our plan to lie offshore for the night. We would go in, but felt thankful that we had the cover of night for our lame return. I was worried. Was there something about me which doomed marine enterprises?

It was a very black night. We peered anxiously at the coastline. I thought I had got my bearings and felt apprehension when Jim started to head in on a different line to the one I would have taken. I thought I knew the entrance better than he did and was convinced he was wrong. But I was. We dropped anchor safely in the bay and I felt glad that David and I hadn't headed for Cape Praso Nisi. We might have got there.

We left early next morning and learned later that no one had known of our return. The weather forecast was winds force 1 to 3. In fact the wind quickly became a force 8 westerly and later northwesterly. Jim decided to abandon our original sailing plan and to go south of Crete instead, which meant my long hoped for sight of Santorini would have to wait for another occasion. The weather grew worse and we were forced to take shelter in Amorfos bay, Carpathos, where we spent an uneasy night. The only other sign of life we had seen all day was a large yacht in the distance making for shelter further along the coast of Carpathos.

When we set off again our companion took his first turn at the wheel. After about ten minutes he asked to be relieved because he felt too ill to continue. Jim and I soon came to admire the selective nature of the seasickness from which he suffered, a type which allowed him to eat only the choicest items among the stores on board. We discovered after he had left *Nyata* that he had spent a lot of his time below doing some very solid solitary eating. I suppose there wasn't much else he could do with the time on his hands. He did no more work of any kind after his brief turn at the wheel.

We had thought that by going south along the coast of Crete we would get the benefit of the island's lee. In the event the wind changed and we found ourselves heading into dirty weather most of the time. One soon learns that one of the peculiarities of Greek waters is that the winds contrive, more often than not, to be in your teeth.

But it was not all rough water, bad weather and struggle. Even during some of the worst seas the sun often shone and it was warm in the shelter of the deckhouse; and it was possible also to wedge oneself securely in a corner on deck and sunbathe. I gradually learned to relax at the helm, to balance *Nyata* and let her settle to her fashion. Instead of turning the wheel like a coffee grinder I began to get the feel of it in response to the run of the sea and *Nyata*'s reaction to it, helping her to keep on course with an occasional touch, a reminder not to stray rather than an imposition of my will. She responded like the lady she is, willing to be courted but not forced. I got the hang of adjusting myself to her plunge and roll, moving with it, and became absorbed in watching the rise and fall of the bows. The world was a welter of water cut by the resolute geometry of the bows, a place of shredded clouds snatched away and thrown behind us, and the punctuating divisions of the compass moving from their place if one's attention wandered.

The feeling of isolation was intense, especially at night when Jim was below, off watch and resting. I began to feel an identity with the ship, a satisfaction in holding her steady on course. Muscles ached as the hours wore on, my eyes became heavy and their involuntary closing had to be fought but there was the feel of the wheel's smooth polished wood, rounded spokes, the feel of the stiff hardness of identifying rope round one, the kingspoke, the awareness of a complicated and living structure in one's care to sustain the spirit against the erosions of tiredness. When Jim came up to take over I felt regret at having to give up the wheel and a reluctance to go below and rest.

We stood in close to Crete. It was the first time I had seen the island and found it frustrating to pass so close along its whole length with no chance of going ashore. We passed Massara where an international colony has established itself in the caves which riddle the cliffs there—people living no less distraught lives in their simple surroundings than if they had been imprisoned in the ghetto of some large city. Inevitably, the sight of the place triggered off a philosophical mood. There could be no greater contrast than that between a yacht embattled against wind and waves and the self-conscious 'primitive' living of the distracted community in its caves. How many of them living there must have been quickly disillusioned with the life. Couples come to Lindos looking for the simple life—'a shepherd's hut will do' but it often turns out that the hut must have running water laid on and electric light. There is no easy way to revelation whether by way of cave, trips or any other stimulus which doesn't extend the spirit of the individual.

We rounded the western point of Crete and turned north towards Kythera, one of the islands that became a centre of the Aphrodite cult, brought there from Cyprus by the Phoenicians, and entered Kythera's port, Kapsali, in the dark. We had been tempted to carry on and make straight for Kalamata in the Peloponnese but we needed fuel and water. We learned in the morning that there wasn't enough depth for us to come alongside the fuelling berth and, to our dismay, that the island was out of water. It is the great problem of so many of the Greek islands' water. And it is a mystery why more use is not made of distillation plants. Kythera was completely out of water. There was not a drop to spare for us—even the hotel had none. We learned this in a shouted conversation with a bearded Englishman ashore, one of the itinerant seafaring community which has made the Mediterranean its stamping ground. They are men and women, footloose, but who stand apart from the Beats and the Hippies and the Flower people, the tourists and the holiday makers. They work. They crew yachts, leave them: join others. They are the fringe which feeds off the pickings to be had from the banquet table of rich men's boats. They are mines of information. They know who is where and on what yacht, the personality traits of skippers, the foibles and weaknesses of owners and their wives. They are the guide books and gossip columnists of the community of Mediterranean yachtsmen. And what a community it is! As capable of far-out freak-outs as any—but always held to some reality by the exactions of the sea.

Jim knew the Englishman ashore and got from him all the latest gossip as we moored. The Mediterranean, I realised, is not just a sea. It is a parish and a club. They exchanged their in-talk as we busied ourselves getting out fenders, warps and attending to all the minutiae involved in bringing a boat alongside and securing to a wharf. We stepped ashore, shook hands with Jim's friend, and were guided by him to the best place for a drink, shown where to get supplies, stamps and the host of things one develops a need for immediately one steps ashore. Our companion asked me to keep an account of what I spent on stores so that he could settle with me later for his share. He had said the same thing before we left Lindos.

Jim, once he had satisfied himself that there really was no water to be had, decided not to refuel at Kythera. We would wait and get both fuel and water at Kalamata in the Peloponnese, our last stop before heading west across 400 miles of open sea to Malta.

I would have liked to have stayed and seen something of Kythera, gone up the hill to look at the town and visited the strangely shaped monastery which clings to the hill above the port. But we decided against dawdling. The voyage ahead was already pulling us back to the sea from whose turbulence we had so recently been only too glad to find shelter.

21

We left Kythera in the early morning when the colour of the hills is still muted and the painted houses are not yet struck to vivid colour by the touch of the sun. We were making for Port Kaio which would, in case of need, be a suitably sheltered anchorage on the way to Kalamata. Port Kaio lies on the eastern side of the central prong of the Peloponnese; the Mani, about which Patrick Leigh-Fermor has written with such compelling grace.

We nosed out into a troubled sea and a NW wind of force 6. The wind piped shrilly among a group of rocks fantastically twisted into strange shapes and pierced with holes. Liquid, wild and free the sound agitated the air and disturbed the senses. It was diffused and yet specific in its direction, immanent but as tangible as a radio beam. It was the siren's voice inviting, a lure extended to turn the bows of our boat towards the turmoil of water about the rocks. It was a sweet enticement and a shrill warning.

Once again, I cursed my lack of knowledge and resolved to learn more about the islands and their history. How little one knows and how imprecise it is, just enough to tease the mind and evoke dimly remembered things. How one longs for the capacity to conjure clear detail from one's palimpsest of jumbled recollection of their legendary history, to pick a clear way through (as though one ever could) the tangled relations and metamorphoses of the characters with which their history is peopled. And now that I was so soon to see the Mani there was much in Patrick Leigh-Fermor's book that I would have liked to have been able to recall clearly.

The main engine had for some time shown signs of not being happy. Jim nursed it and we kept going. But we were not surprised when it stopped completely. A fuel pump valve had stuck. We changed to the auxiliary engine and Jim left me to keep *Nyata* on course as best I could against a cross-sea and a buffeting wind while he worked on the engine. We barely kept way on and were losing the fight to keep on course when the engine started again.

The water in Port Kaio bay was clear and still, a mirror for the surrounding hills, crowned with the square towers which are so distinctive a feature of this part of Greece, remote from government control, where until recently men made their own laws. As in Corsica, and for probably the same historic reasons, the vendetta became the instrument for settling accounts in the Mani between men who could not look to a law, made to promote the interests of foreign overlords, for justice. The square towers were fulcrums of family power, their height not inspired by *folie de grandeur* but by highly practical considerations—the man with a tower high enough to dominate his neighbour's gained an important advantage: from its superior height he could plunge a lethal fire down upon his disadvantaged enemy.

We were tired and glad to do nothing much but cook and tidy up, rest. We went to bed early. The night was dark and mute, heavy with lack of sound. A light shone out from the shore and a faint smell of wood smoke floated in the air. *Nyata* lay at anchor in the inert water without movement or creak of timber, dead.

In the morning the bay was covered with a smoke of mist which softened the outline of the surrounding hills. Nothing moved. The towers pointing at the sky were memorials to the past in a frozen world of silence. A small boat crept across the water like a water beetle. There were two men and a boy in it. The man at the tiller stood up as the boat approached and raised his arms briefly in greeting. He had no hands. The boy took the tiller and the man remained standing, looking towards us. His torso was bare and the resemblance to a Greek classical statue was striking.

Men with a hand or an arm missing are not uncommon in Greece where the habit of fishing with dynamite and other explosives is widespread. And explosives are dangerously temperamental in amateur hands. I had heard of men who had lost their arms using old British hand grenades for fishing, but whether this man had lost his hands while fishing with explosives, or through some act of war, there was no way of finding out. He bent down and busied himself with a yellow nylon net in the bottom of the boat, and then straightened up holding part of it in his teeth as he disentangled fish from its meshes. As he worked, his body assumed poses one sees in museums all over the world.

Our last sight of the Mani was the fisherman watching us as we sailed off, a stump of arm held up in farewell. A ruined tower on the skyline duplicated his mutilated gesture.

The sea was not too wild as we rounded Cape Matapan on our way to Kalamata. There was time to look at the headland and think of the great naval battle that had been fought here with such devastating consequences for the Italian fleet, mauled so badly by the British. So much violence and concentrated power had been deployed in these waters on that occasion that the long-running waves should, I felt, show some signs of the agony. And, before, how many other men had, through the centuries, found death in battle off this coast? Venus took Adonis' blood and, mixing it with nectar, made the anemone. Had other gods found compassion enough to mourn for men who had met violent deaths in this sea through the long ages, metamorphosing their substance in similar tribute, the Mediterranean would today be a garden of flowers.

The Port of Kalamata is a good anchorage for boats of some size. A sailor appeared as soon as we poked our nose into it and showed us where we should berth, indicating by peremptory gestures exactly where he wanted us; a position that involved coming in at an awkward angle at the end of a row of fishing caiques.

We ran out of gangplank and with that manoeuvre once again became bondsmen to the paper formalities governments impose on travellers, understandably, but they are irksome for all that. Even before we had tied up the sailor was shouting 'Passport, passport' at us. His intention was, I think, to be helpful. An official arrived on a bicycle after we had resisted the sailor's demands that we set off for the Port Office at once. He demanded the ship's papers and the log. Jim looked at him stonily and gave him the ship's papers. There was no further mention of the log.

I went ashore to do some shopping and Jim went off to arrange about fuel and water. Our travelling companion set out to see if there was any transport going to Athens, though he might, he reassured us, come on with us to Malta. One of the reasons why Jim had hesitated about letting him come with us was because he had a leg injury which made it difficult for him to walk. This had made us forgive him much but we had noticed this disability seemed, at times, much less crippling than at others. While I was out shopping I came out of a side street and saw him ahead of me. He was striding along without any sign of there being anything wrong with him—strange to practise such elaborate duplicity in the circumstances.

When I got back to *Nyata* it was to find Jim disgruntled at the information that there would be no water or fuel to be had until the following day. Our companion arrived shortly after, walking with painful difficulty. When he heard we would be staying until the following day he said he would decide then whether to stay with us or come on to Athens.

There were plenty of things to do on board *Nyata*, and a beach nearby; and there was a boatyard close to us where they were building a caique. We were not short of things to do to pass the time. But the delay in getting off to Malta didn't worry me: for me, everything about our journey had the interest of novelty, even the formalities and official hoops we had to jump through. One day I hoped to be put through them myself while in charge of a boat of my own.

We took 250 gallons of fuel on board and 2 tons of water, and only discovered when it was too late that fuel is more expensive in Kalamata than anywhere else in Greece. Our passenger was still uncertain about his moves. His bags were packed but he seemed incapable of making up his mind: and then, in a great flurry of gathering up belongings, he pointed to a bus which had stopped across the street from us. It was his. Hurried farewells, handshakes and he was gone. Just before leaving he had taken Jim aside and told him that he had settled up with me for his food and other expenses, and had told me that he had given Jim money to cover everything, and a contribution towards the cost of fuel besides. It was not until the day after his departure that we learned how simply he had got out of paying his share. We were lucky to have got off so lightly—he hadn't got any money out of us, as he had out of a girl in Lindos. Asking her to settle up for him in the village, he had given her a cheque that bounced. He had used the same technique in Lindos as he had at Kalamata—uncertainty about whether he was or was not leaving. And then there was a last minute flurry and no time to settle bills. Someone had to do it for him. It was, I suppose, his way of getting kicks, he would say. The con man always has to con himself into believing that his motives are less shabby than they are. We only discovered when we were well out to sea again the extent of our ex-companion's depredations in the food locker: he must have done some really concentrated eating when down below on his own. How, we wondered with some admiration, had he tucked so much into so slight a frame?

We sailed south from Kalamata, then due west, turned north up the western prong of the Peloponnese and headed for Malta, setting our course west when we came level with the great hulk of a ruined Venetian fortress.

The weather was overcast and uncertain, the sea wayward. But we had fallen into a confident routine and the stop at Kalamata had refreshed us. It was just as well. The next day we had to reduce our speed because we were taking such heavy seas over our bows and too much water was coming below. How do boats stand up to the pounding they have to take? How can anything stand up to the power of the immense, indifferent sea? On the map the Mediterranean looks such a little sea but sailing it in bad weather in a small boat extends its dimensions. *Nyata* was old but she was soundly built and she had two engines besides steadying sails. And yet, in the empty stretches of moiling water, in whose peaks and troughs her bows lofted and plunged, in which she rolled from side to side, she was a chip of wood. And at times she trembled and hesitated, shuddered, and then shook the creaming water off herself and moved forward stubbornly. But men had sailed much greater seas in much smaller craft, without engines, sextant, weather forecasts and all the other advantages we had. It was a thought with which to reproach myself for my occasional misgivings.

The engine failed. A fuel blockage. We kept going for a while on the auxiliary. But it was no good. We had to heave to. While Jim worked below I stayed at the wheel and did what I could. It seemed a long time before the engine started again and we were once more on our way, on course and butting forward against head seas. How one takes machines for granted! And how sweet their music is when it has been silenced for some time.

The weather became quieter and we decided to set a line, securing it to one of the shrouds. Jim ingeniously arranged a matchstick so that, by breaking as the strain of a fish came on the line, it would signal a catch to us. We were both watching it when it broke. The tunny was a small one, 29 inches long and weighing 20 pounds, but in superb condition and very beautiful. Surprisingly, there was no fight in it. It gave up immediately we hauled it in and brought it alongside: a strange docility in so strong and vigorous a fish. Its body was hard and smooth with a subtle fusing of colours which changed as it died; and its blood was a full, rich red and heavy flowing. It was very clean. None of the messy confusion of bulging offal I associate with cleaning fish. The stomach held practically nothing and the flesh when cut into steaks was more like the meat of an animal than the flesh of a fish, but dryer. We had caught it for the pot—no other reason could justify catching and cutting up so beautiful a thing. The bloody lumps lying on the deck were a reproach to the triumph we had felt when we had seen it threshing helplessly on the end of our line as we pulled it in. We never had a chance to eat it. Neither of us felt like eating fish in the weather conditions we encountered after catching it, and when we got to Malta it was off.

But the skies cleared a little after we caught the tunny and Jim got two good sights. I had hoped to learn some navigation from him on the trip but there was never a suitable opportunity. The sea grew quieter and then, unexpected, there were dolphins playing round us, racing along beside us and veering away in arcing plunges, surging to the surface and breaking clear of the water in burnished rushes, airborne. They saw us watching them and started a show-off criss-cross game in front of the bows, timing their passes with the precision of gymnasts sure of each other's nerves and control. And then they were gone and the weather came up again.

Malta appeared exactly where it should have been. The Grand Harbour was empty. When I had last seen it it had been full of grey ships of war, crowded. But there was a great flag flying above a battlemented tower, its white folds barred with red as it streamed in the wind. And tucked away, huddled together, were two small grey shapes which, with the flag, were all that remained to remind one of the presence which had once filled this harbour with life.

When the Knights of St John, driven from Rhodes, first saw their new bailiwick of Malta they wept, or so it is reported—and well they might at seeing the barren rock they had acquired in place of the green island of Rhodes which had so flowered under their care. Typically, their moment of weakness didn't last long and they set about transforming Malta. It, like Rhodes, is an island stamped forever with the seal of the Knights of St John: the shadow they cast in both places was a very long one. And, again like Rhodes, Malta has become a centre of tourism—and much that draws the tourist is a legacy left by the Knights.

We had left Lindos on 24 August and we tied up at our berth at the old Torpedo Jetty in Malta on 1 September. We had come 835 miles. It was the Feast of St Julien. Malta was full of the sound of explosions and as night came processions filed along streets thick with people, headed by priests. Perhaps the Knights of St John are responsible for the Maltese love of fireworks: at the slightest excuse they set them off. Although bangers are, officially, forbidden the prohibition is totally ignored. One would have thought the much-bombed island would have had enough of explosions in the last war. A returning knight might well have been excused for thinking a major military engagement was taking place on the island the night we arrived, instead of a celebration in honour of a saint.

Jim seemed to know everyone in Malta. Approaching the island he had looked at his watch, said 'time to Listen with Mother' and switched on the radio telephone. The air at once filled with the sound of voices demanding information, asking questions, giving advice. Occasionally he would cut in and supply the answer to something somebody wanted to know. Everyone was on Christian name terms and they all seemed to be making extremely incontinent use of the air. We Listened with Mother every morning I was in Malta, and gradually all the Charlies and Harrys, Dicks and Johns and Pamelas and Barbaras and Marys became people one met in bars and clubs or on board their boats. And what boats there were in Malta! Sailing boats were always heading out to sea in weather which would have kept everyone firmly in harbour in Greece—by order of the Port Authorities. But the main boat population remained crowded thickly at their moorings—yachts of every conceivable shape and size from vast motor yachts to semi-derelict sailing vessels left forgotten at a mooring and gradually disintegrating. And the people aboard them were as varied as the craft: professional yacht captains, sea bums, rich men escaping UK taxes, poor men escaping, women left deserted on boats by men who had taken off for other pastures. And what they all had in common was boats, an addiction to boats and the sea which was obsessive: the lavatories in a club I was taken to were labelled Mermen and Mermaids, nearly as perverse a conceit as the vast Madame de Pompadour bed I saw on one yacht in which the owner and his wife created the illusion of being in some noble house in France. There was an ersatz flavour about Malta, something as denatured as Maltese wine, a fearsome concoction—a 'reconstituted' wine. When the Italians have got everything there is to be got out of the grape after the wine harvest they take the residue, dry it and grind it to a powder. From this the Maltese make wine. The curious thing is that it does bear a resemblance to wine, about as strong a one as Spanish champagne, that acidulous alcoholic lemonade, bears to the real thing. I have only once in my life tasted a nastier beverage—a bottle of what was pleased to call itself a 'port type' wine.

I had learned a great deal on *Nyata*. I learned a great deal on Malta. I wonder how many owners of yachts are aware of the hundred and one ways in which they are done silly by the captains they employ and the yards who carry out work for them? But the most surprising thing of all is the salaries which some of the captains are paid for doing nothing most of the year, and the number of men who, it seems, can afford to keep large yachts and crews doing nothing for long periods. One thing they don't get for the money they spend is the regard of their captains—most of the ones I met made no secret of the low opinion they had of their owners. And they seemed to look on the yachts they captained as their private property, something they allow the owner to use as a favour granted on rare occasions. It was not an aspect of the world of sailing over which one could raise any enthusiasm. But there was, to compensate for this, the more wholesome world of working yachts like *Nyata*, and all the others run by people just because they like boats: and Malta has a flavour of working boats and the working sea which neutralises the clip joint taste of the luxury yacht world.

There was work to be done on *Nyata*, washing and cleaning and making good the effects of the journey from Rhodes. When it was done, I felt it was time to get back to *Aeolus* and the task of finding someone to come with me for another attempt at Symi and the Turkish coast. This time I was going to make the try by way of Cape Praso Nisi, I had resolved. And there was another reason for leaving. When one travels with a lady like *Nyata* a certain affection is bound to develop. It was time to say goodbye.

22

'Mo-omm, I wanna Tootsie Roll,' were the first words I heard when I got back to Lindos. 'Mo-omm, I wanna Tootsie Roll.' And for all I know the child may well have got one. And if it didn't, then next year most certainly it probably would be able to.

I had travelled from Malta by boat to Syracuse, from Syracuse to Brindisi in a train that called itself a *Rapida* and was anything but, in the company of a sable of nuns. Where were they going in such numbers? An outing? A convention? A mass migration to a new establishment? I will never know. They were highly vocal, in good appetite and absolute masters of the long tram-like compartment. One of them was young and had a lively eye. Another applied herself virtuously to a book filled with highly coloured religious pictures of painful sentimentality which she showed to anyone whose eye she managed to catch. She failed to catch mine—I hadn't forgotten the lessons learned at my psychiatrist's knee about the arts of evasion. When night came I passed it enfolded in black robes, an island of masculine unbelief in a sea of feminine redemption. There is, I believe, some sort of Queen's Regulations which establishes a canon for a nun's behaviour and general conduct. I wonder if it provides guidance for occasions such as passing the night in the company of a man so devoid of decency as not to abandon his seat and go elsewhere? But the train was crowded. I had passed a whole day wandering about Brindisi in the company of a large Japanese gentleman—I even sat through an Italian made Western in his company. It was a film full of blood, killing and sex. When it was over and I stood up to go he remained seated. He intended, he said, to see it through again. To do so he was prepared to miss his train and catch a later one. And I had spent a disturbed night before that trying to get some sleep on a wooden bench in a waiting room in Brindisi station. I needed my seat and I was not going to do the decent thing even for a nunnery. I hope they have forgiven me.

And now I was back in Lindos. 'Momma, I wanna Tootsie Roll.'

The world was back in its place and I was sheltered once more from Japanese film fans, peripatetic nuns and all the other hazards of uprooted man. I could relax. From the top of the hill above the village, where the tourist buses usually stop to let people out to take pictures of Lindos below, I had seen *Aeolus* lying quietly at her mooring. All was well. No need to hurry to her. I had time to look about me.

The Platea was jumping with tourists and, at the donkey stable, donkey boys were heaving fat ladies aboard. Scarlet in the face, giggling and clasping expostulatory hands to pillowcase bosoms, they hoisted their skirts crutch high above jellied white thighs as they settled astride the docile animals. Now was the time, if ever there was one, when any right-minded donkey should bray. But I have never heard one to do so when invested with a rider.

The donkey boys sweet-smiled their cargoes as they heaved and pushed at unstable flesh, exchanging salty witticisms amongst themselves before starting up the Acropolis. No sooner there than they would hurry back. There were a lot of tourists today. On such occasions the road to the Boat beach becomes a hazard. The donkey boys want to get back to the Platea fast, and come down from the Acropolis hell for leather, the Lindos cavalry really rides on these occasions, elbows pumping, legs urging, to get the last ounce out of their mounts. The charge has weight behind it as it thunders along the blind turns of winding cobbled streets. Be ready to leap like a cat and flatten yourself against a wall or to dive into a courtyard. It costs 20 drachmas to ride up to the Acropolis on a donkey. There is loot to be made. Nothing can stop those terrible riders when the scent of money is in their nostrils. But they are Greek riders so they are never so intent on mining gold that they haven't got time for a laugh or a greeting to a friend.

The days passed, sailing locally across Viglika bay and the bay of Malona to the castle of Phereclos and beyond, where there are little beaches and, on the furthermost tip of an arm of rock looking straight across to North Africa, a natural armchair very conducive to thought: or in the opposite direction, to the island once known as Goat Island and now called Shark Island; to Lust Ledge—an accommodating shelf in the ragged edging of sharp rocks along the shore of Lardos bay and past caves, hacked out with a giant axe in the cliffs before the mushrooms, stone formations standing in an enclosed bight secluded from the sea. But these were for the most part short expeditions made when the fiercest heat of the day was over, after work was done.

My visit to Malta had given me time to absorb lessons learned from *Aeolus* earlier in the summer, and *Nyata* had added to my experience. My movements had acquired leisure, were surer and without the haste that betrays inexperience whether it is in handling a boat, a gun or anything else calling for coordinated skill.

But the summer was spending. Soon the winds would begin to turn, sweeping round the compass to blow from the opposite direction, coming from North Africa instead of blowing towards it. This is what, in the days of sail and oars, controlled the pattern of trade in the Mediterranean—sending ships to Africa in the spring and bringing them back in the autumn.

I was still looking for crew although I had, without knowing it, already found one. Tina had sailed with me a few times on short trips about the vicinity of Lindos when *Nyata* was anchored in the bay. She liked boats and seemed content to sail quietly, enjoying sun and sea in the uncomplicated way that people can when it is blue and the sun bright, and they are on holiday. It had never occurred to me that I might find myself with her as crew. I had been looking for a man but there didn't seem to be any around Lindos with much interest in sailing. I soon found out that Tina knew more about sailing than I did; about dinghy sailing at which she had represented her university. The possibility of her crewing was first mentioned *en passant*, not as a serious proposition at all. It cropped up again later, once more in general conversation, and then it was settled that she would come to Symi. And now the only thing left was to chose one's time—and that depended on the weather.

The Melteme blows usually for from two to four days at a time. A Melteme began the day before the one we had provisionally chosen for our departure. There was a party that night at English Villas. Tina was going to it and so was I. The wind hardened as the evening wore on. Each time one of us went outside to inspect the weather the branches of the trees lining the road in front of the house were tossing more wildly. Those of us who knew about things like the Melteme said to anyone who would listen 'they usually last from two to four days', and felt irritated when someone replied 'but they can last longer'. They can. This one did. A week went by. Another. It was a most unusual summer. The local people were dismayed and the visitors increasingly put out.

Friends who were leaving Lindos lent me their house. From its courtyard you could see the whole bay and beyond, right clear across distances of sea and sky to the hills of Turkey. From the vantage point of this observation platform every quirk of wind and sea could be studied.

The wind blew and drove the sea, turbulent, to the land. 'When are you leaving?' we were asked with increasing frequency. We could only point silently to the play of the sea and the welter of breakers on the beach.

And then the wind died. I met the oldest, the steadiest, of the fishermen as I walked down to the boat beach.

'Kalimera,' he said. 'Good morning.'

'Kalimera,' I replied and pointed to the sky enquiringly.

'Kala,' he said. 'Good.'

'Good,' I repeated and added 'orea' to emphasise my satisfaction.

'It will be fine for ten days' he said and his long face smiled. He eased his cap on his head, looked about him and smiled more widely, deepening the creases round his mouth into deeply incised cuts in his face.

I left him and went in search of Tina.

Friends watched with interest as we laboured to get everything together that we would need, dispersed by the delay. They helped us to get it all down to the beach and on board *Aeolus*. The sudden end to the Melteme had caught us unprepared. There was shopping to be done, all sorts of last minute arrangements to be made. By the time we cleared the entrance to Lindos bay and headed SW down the coast it was already late afternoon. The sea was calm and there was a polite, gentle wind which quickly died away. We started the Seagull and then, without any rhyme or reason that we could see, ran into a heavy sea. I knew this part of the coast. There was nowhere to shelter. We kept going, taking spray on board, and I reproached myself for not having postponed our departure until next morning—it would have been wiser to have started off at the beginning of a day. The light began to fail. We had to find somewhere for the night and drew in towards the coast. White swirls warned us of rocks just beneath the surface of the water. A reef barred our way. We skirted it and found, tucked away in a fold of rock, a cove. The water was troubled right up to its entrance but, inside, was as smooth as glass. Only a boat like *Aeolus*, with a draft of 10 inches with the centreboard up, could have got in.

We lit the little Bleuet gas stove, a single burner, and started a stew, opening tins with reckless improvidence, more than a little carried away by having actually started off for Symi. That meal set the pattern our cooking was to follow. With a packet of soup as a base, retsina and plenty of brandy—Greek brandy, robust brawling stuff—our stews, whatever they had or didn't have in them, were always full bodied. We never again quite reached the standard our first one attained but we got near enough on more than one occasion.

The stars were bright and their constellations stood out as clearly as if they were drawn on a map of the sky. The sea squabbled with the rocks outside the entrance to our haven. We were tired and went to sleep immediately we had eaten, one of us on either side of the drop keel casing. It was cold enough to make us glad that we had sleeping bags with us.

Before going to sleep we had decided we would, before trying to make it round Cape Praso Nisi, take a good leisurely look at things first and then make our decision.

The sea was quiet next morning. We swam and then rowed *Aeolus* clear of the reefs. I started the Seagull and it ran for a short time, backfired, coughed, died. By the time I had finished the ritual cleaning of the sparking plug the sea had begun to get up. The Seagull started first pull and we pushed steadily on for most of the day against a rising wind and sea, taking a lot of spray over the bows until we were soaked, and occasional spats of rain. We were making water through the top of the centreboard casing, where it had lifted a bit. We used our sails when we could and on one occasion, furling the jib, the roller reefing line broke. A little maintenance was needed. We made for the shore, heading for a crescent bight in the coastline. The keel touched lightly. The water was shoaling rapidly. Steep, short waves swept in towards the shore, a lee one. We ran into the beach on the stern anchor and secured a line ashore. The sandy bottom off the beach was, we found, strewn with rocks.

It was the beginning of October, an uncertain month when the long dry summer is broken by the first rains of autumn. Low, dark clouds moved overhead. We gathered driftwood and moved our things into the shelter of an overhang, a shelf of rock thrusting out from an earth bank among the dunes running inland from the beach.

The wind blew more strongly and sand began to fly so much that we had to build the windbreak which protected our bonfire higher, and shield the cooking with our bodies. The fire's agitated flames, reflected off the walls of our shelter and our crouched bodies, must have from outside given the scene a thaumaturgical look. But there was no one to see us. The world outside was empty.

It rained during the night and blew harder. In the morning the bay was a white welter of racing waves. *Aeolus* was in the lee of a shallow spit of sand and rock, slightly protected but moving uneasily, straining with restless sideways movements against the line secured ashore. We decided we should get out of the bay, an unwise decision on my part. *Aeolus'* high freeboard acted, in this wind, like a sail. We found great difficulty in keeping her bows on to the sea and wind, and there was a danger of her broaching. We had a long and tiring fight before we got her back to the beach and safely secured again. I laid the main anchor out aft to reinforce the stern one, wading up to my neck and then diving to see that it dug well into the bed, and another line ashore. Then we found *Aeolus* was pounding on a rock flush with the sandy bottom. The only thing to do was hold her away from this underwater hazard with another line. We unshipped most of the stores and the Seagull to lighten her.

In spite of all our exertions we were very cold. And we were very wet. We crouched for shelter under our ledge. Tina got up and walked purposefully over to *Aeolus*, her fair hair dark with rain hanging loose down her back, stringy with moisture. She climbed on board and busied herself with something in the bottom. When she straightened up she had one of the forward sections of the floor-boarding in her arms. She walked away to a part of the beach where the waves drove straight in from the sea. Breasting the waves doggedly, she walked steadily out to sea holding the floorboard high above her head, then turned and launched it upon the shoulder of a wave and rode triumphantly towards the beach. She sank in a welter of foam, recovered the floorboard and once more set off seawards. It was irresistible. I joined her. But the board wasn't buoyant enough to bear my weight and I floundered. Then the rain came down and warmed the water, but it was still too cold to play for long and we were glad to get back to the shelter of our overhang and the comfort of a hot drink.

The wind dropped during the night and, next morning, the sea was much quieter. We got away from the beach just after five in the morning, resolved to take a cautious look at Cape Praso Nisi before deciding what to do. We would, we decided, spend the night somewhere close to the Cape so that, if we decided to have a go at rounding it, we would have the whole day before us for the attempt: the Cape's reputation induced a respectful caution in us.

The sea got up wildly just before we came to a place where the land fell away to an open stretch of water, whose surface was streaked with tattered shreds of spindrift, before rising again, whale-backed, to run down to the sea in a spit. There was a lighthouse on a shoulder of rock.

The suspicion I had had for some time was confirmed by the sight of it —or should have been, but I was reluctant to admit what had become increasingly obvious. There were lumping seas ahead, a grey heaving uneasy mass reaching for the sky and falling back, a marine landscape of watery alps stretching away as far as the eye could see. Without the shadow of a doubt we were already at Cape Praso Nisi. The coastline of Rhodes had mysteriously shrunk during the night and we had reached crunching point much sooner than I had bargained for. I had in fact misread the chart. We decided to carry on. I had my doubts about the wisdom of doing so but we would be no less uncomfortable going back than we had been coming forward.

We cleared the land and the waves rose at us in slabs, massively rising expanses of water which seemed to be coming at us from every direction. *Aeolus* rose to them, slid them under her stern, and headed down slopes with a steadiness that was very comforting. I glanced back at the gap of water we had passed. The spindrift driving across its surface looked like smoke.

The further we left the land behind the more we felt the full force of wind and water. When we were well out from the Cape we turned north and met the weather head on, or nearly so—we were never steady on one course for long. The water here was in jumbled disarray and we had to meet it as its nature dictated. Exactly opposite the point of the Cape the Seagull stuttered, picked up, and went on; stuttered again. I handed the tiller over to Tina and slithered my way aft clumsily on my seat, cursing the film of oil on the deck from spilt fuel. We had put on our life jackets a short time before but I found mine hampered my movements so much that I took it off, sweating with the effort of getting it off as I clung to the mizzen mast, my legs braced for support against *Aeolus'* side. I watched the outboard anxiously, listening to the engine with rapt attention, tools and a new spark plug ready in my hands. The water in the outboard well was only inches below me. I stared at it with increasing fascination as I relaxed my attention on the engine, reassured by its steady, regular sound. Each time *Aeolus* rode a wave and started down the other side she tucked her stern well down. The sea appeared to rise vertically away from beneath her, a wall blocking out the horizon.

I had from the outset of our voyage refuelled to a strict routine, filling up every hour and a quarter to make sure of never being caught out with a tank either empty or nearly so. It was time to refuel again. Even with gallon cans of fuel, ready mixed, wedged conveniently to hand between the bumpkin and the side of *Aeolus*, it was an awkward job and impossible to avoid spilling some fuel as *Aeolus* moved to the waves. A square funnel would have helped and so would tops attached to the containers. Why do all petrol companies make cans with such wretchedly flimsy screw tops? They distort if you look at them and getting them on again can be infuriatingly difficult. I was too much engaged with the task of refuelling to pay much attention to anything else for a while. I screwed the top of the petrol tank back on and wedged the petrol can firmly in its place, then glanced at the sea just as a mass of water rising steeply upwards and away rose from beneath us. I had been warned of its size by the extra pressure I had had to use to brace myself, alerted in advance that it was a specially big one. What had Tina felt when she had watched that one bearing down upon us? I slithered back inboard towards her. She handed me the tiller. It was a manoeuvre which required careful coordination between us. When it was completed we both sat huddled on either side of the tiller peering anxiously at the ravage of water ahead, apprehensive, but exhilarated too, at being alone abroad in this convulsed waste.

We drank some brandy to warm us.

Nursing her mug gratefully against her Tina said, her eyes on the seas ahead of us, 'There was such a wave while you were back there looking at the engine. When I saw it coming I said to myself, help! I didn't think we were going to make it.'

'I saw it going the other way. I wondered how we had made it.'

Tina patted the deck, a gesture of encouraging congratulation to *Aeolus*.

I poured a libation of brandy into the sea.

We had hoped to find shelter, once round the cape, on the western side of Rhodes but there was nothing, only harsh rock faces against which the sea dashed itself, climbed up and dropped back from, leaving white streams runnelling down, to be obliterated by a new assault of water before they could reach the sea. We pinned our hopes of finding something near Cape Monolithos which rose, massive and remote, ahead of us but there was no comfort for us anywhere near that towering dark height, guarded by jagged rocky outcrops round its base, their menace veiled in drifts of tossed white spray.

A spur of land seemed to offer some prospect of a lee, but in this veering, wayward wind we couldn't be sure of protection there for long. But it was something. It would soon be dark and we had been going all day. There was a small beach at the base of the landward end of the spur from which a steep cliff rose. There was an incline to one side of this up which we could climb in case of need.

We ran in on both the stern and main anchors and set a line ashore but I came in too close and we rode uneasily, taking in water through the outboard well until I found by experiment the best distance to lie off from the shore. We kept an anchor watch all night, fortifying ourselves with Metaxas brandy. But even with its help we passed an anxious and uncomfortable night.

We headed out into a lumpy sea next morning, glad to get clear of the coast but doubtful about setting off although there wasn't much choice in the matter. The short five miles from Monolithos across to Khalki island were long ones. Rhodes seemed to be holding us back. The way the receding land appears to cling to you is a disturbing trick of the light—there are times when the mountains of Turkey, the Taurus, are so close to Rhodes you feel you could stretch out a hand and touch them.

The sun was shining when we entered Khalki harbour. The clouds had been swept away and the sky was blue. We peeled off layers of clothing. There were houses with their feet in the water lining one side of the harbour, white geometric shapes gay with brightly painted doors and windows, and caiques lay alongside the wharf ahead of us. There were shops and tavernas. People waved as we approached and others trickled out of side streets on to the waterfront to join them. And then there was a sudden stir among them, an uncertain movement spurred by quickening interest. We could see people turning to each other and talking among themselves, glancing at us. I realised that they must have noticed one of us was a woman.

When we had secured alongside the quay Tina pushed the hood of her sailing jacket back. This triggered off a burst of excitement. Small children started running about, gyrating among the adults and shouting as they pointed at her. The effect of blonde hair is always considerable in Greece. The effect of Tina's sudden disclosure of her fairness was electric—the taut, quick edge of interest it aroused was tangible. When she stepped ashore women surrounded her and bore her off like a prize. They made much of her and smothered her with kindness. She was away a long time. When she got back she looked as though she had just come from the hairdresser's, which was precisely where she had come from. One of the welcoming women was the hairdresser's wife and she had shut the shop and put its facilities at Tina's disposal.

My own reception, though more restrained, had also been warmly cordial—even the Customs official merely smiled when I admitted that

I hadn't got any papers of any kind with me for *Aeolus*. It must have been a disappointment to a man as underworked as he evidently was but he bore it well.

We spent two days at Khalki cleaning up, drying out and resting in the brilliant sunshine. I fitted some extra cleats and stronger eyes for the jib furling line to run through. *Aeolus* had changed during the course of our voyage and was beginning to look more functional, less an ornamental lady and more a housewife. I secured everything and went over all the gear while Tina rearranged and stowed the stores so that we could get at things more easily. We were never without a group of interested watchers while we worked. And whenever we wanted anything there was someone to spring forward and see that we got it. And if it wasn't available efforts were made to provide the next best thing. I only discovered in the nick of time on one occasion that the empty petrol cans were being filled with paraffin. We were told when I rejected the paraffin that we would find petrol at Symi and, in the next breath, urged to abandon the idea of going there.

We left Khalki in the silent early morning when every waterside house has a mirrored upside-down image of itself lying in the water at its feet. The sea was crystal clear, magnifying things lying on the bottom. Getting to a place like Khalki is not easy and this is a pity for little islands like these are very attractive and deserve to be visited.

Before turning to head for Symi we decided to look at Alimnia, the other inhabited island of the group which lies off the west coast of Rhodes, known mainly for its almost completely enclosed bay. We sailed round this but decided not to land, put off by the mournful desolation of a featureless beach and a sad couple of shuttered houses.

I had plotted a course from Khalki to Symi before leaving Lindos although it had seemed a needless precaution at the time. We could hardly fail to hit the Turkish coast somewhere along its length, and when we did it was only a matter of turning sharp left and following it along until we came to Cape Alupo, thrusting like a sword at Symi. I was soon glad that I had laid a course. The telescoping effect the light in Greece has on distance is confusing. Islands, instead of keeping a decent distance between themselves, crowd each other, confounding perspective and complicating the interpretation of charts. I was glad too of the compass mounted on the top of the centreboard casing, though I had cursed it on many an occasion for getting in the way.

We saw the warships just as I was getting worried about where Symi was. Should I trust to the course I had laid and just follow the compass blindly? Had some weird combination of variation and deviation got together to create some special bedevilment? When you are as low in the water as we were the appearance of things alters. Those nine grey shapes gave me something else to think about. Nine! I had been surprised at the number of warcraft we had seen when sailing with *Nyata* to Malta, sailing singly upon their way. But nine together! They were heading in our direction. How to keep out of the way? There was only one thing to do: hold the course and ignore them— but dip a courteous flag in salute as we passed.

They went by not very far from us, flying no flags; grey Russian wolves now free to rove in packs in a sea they would once not have dared enter. Shades of whips and brooms! A small boat plucked aboard one of those wouldn't be able to do much in protest about it. A warship detached itself from the fleet and headed for Rhodes, executed a few turns, and rejoined the others. Coat trailing? Beaming radio apparatus for information?

Trambeta and Seskli islands lie off the southern end of Symi. Between Symi and Seskli is the Seskli straight. Once through it you are in the channel between the coast of Turkey and Symi, a lane of water separating an outpost of Europe and the land mass of Asia, which leads to all the vastness of the eastern lands. Or you can enter the channel between Cape Vulpe and Symi.

Suleiman the Magnificent, Sultan of Turkey and conqueror of Rhodes, wrote a letter to Villiers de l'Isle Adam, Grand Master of the Order of the Knights of St John, about a matter of piracy executed by one of his captains against the Order, in which he described himself as 'by the Grace of God, King of Kings, Sovereign of Sovereigns, Very Great Emperor of Constantinople and of Trebizond, Very Powerful King of Persia, of Arabia, of Syria and of Egypt, Prince of Aleppo, Guardian of Mecca, Possessor of Jerusalem, and Ruler of the Universal Sea.'

He had other titles: Sultan of the Ottomans, Allah's Deputy on Earth, Lord of the Lords of this World, Possessor of Men's Necks, King of Believers and Unbelievers, Emperor of the Chakans of Great Authority, Prince and Lord of the most happy Constellation, Majestic Caesar, Seal of Victory, Refuge of all the people in the whole World, the Shadow of the Almighty dispensing Quiet in the Earth.'

He wouldn't have sent his fleets skulking around the seas in shadowy anonymity.

His letter to the Grand Master ended: 'on the conquests we have made in Hungary, where we have subjugated the important place of Belgrade, after having put to the edge of Our redoubable sword all those who ventured to oppose.' This was calculated to impress the Grand Master.

Unimpressed, the Grand Master in his reply referred to the capture of two merchant ships under his protection. '... but the galleys of the Order which I sent in pursuit beat him, put him to flight and made him disgorge what he had already taken from the merchant ships.'

Those 'galleys of the Order' used to be built on Symi and were manned by men from the island. The people of Simi are sometimes called Simians—the island's name is often spelt Simi. They don't like this but there are mythical grounds for it: Prometheus is said to have created man on Symi by moulding a piece of clay there. This enraged Zeus who, as a punishment, changed Prometheus into a monkey.

We were tempted to land on the Turkish coast. It was frustrating to be so near and not be able to do so but there were too many warning stories to discourage the attempt: the Turks have a reputation for not standing on ceremony with boats without proper papers.

The weather, which had closed in after the warships had steamed on their way, suddenly cleared completely, but as we entered the long fiord-like approach to Symi, made a last petulant gesture by aiming a scurry of wind at us which sent white crested waves to take us on the beam with flung spray. Not so long ago this would have drawn a certain respectful attention from us. Now, we did no more than take note.

The town of Symi is spread over steep hills that rise sharply out of the sea, curving round at the end of the gullet of water that forms the port, to fall away behind the boat building yard which was what had first made me want to visit Symi. On the site of this yard, or somewhere near it, was probably where the ships that went to Troy from Symi were built.

'Niraeus three well-trimmed ships from Syme brought.' The Church World Service Inc. hotel on Symi is called the Nereus and commemmorates the king in worthier, strictly 'contemporary' style than does the ramshackle clutter of the boat building yard: but there are caiques on the slips and a glimpse of their lovely lines is enough to evoke memories of the heroic past. A line of ruined windmills high on a hill, and the empty shells of what were once the houses of prosperous sea captains and merchants, recall the days before Symi began to die.

We took a turn round the rectangular harbour, watched with mild interest by fishermen mending their nets and raising excitement in small boys who pranced about making wild gesticulations, inviting us to come in where they indicated. They all recommended different places. Greek individualism starts early. But they took and secured our line with brisk competence and without resentment at the selection of a place of our own choosing.

We had made it to Symi. I had got my Tootsie Roll.

'Bit far from home aren't you?' an English voice enquired.

We looked up.

'Can't stop now,' he said, pulling at his beard. 'But why not come to dinner tonight?' He pointed. 'My house is over there.' He raised his hand in farewell and went on his way. Wherever you go, a boat is better than any number of letters of introduction as a means of meeting people.

Symi is beginning to show signs of revival. One sign of this is that a small tourist trade is developing, but visitors are given very little time to look around by the tour boats which bring them to the island—just enough for an organised meal and a stroll round before the ship's siren peremptorily summons them back on board. But they have time to get the flavour of the place, and would get more of it if they were shown Symi's native amenity instead of being shepherded to the clinical porcelain and pushpull facilities of the Nereus. I would probably not have paid any attention myself to the small square stone building had I not seen, and appreciated, a similar public lavatory on Khalki. The one on Khalki is better sited; withdrawn and looking out to sea, it induces reflection. Symi's is more metropolitan. Placed at the edge of the water near Mitsou's taverna, it affords a view of all that is going on in the harbour through slits in its thick stone walls. The charm both easements have in common is that they are built over the sea which, when agitated, flings sprits of water up through the holes beneath the occupant. Rabelais in *Gargantua and Pantagruel* missed listing this method in his *Cent façons de se torcher le cul*, an otherwise fairly comprehensive catalogue—there is always something new under the Greek sun. In calm weather both loos provide the simple pleasure of seeing small aquatic life swimming below one.

In the Nereus, of course, the amenities are more functional than picturesque. They were out of order when I was there. In private houses on the island seismic crevasses provide natural lavatories. These, plunging deep into the core of the island, are as effective and sanitary as anything one could devise—opportunist exploitation of the earth though they are. Church World Service Inc., an American charitable organisation, disapproving of these, has introduced a utility which they hope will supplant them, one more seemly to a people who believe civilisation depends on the proper flow of manufactured goods. These portable aluminium sanitary erections stand forlornly about Symi, largely unused and despised monuments to a meeting of cultures.

Church World Service Inc. has also built a solar water distillation plant in Symi, taking over the town's Platea for the purpose. It will take some time, a century or so at least, before the uncertain supply of fresh water it produces convinces the Simians that distilled water is better than the pure, natural stuff they stubbornly persist in preferring. This installation, a concrete and metal expanse of total ugliness, draws its supply of sea water through a pipe lying in the shallow water near the public lavatory, its mouth open like a greedy snake. Church World Service has also provided bus shelters on the island. There are no buses. There are no roads either. Unless someone decides to raze the town and level the mountains of rock upon which it is built there never will be.

The people of Symi are full of horror stories about the Turks. With bated breath and high indignation they tell you what happens to fishermen who drift over to Turkey. I got a strong impression that the drifting is often assisted by outboard engines. Certainly not all the visits made to the Turkish coast by Simians can be unintentional—there is a brisk clandestine trade between Symi and Turkey in coffee for one thing: Nescafé going from Symi to Turkey and Turkish coffee coming back in exchange! I would dearly like to know how the barter rate is fixed. Presumably things like the visit of the Sixth Fleet to Rhodes must affect the going rate. Greek meeting Turk in the conduct of such esoteric business must be a sight worth witnessing.

It is fatal to stay anywhere for more than a day. There are so many tendrils of information which begin to twine themselves round your curiosity, tempting you to stay on, if you do. For instance, what ancient rite clings on under the cloak of Christianity, in the Symi custom of mounting the effigy of a Jew on a donkey at Easter and leading it, pelted and derided, round the town? The custom has recently been forbidden.

We left Symi in halcyon weather. There was no wind at all when we started. We wore bathing costumes and took our ease. Was there ever a time when we had been wet and cold, frightened and glad of tots of brandy? Tina stretched out in the bows, sunbathing.

A mild mannered wind got up, a wind set fair for Rhodes. We hoisted the sails. The wind freshened and *Aeolus* gathered way. When she is going well she makes a thrumming sound which is very agreeable. She made it now. And at times seemed within an ace of planing.

The wind became stronger. We passed Cape Alupo at a spanking pace and pulled Rhodes towards us hand over fist. We were going hard, creaming along, running free in the sun. It was dream sailing. We swept at pace across waters that we had fought our way painfully over so short a time before. We reached Rhodes, going like a charging squadron of lancers, our tan sails turned to scarlet banners by the sun. Should we stop at Rhodes or not? It was late afternoon and it would have been prudent. But, the way we were going, we could probably make Lindos before night came. The temptation was too great. There was no need for a conference about what to do. We were of one mind. We kept going, already living the moment when we would sweep into Lindos bay under sail.

The wind dropped and we dawdled along. It began to grow dark. Half way to Lindos, night came. The wind veered and backed, rose and began to howl in our faces. Gusts slapped at us and the rain came.

> And for the Windes brake, from their brasen beds
> That strooke the mountaines so, they cried quite out
> The thunder child: the lightning leapt about;
> And clouds so gusht, as Iris nere were showne
> But in fresh deluge, Heav'n itself came down.

We hauled down the sails, blinded by assaulting water, fighting them as they billowed and struggled under the rape of the wind.

The Seagull started first pull.

There was a cove somewhere along this coast which, when I first saw it with David, looked to me as though it would afford shelter from any weather. *Aeolus* could get in through the narrow gap in the rocks encircling it. But to do so meant sailing straight at the coast and then doing a sharp right-angled turn. Careful allowance had to be made for the set of the sea and the effects of the wind on *Aeolus'* hull. If only the moon would show. Clouds covered it, but an occasional glimpse of light shone through them. Even the outline of headlands were difficult to distinguish against the murky darkness of sea and sky. We were wet and hungry and all the fine exhilaration of the day had gone. I probed at the coast, hoping to strike the right place but uneasy about getting in too close to a lee shore and being unable to get off again. The moon brushed herself free of cloud and I saw what I was looking for.

The anger of the sea was behind us. Our turn and angle of point had been right. We slipped through the gap and were in stillness. There was a sandy beach, gently sloping, and a flat surface of rock. We lit a bonfire and when we had eaten zipped ourselves gratefully into our sleeping bags.

The sky cleared and the stars came out.

We made Lindos at our leisure next day.

When we reached the top of the path leading up from the Boat beach we looked across the bay. The Tourist beach was animated and people were playing in the magic sea. And then we looked down at where our sea blue boat *Aeolus* lay quietly like a lady in the sun.

On the Acropolis high above us is a ship in sail carved in the rock.

Rhodes and London, 1970